I0432075

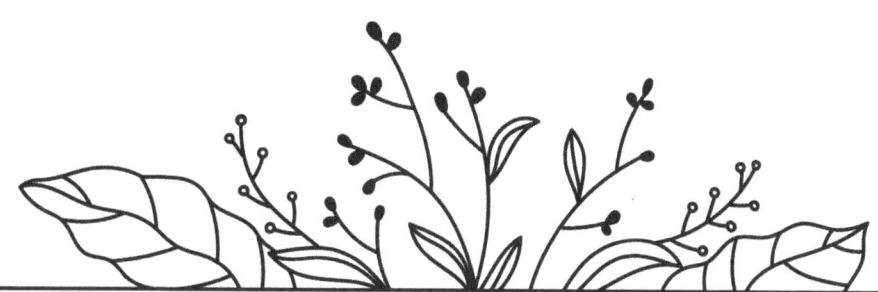

These religious paper bookmarks
can be cut out and stuck on card,
colored in treasured or given
as gifts. Each contains a bible verse or quote.
Suitable for adults or older childrens art and crafts
activitites for church, sunday school or personal use.

Thank you for your purchase.
We are a small company,
so really appreciate your feedback.

Copyright of Artkton Print

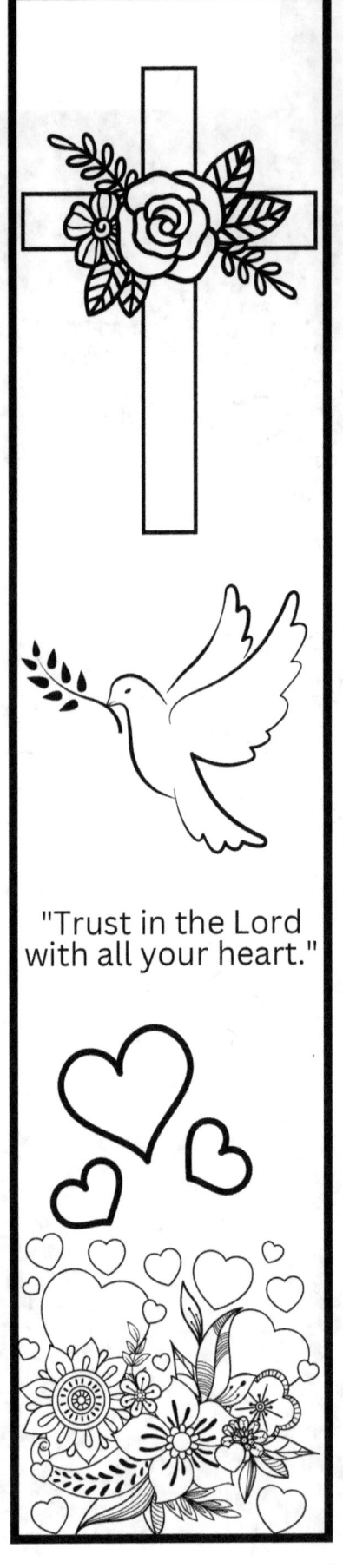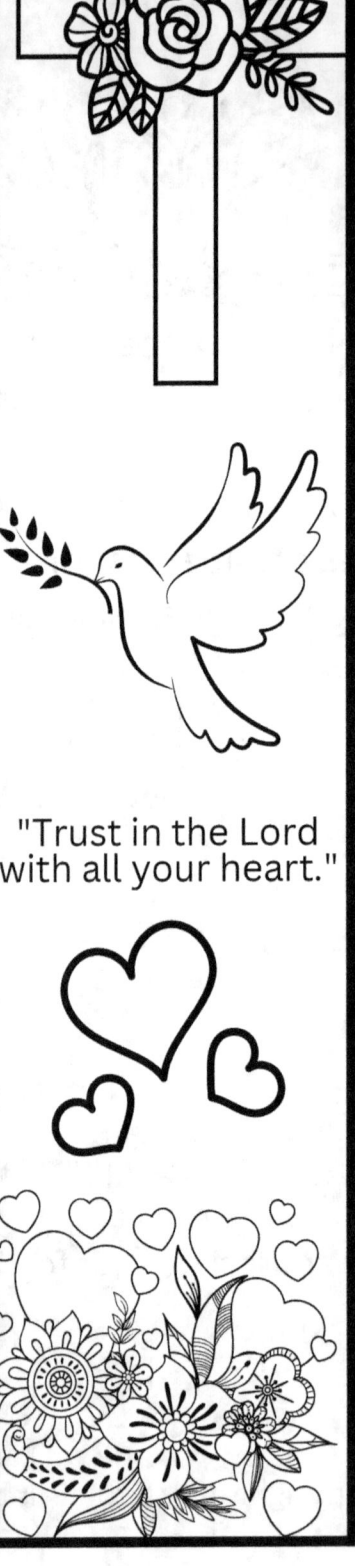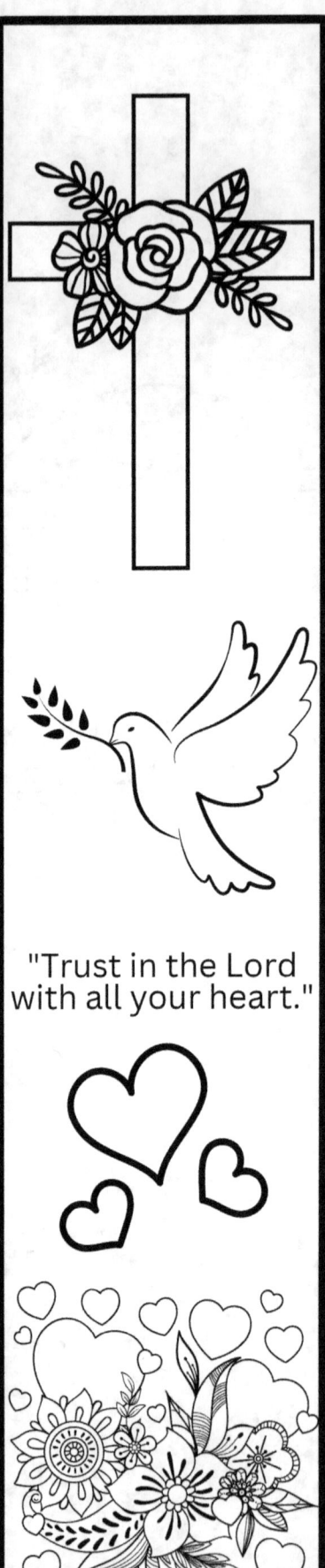

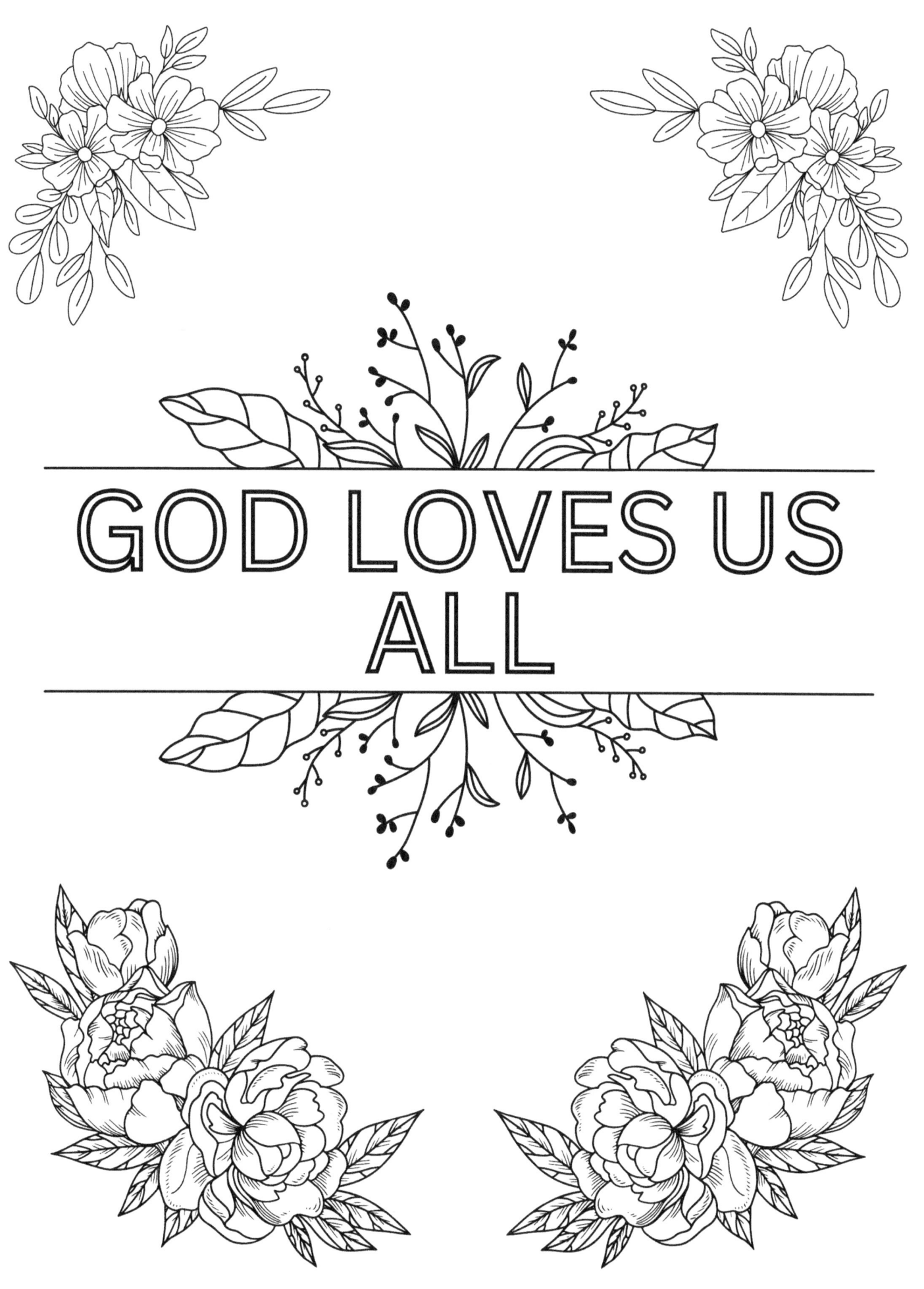

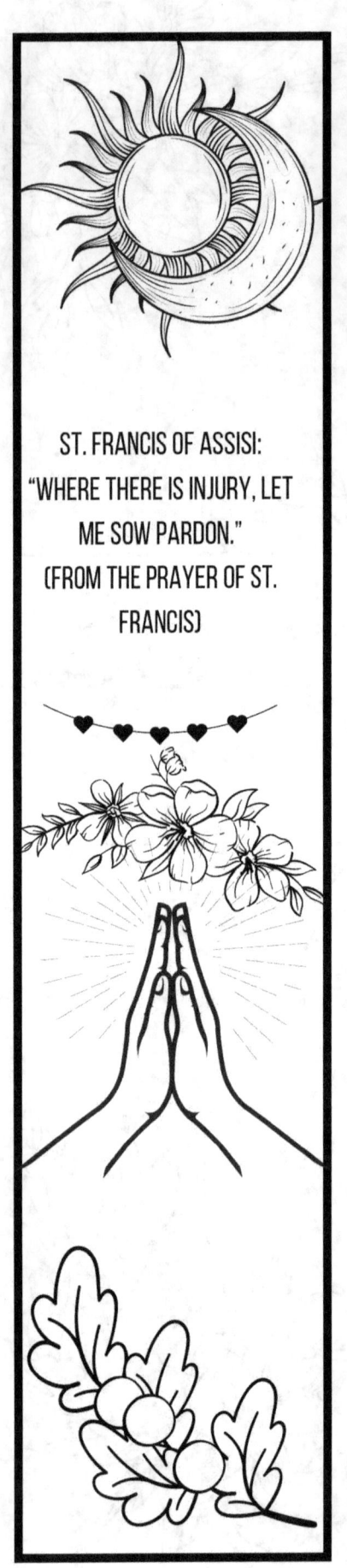
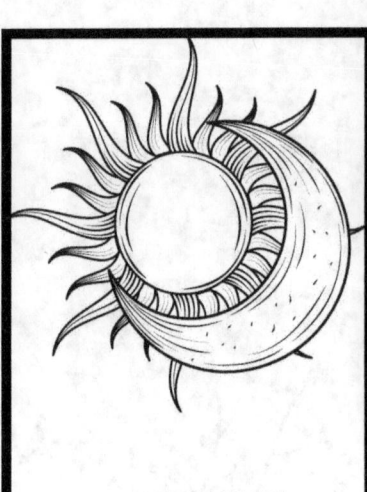
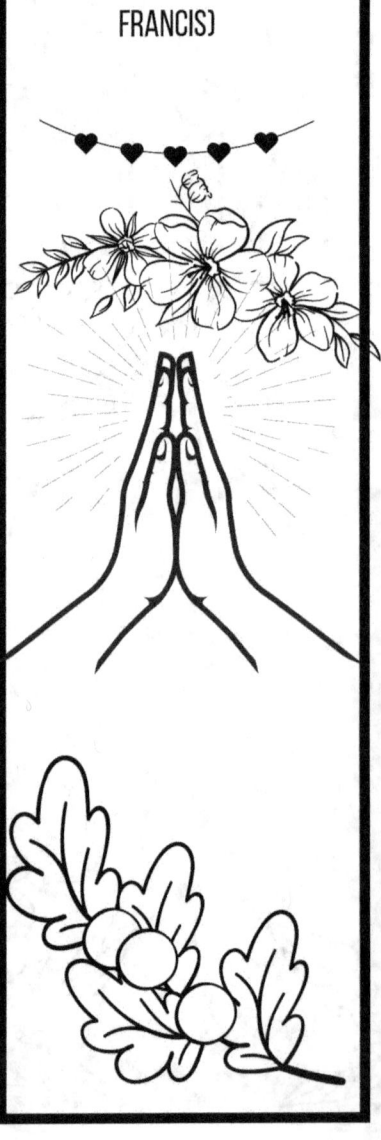
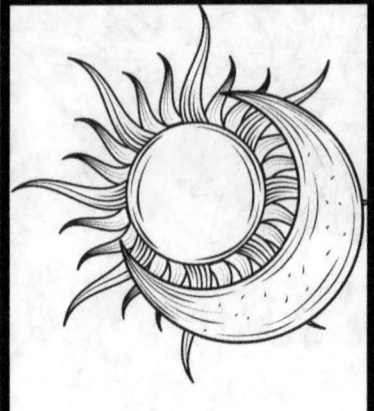
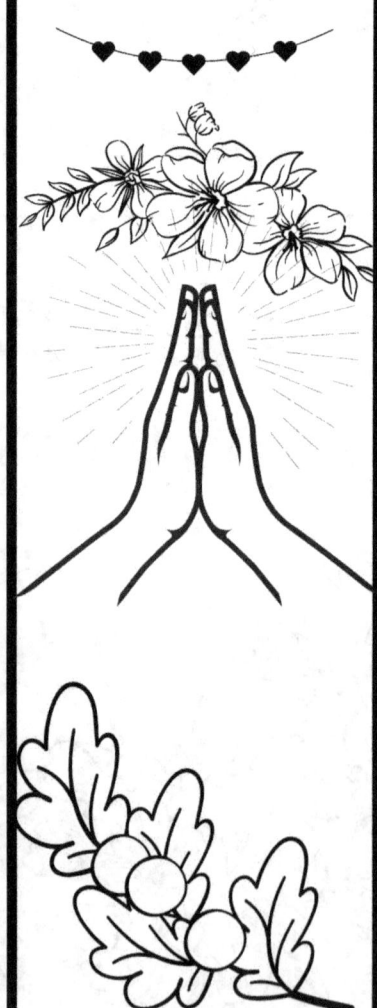

ST. FRANCIS OF ASSISI: "WHERE THERE IS INJURY, LET ME SOW PARDON." (FROM THE PRAYER OF ST. FRANCIS)

ST. FRANCIS OF ASSISI: "WHERE THERE IS INJURY, LET ME SOW PARDON." (FROM THE PRAYER OF ST. FRANCIS)

ST. FRANCIS OF ASSISI: "WHERE THERE IS INJURY, LET ME SOW PARDON." (FROM THE PRAYER OF ST. FRANCIS)

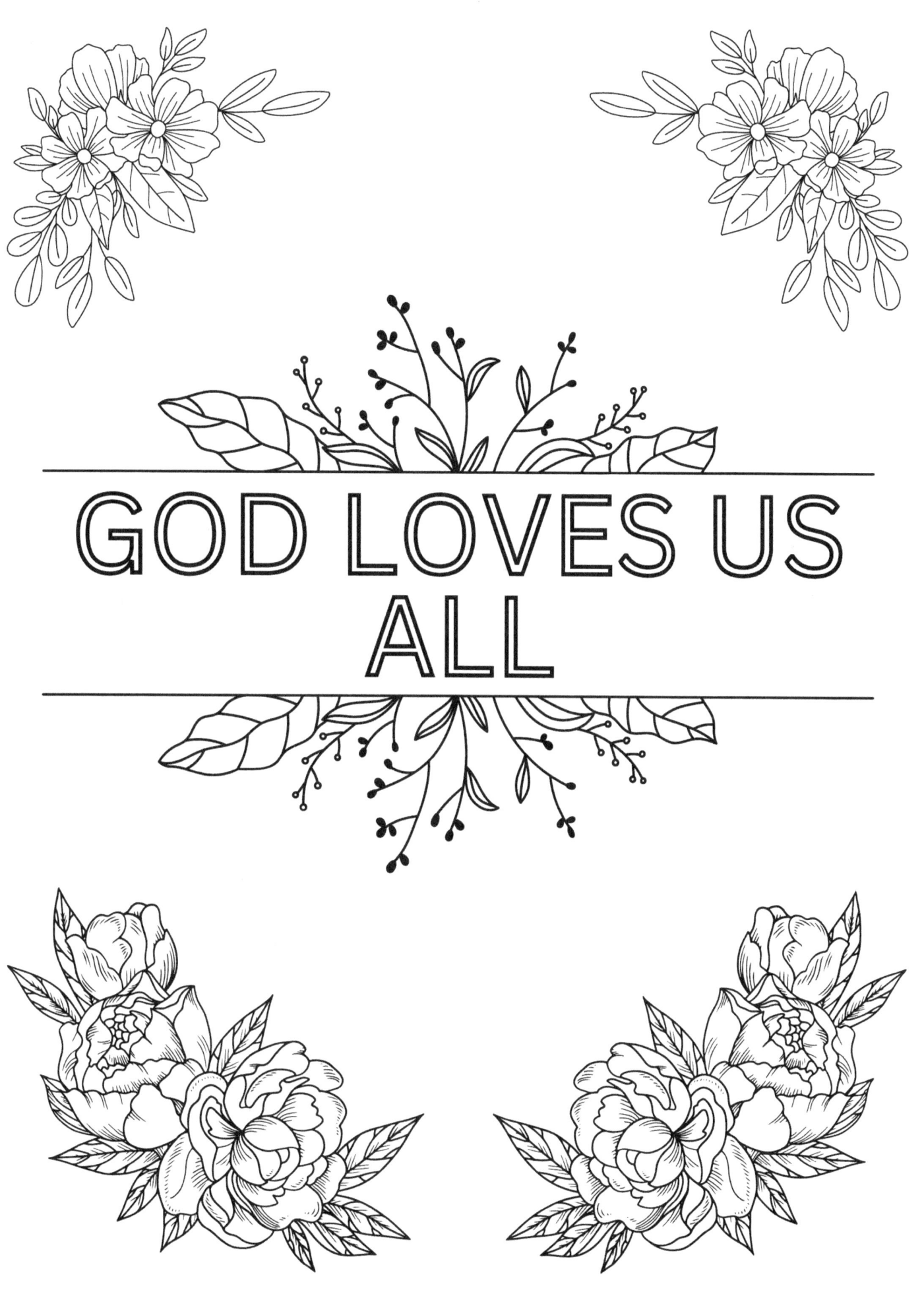

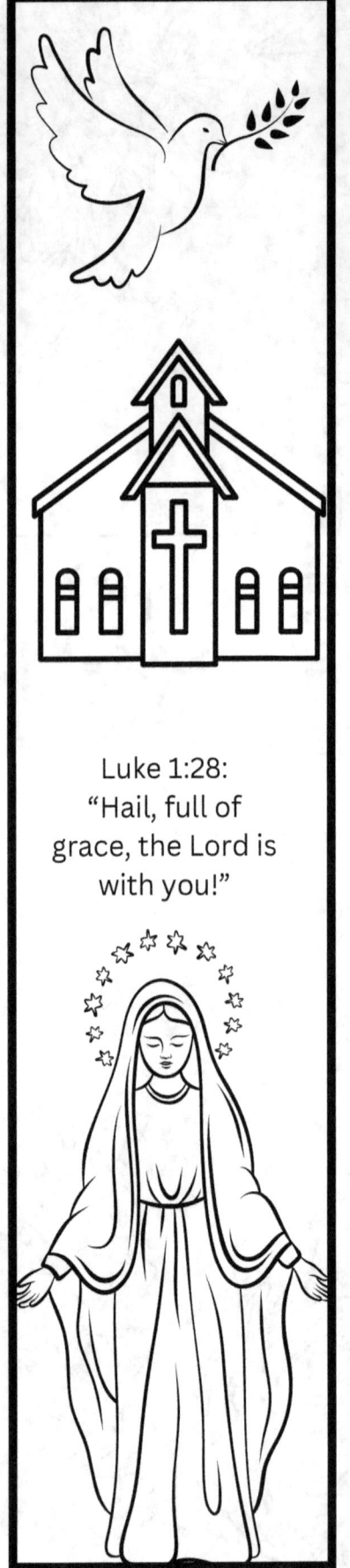 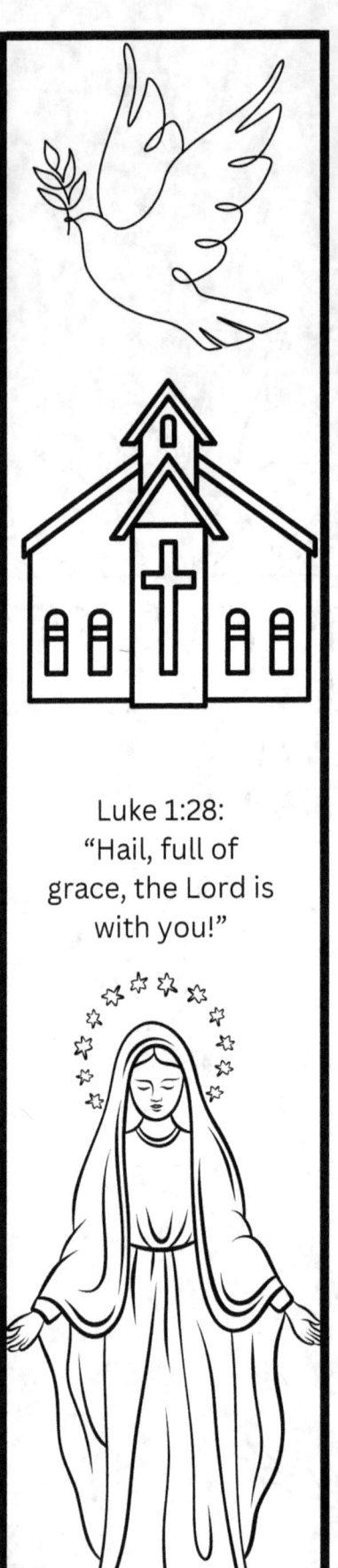 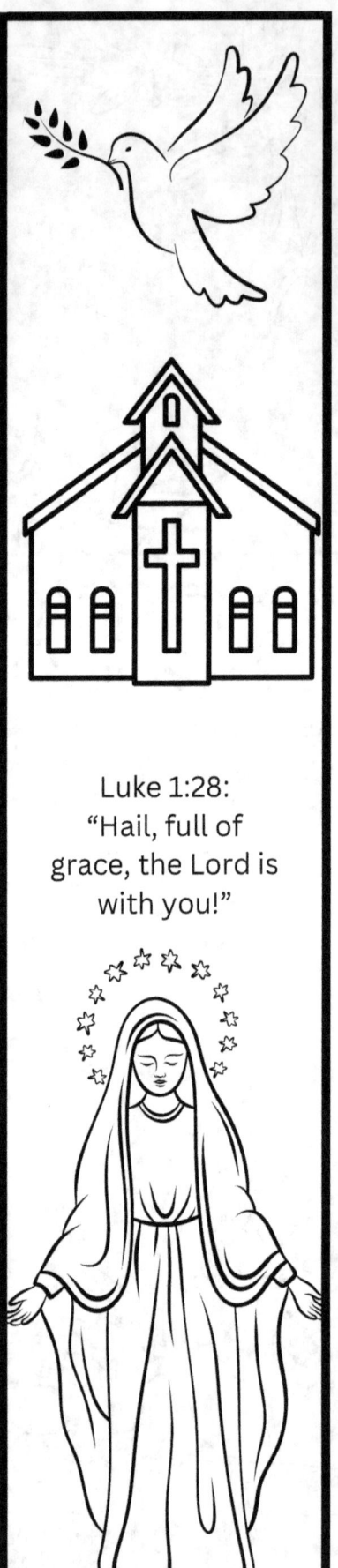

Luke 1:28: "Hail, full of grace, the Lord is with you!"

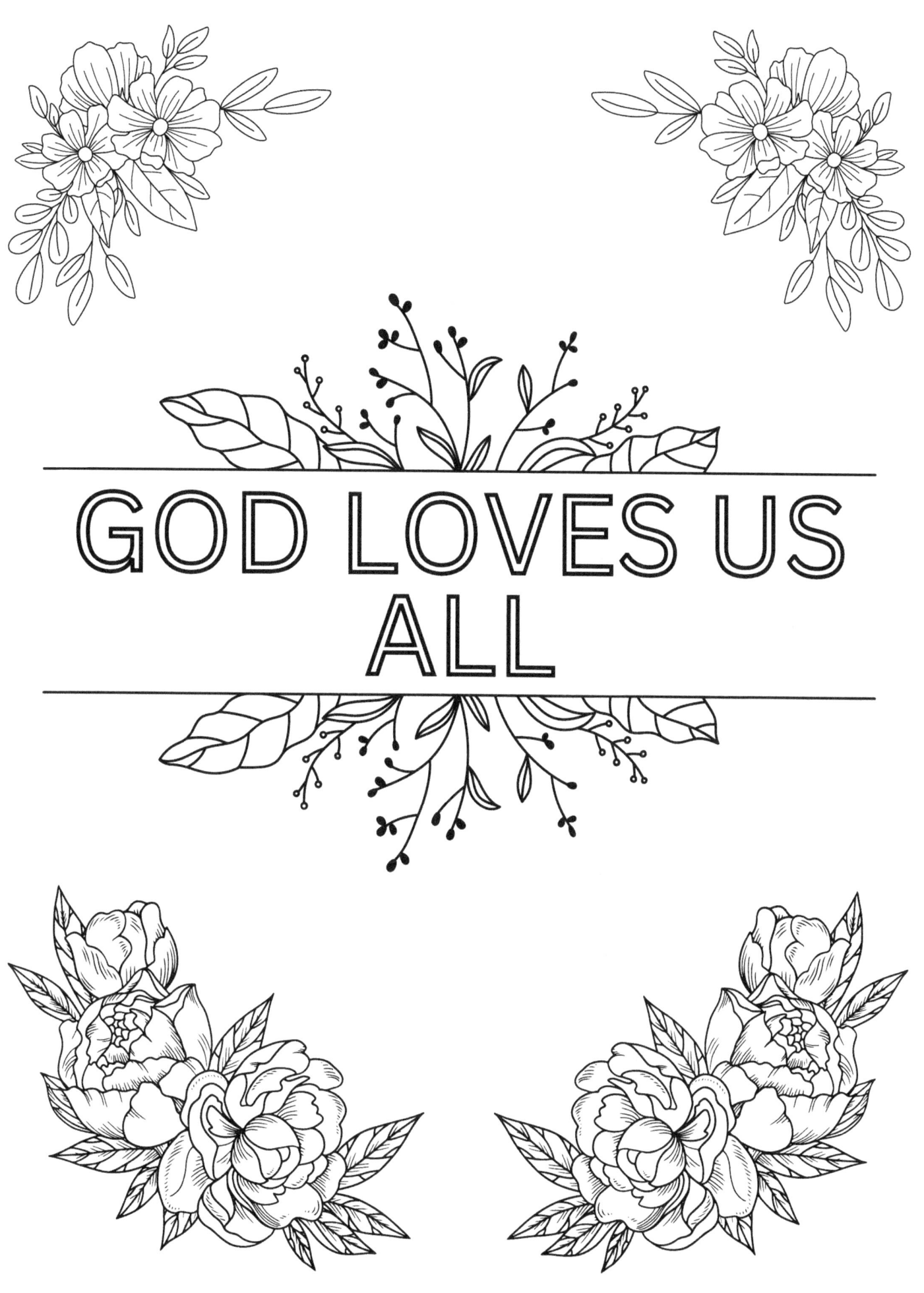

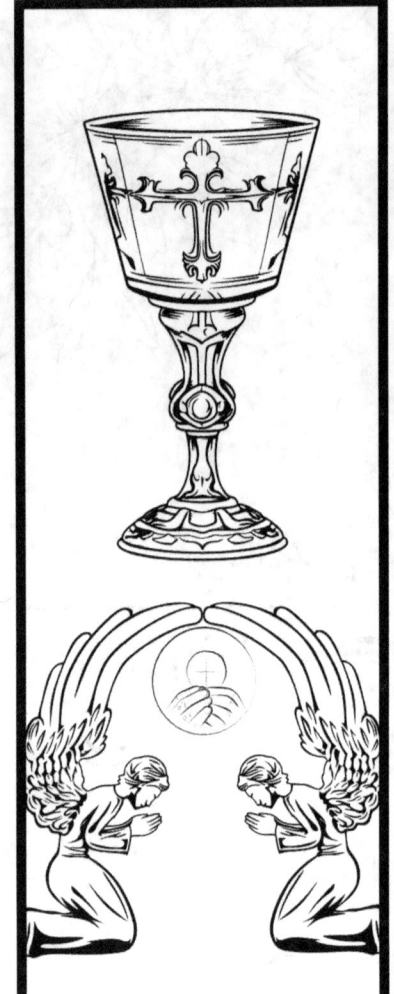
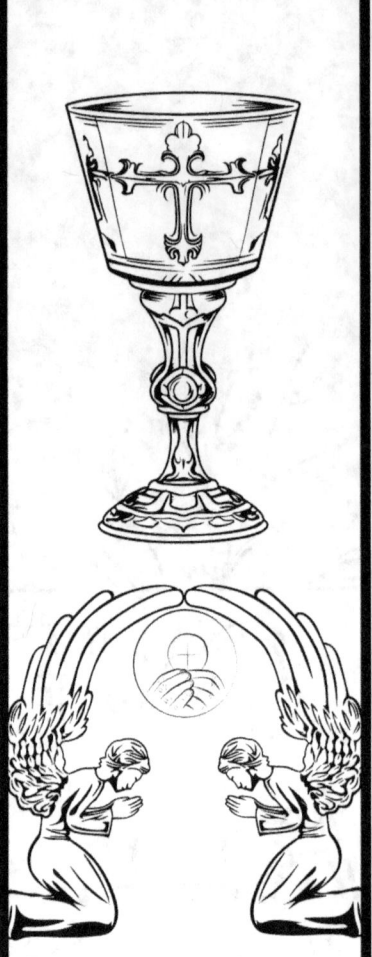
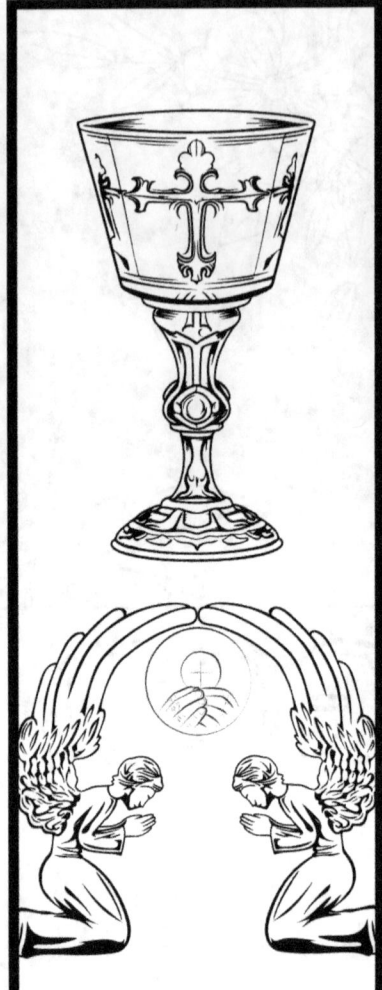

"Because there is one bread, we who are many are one body." – 1 Corinthians 10:17

"Because there is one bread, we who are many are one body." – 1 Corinthians 10:17

"Because there is one bread, we who are many are one body." – 1 Corinthians 10:17

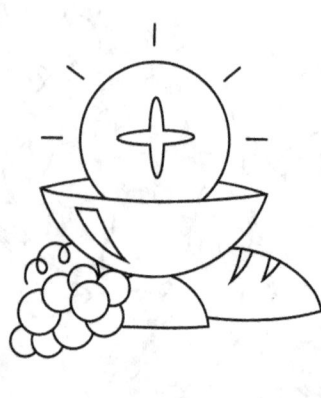
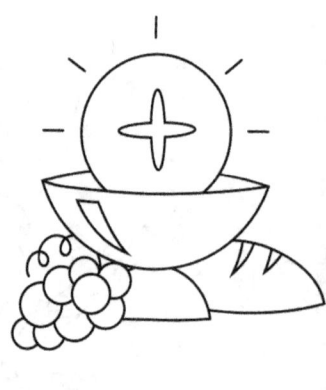
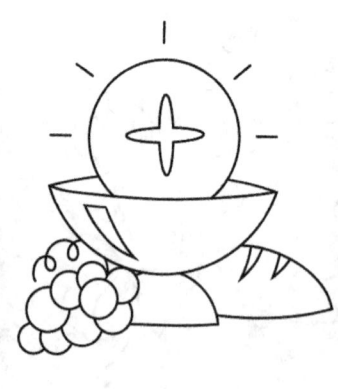

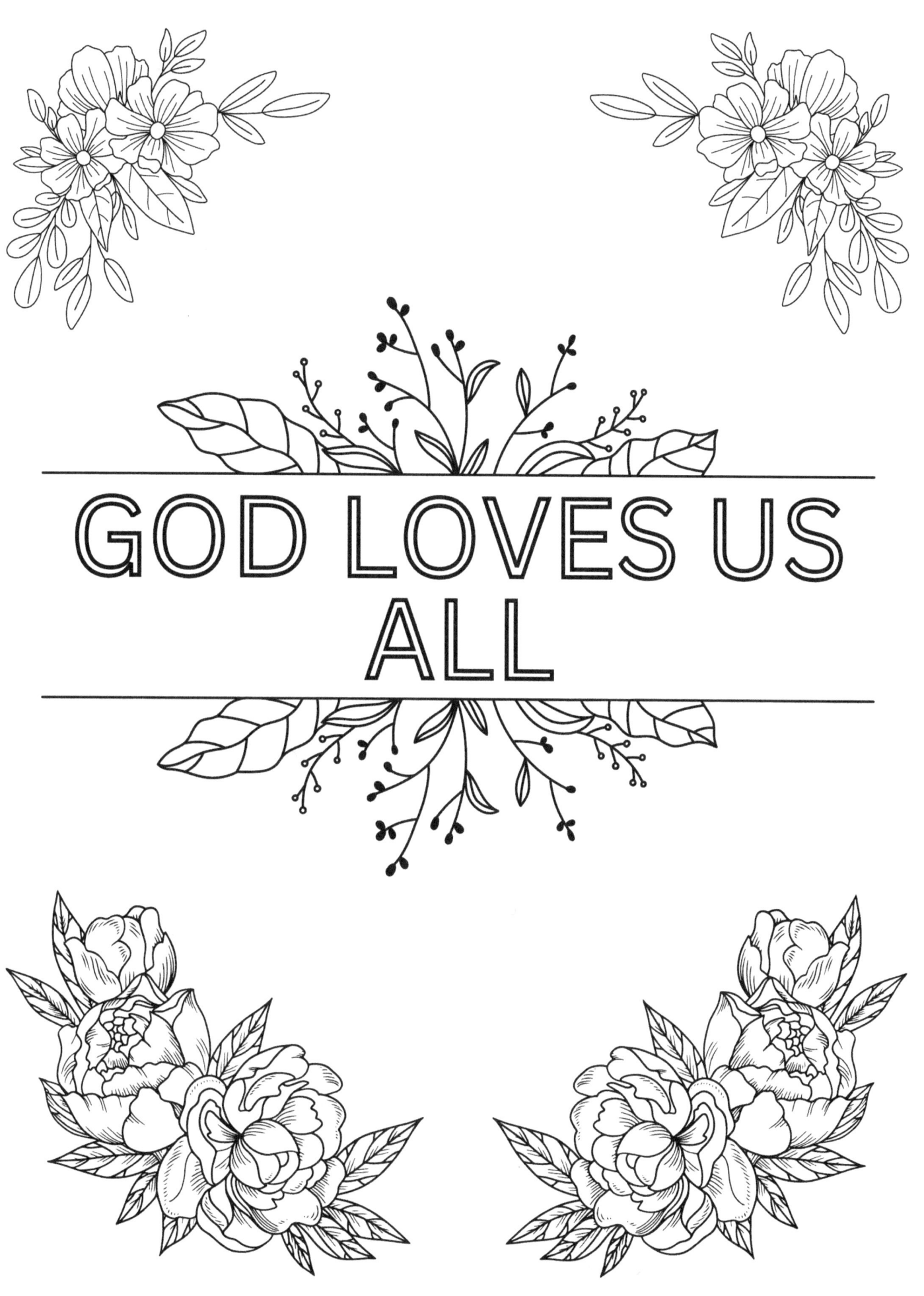

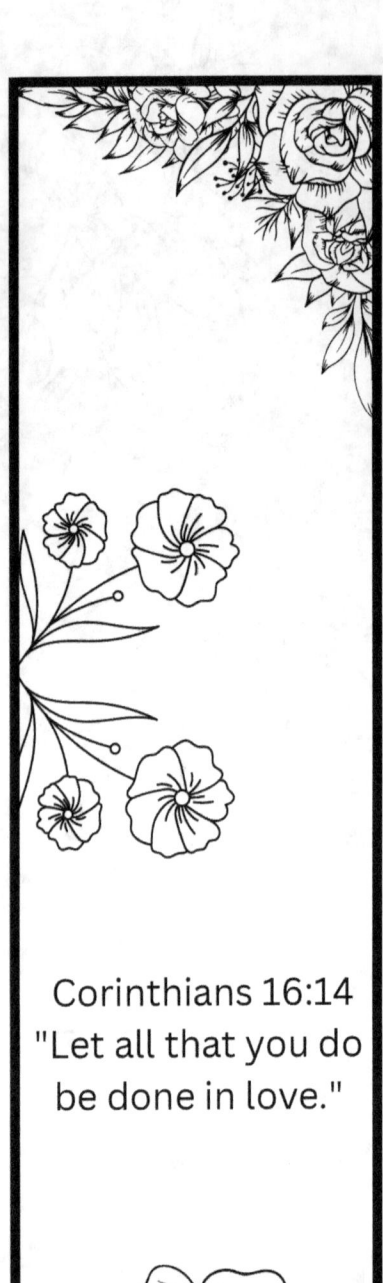
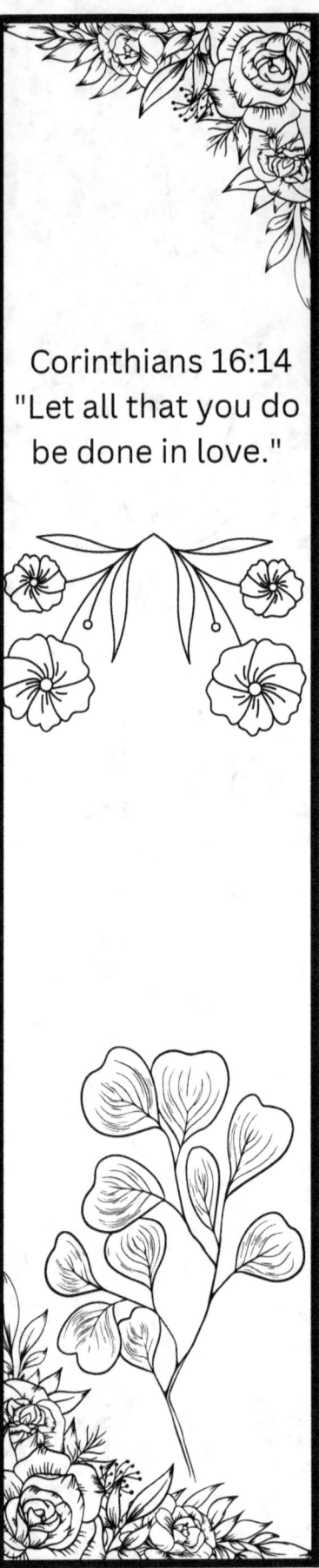
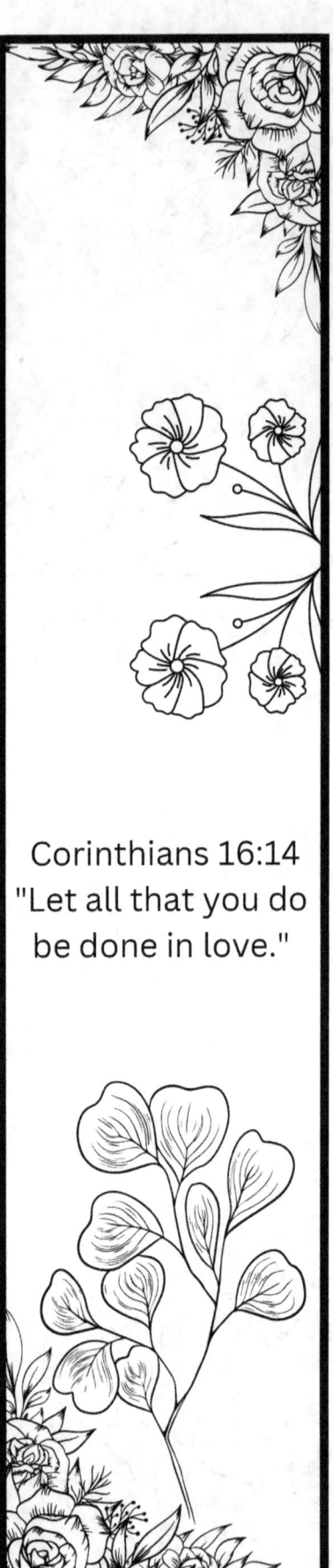

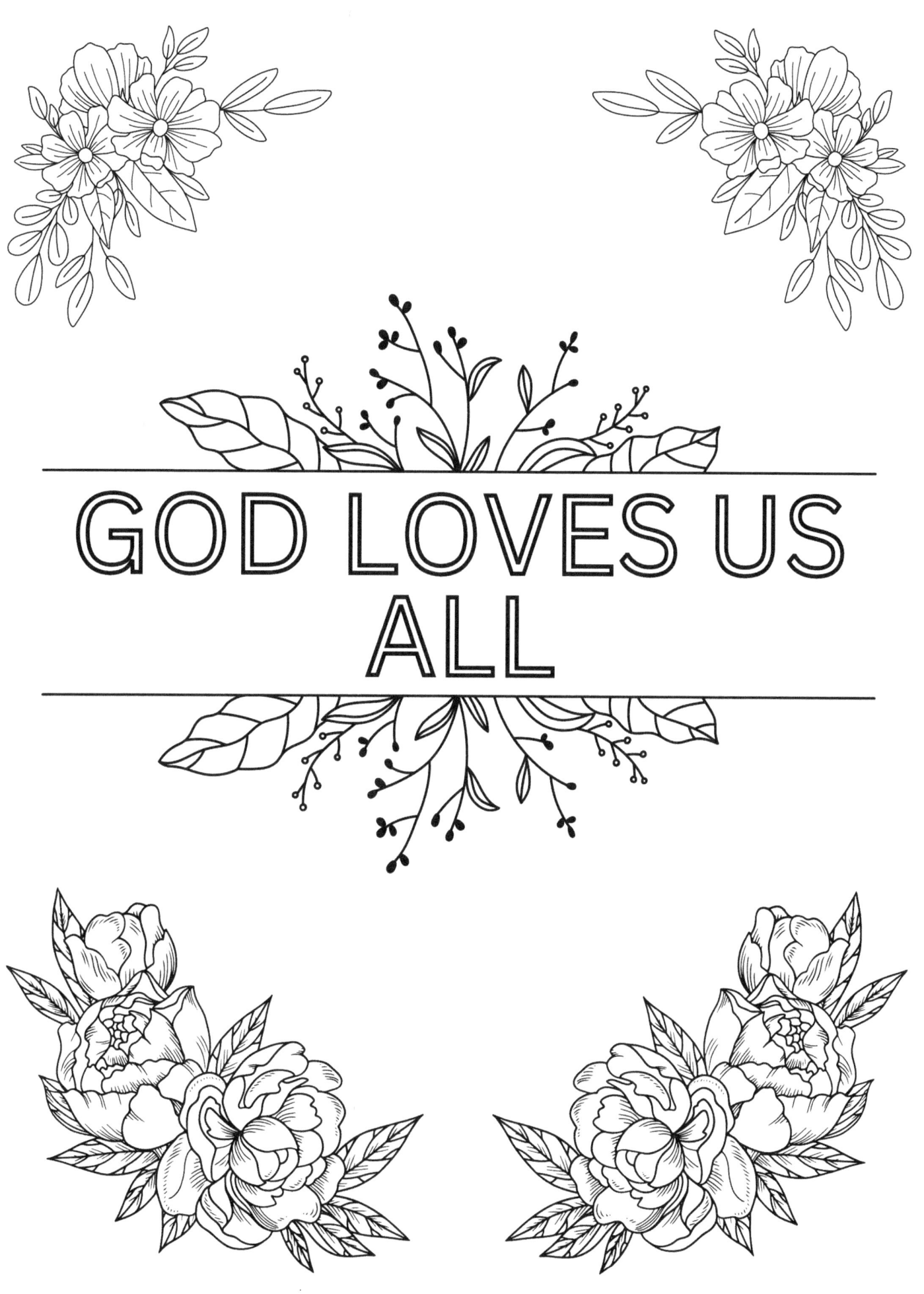

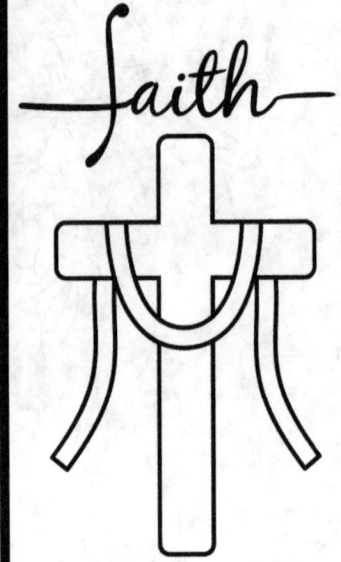

Philippians 4:13
"I can do all things through Christ who strengthens me."

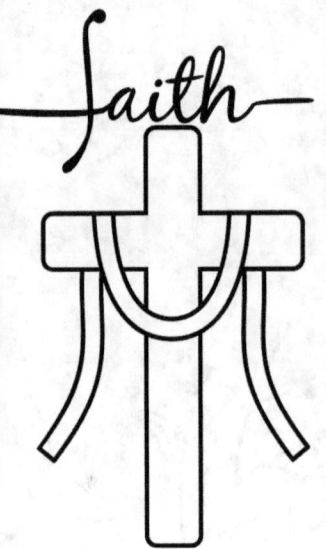

Philippians 4:13
"I can do all things through Christ who strengthens me."

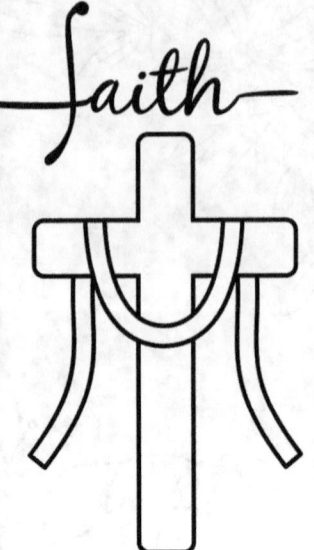

Philippians 4:13
"I can do all things through Christ who strengthens me."

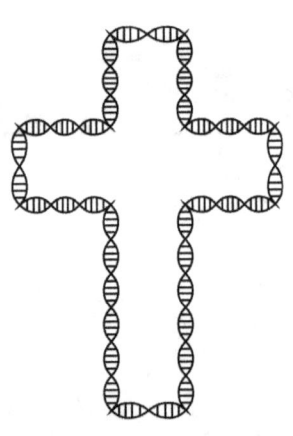
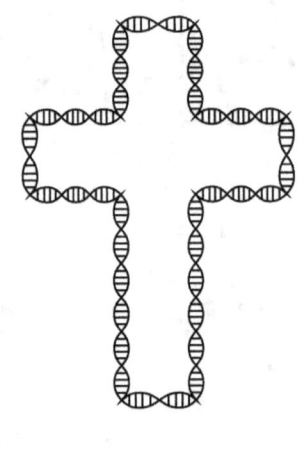
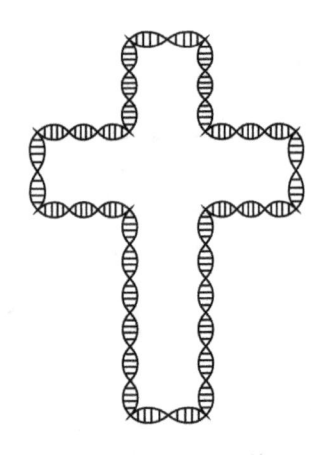

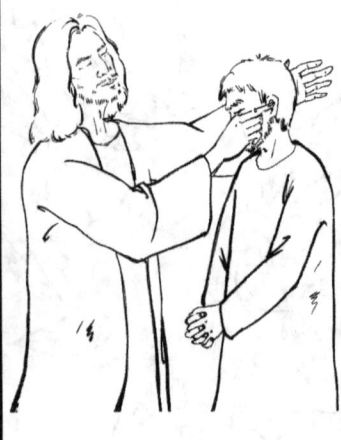
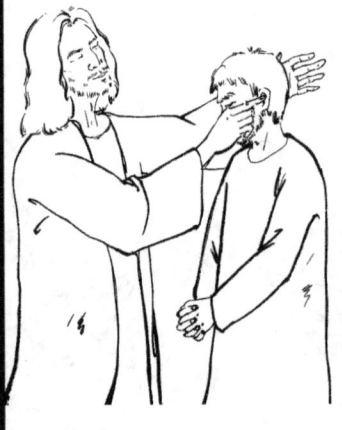
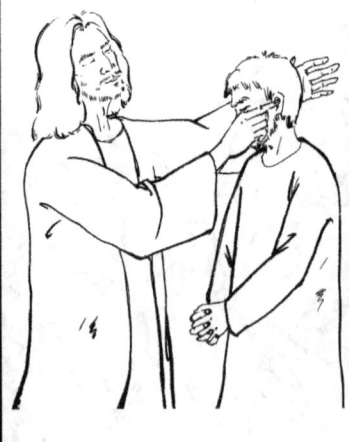

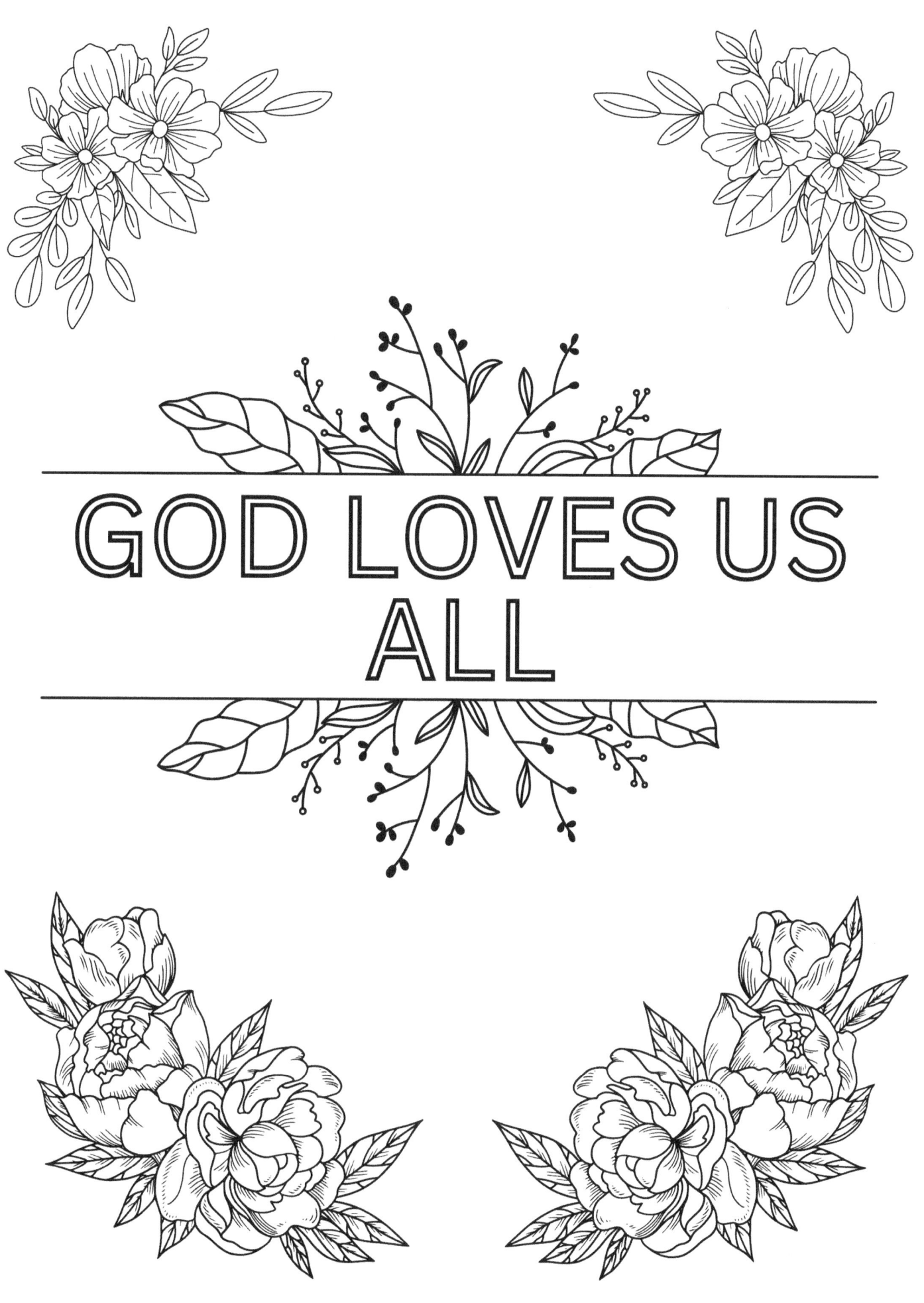

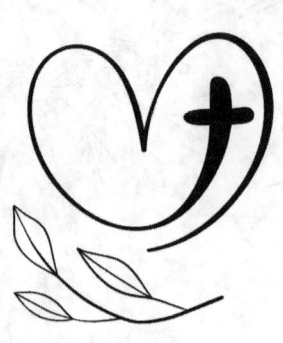
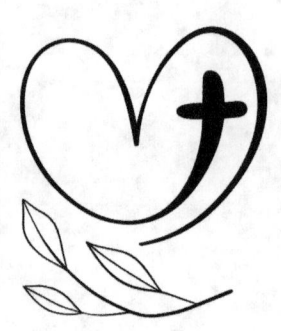
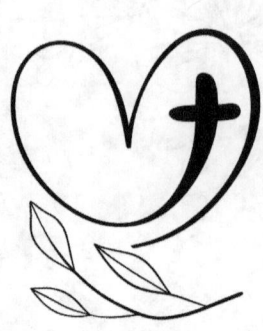

Romans 12:2
"Do not conform to the pattern of this world, but be transformed by the renewing of your mind."

Romans 12:2
"Do not conform to the pattern of this world, but be transformed by the renewing of your mind."

Romans 12:2
"Do not conform to the pattern of this world, but be transformed by the renewing of your mind."

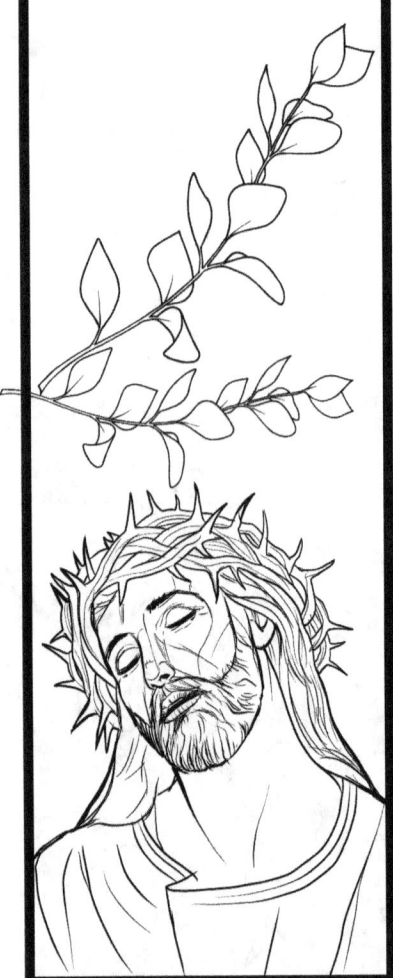
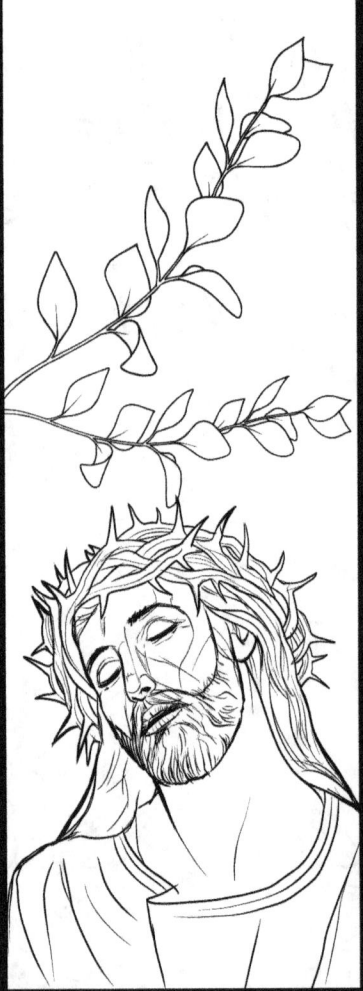
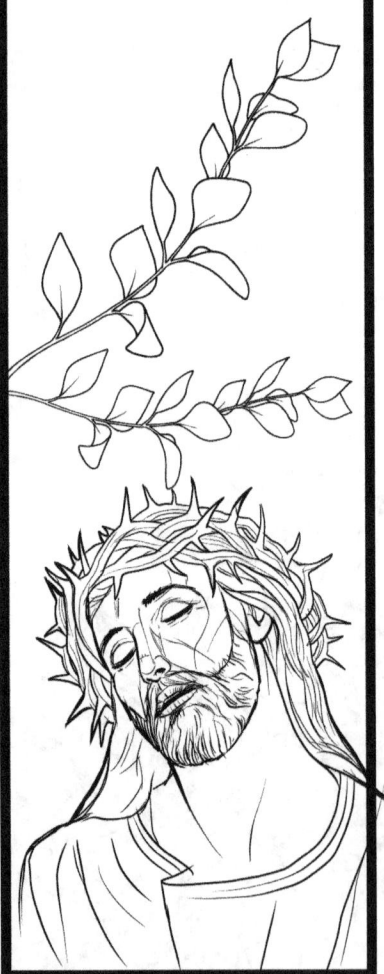

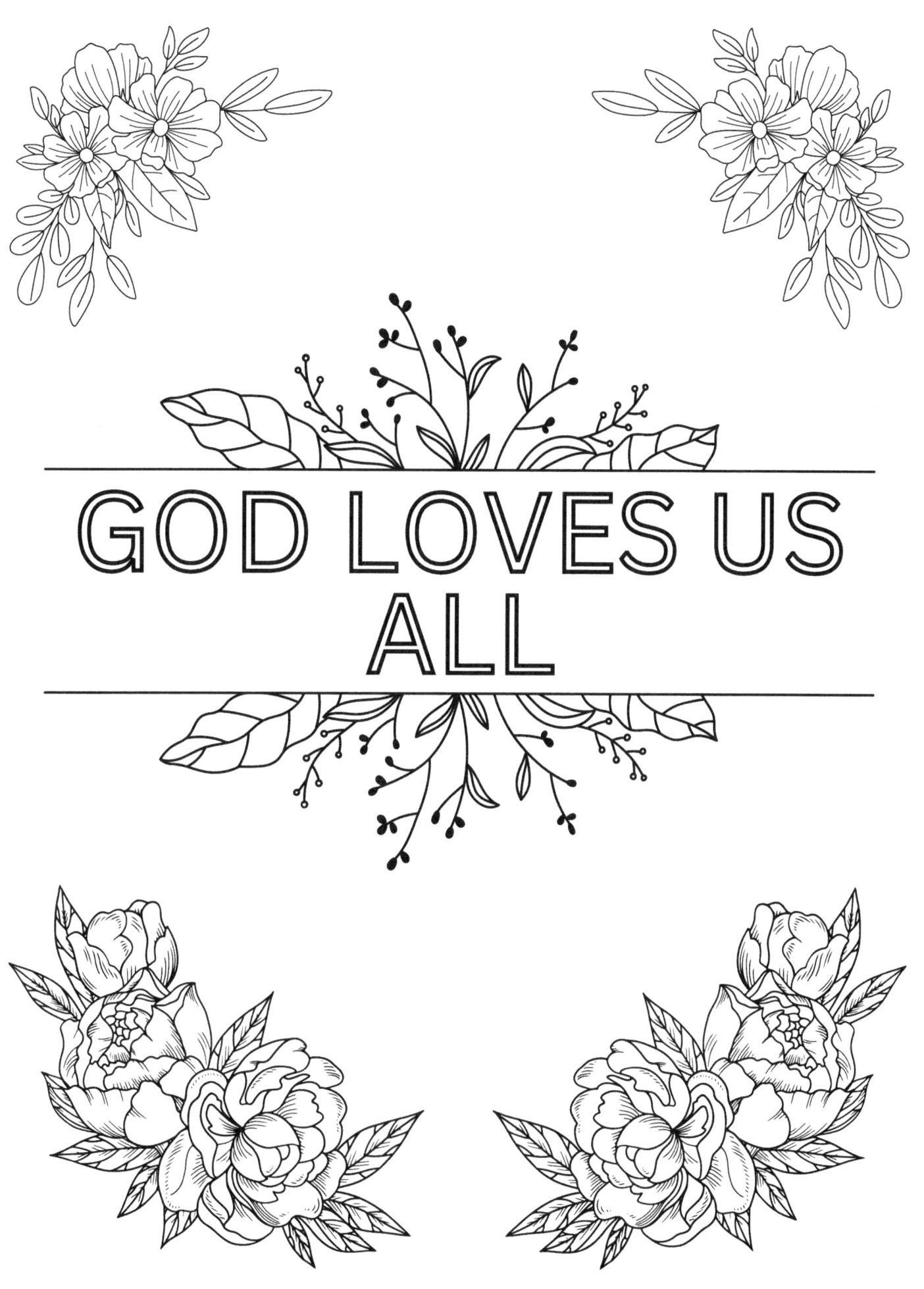

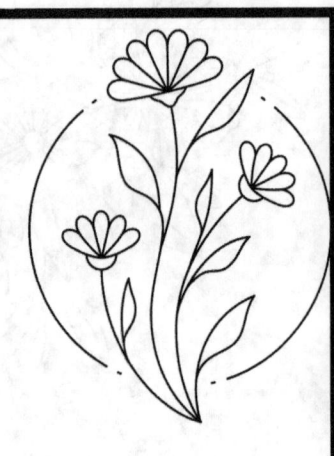 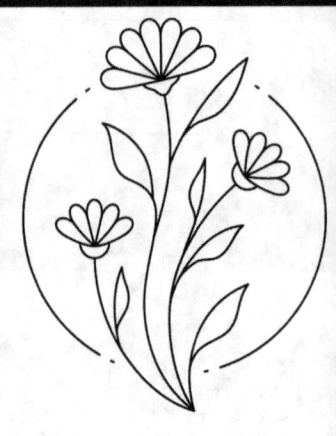 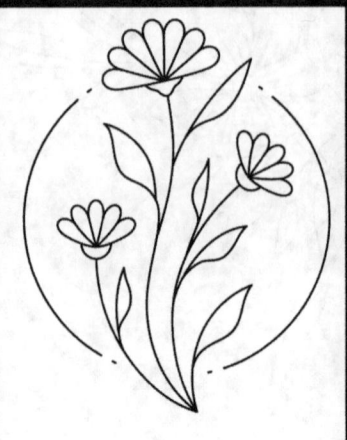

1 Corinthians 16:14** "Let all that you do be done in love."

1 Corinthians 16:14** "Let all that you do be done in love."

1 Corinthians 16:14** "Let all that you do be done in love."

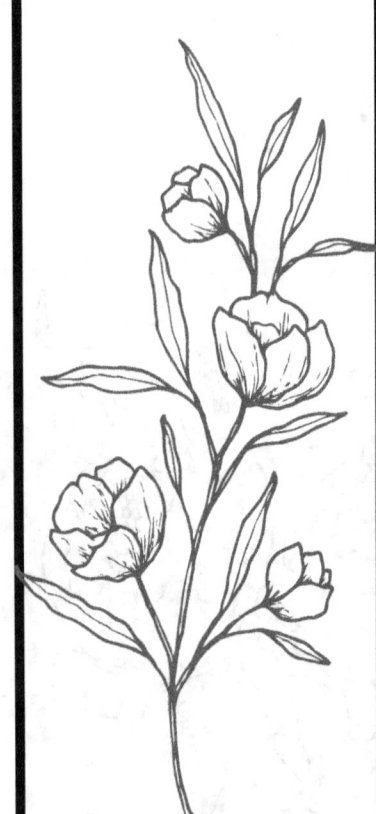 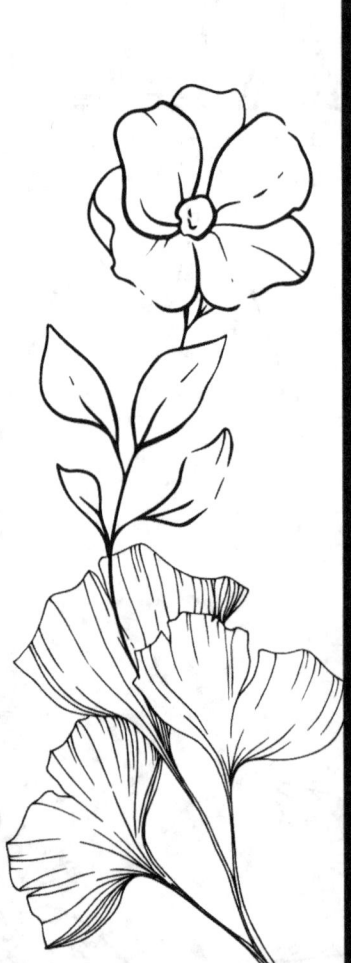 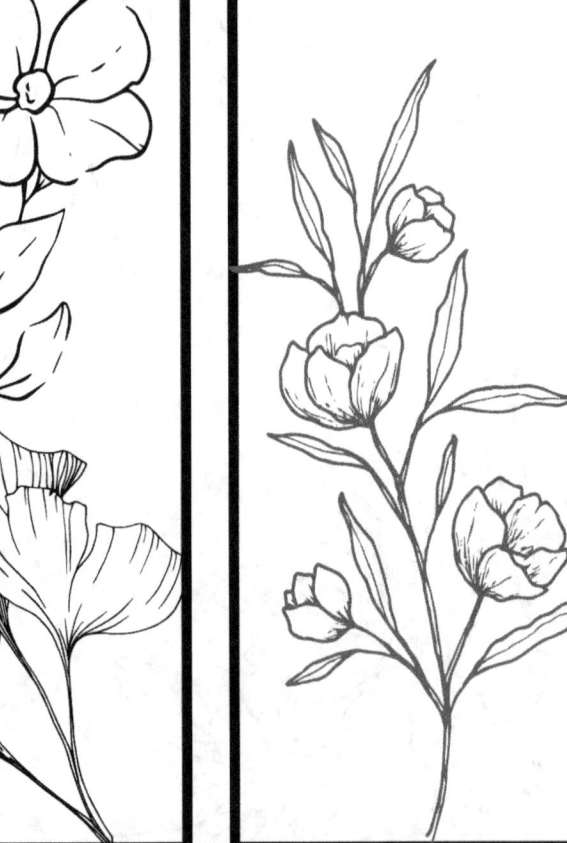

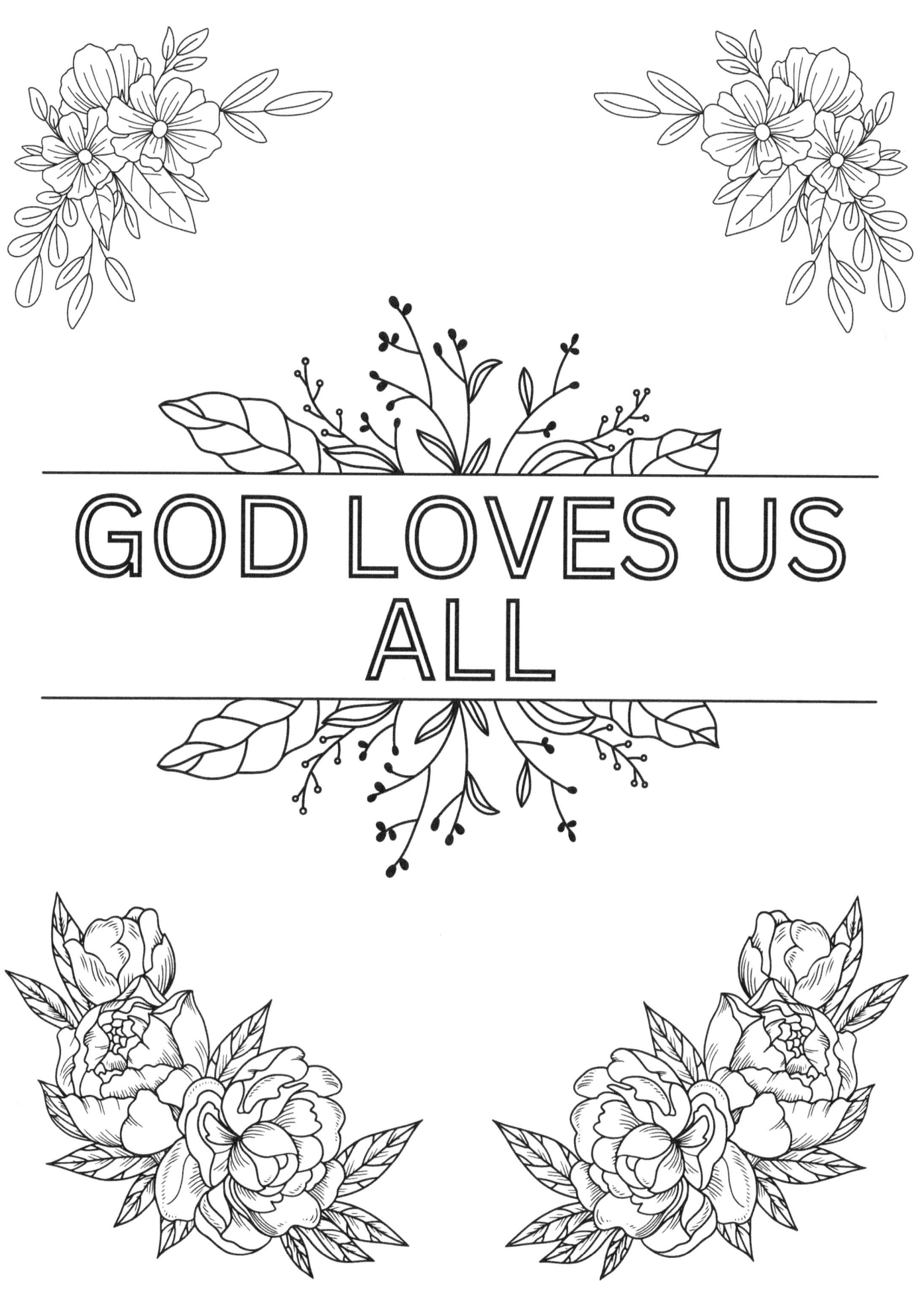

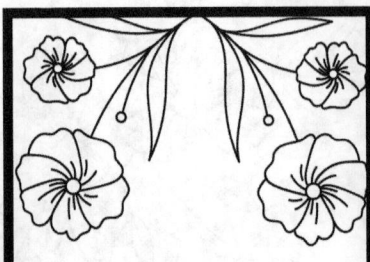 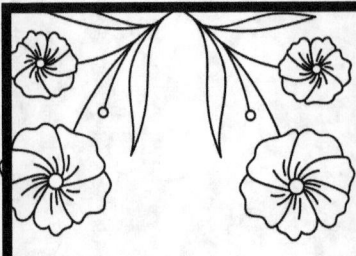 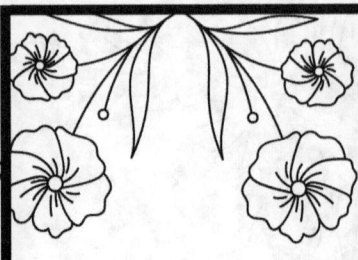

Matthew 19:26
"With man this is
impossible,
but with God all things
are possible."

Matthew 19:26
"With man this is
impossible,
but with God all things
are possible."

Matthew 19:26
"With man this is
impossible,
but with God all things
are possible."

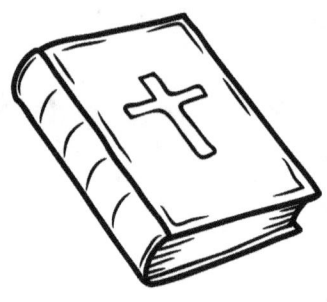  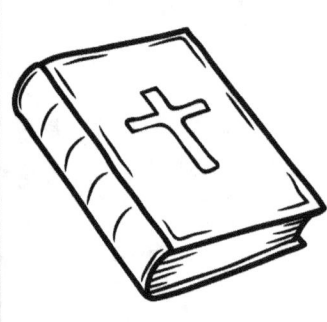

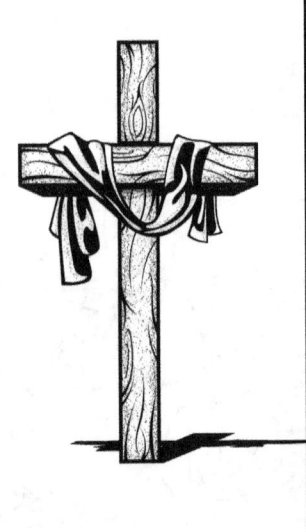 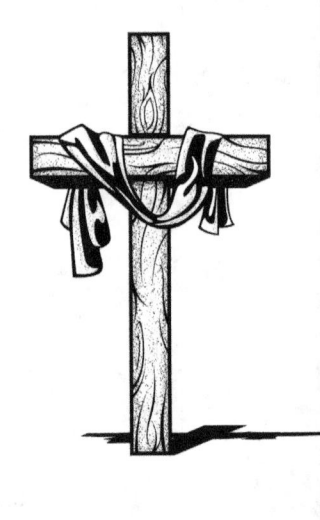 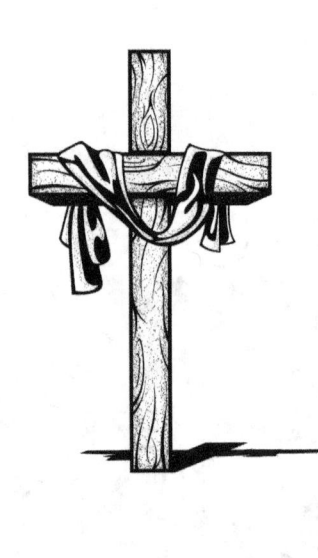

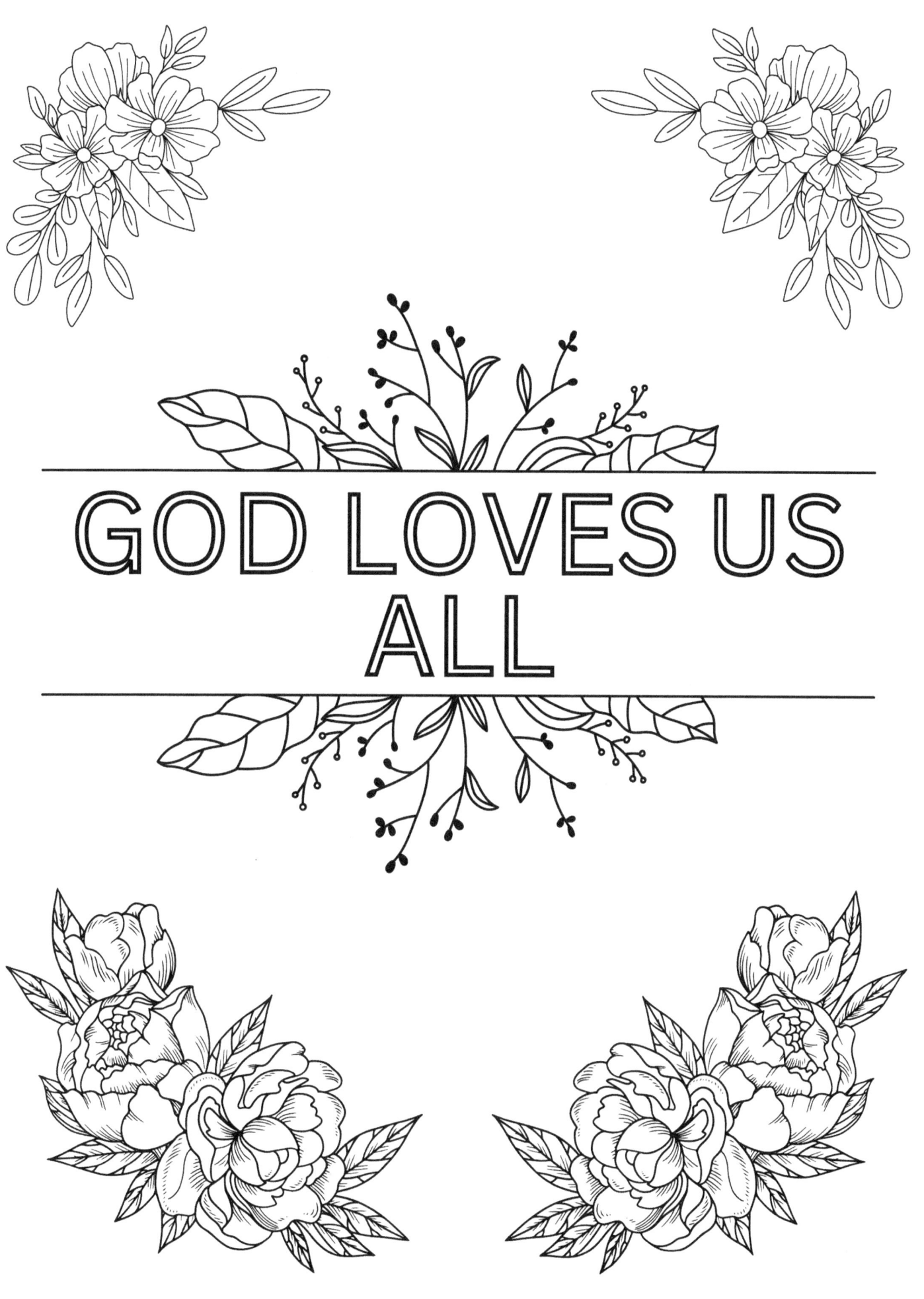

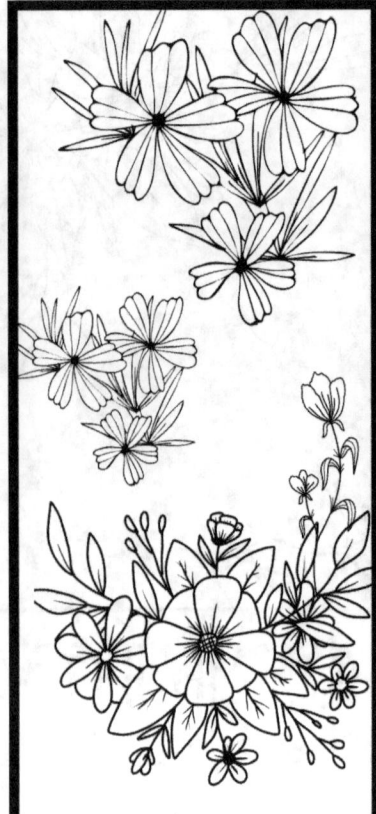
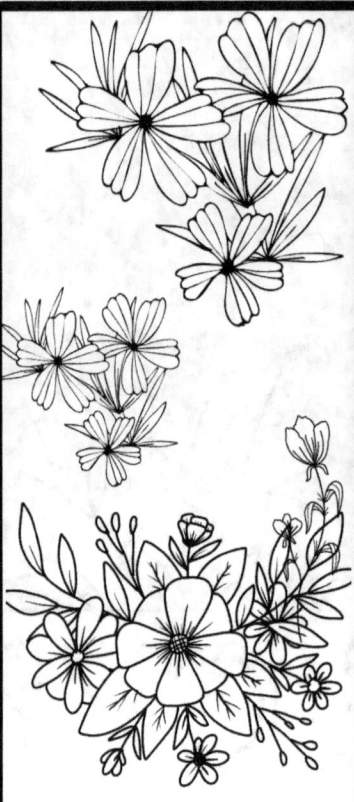
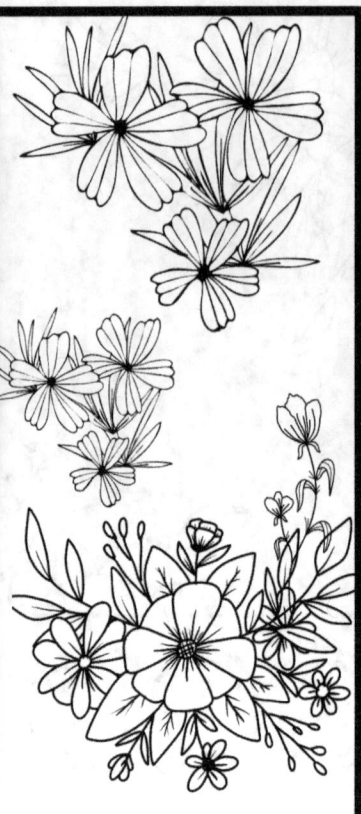

Luke 6:27-28
"But I say to you who hear, Love your enemies, do good to those who hate you, bless those who curse you, pray for those who abuse you."

Luke 6:27-28
"But I say to you who hear, Love your enemies, do good to those who hate you, bless those who curse you, pray for those who abuse you."

Luke 6:27-28
"But I say to you who hear, Love your enemies, do good to those who hate you, bless those who curse you, pray for those who abuse you."

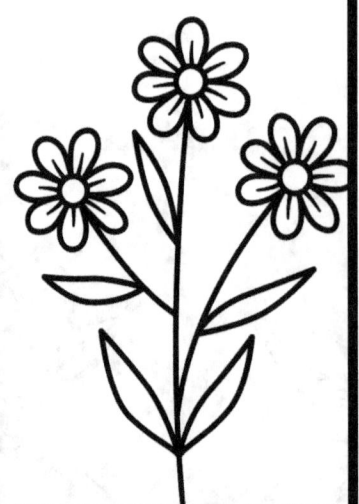

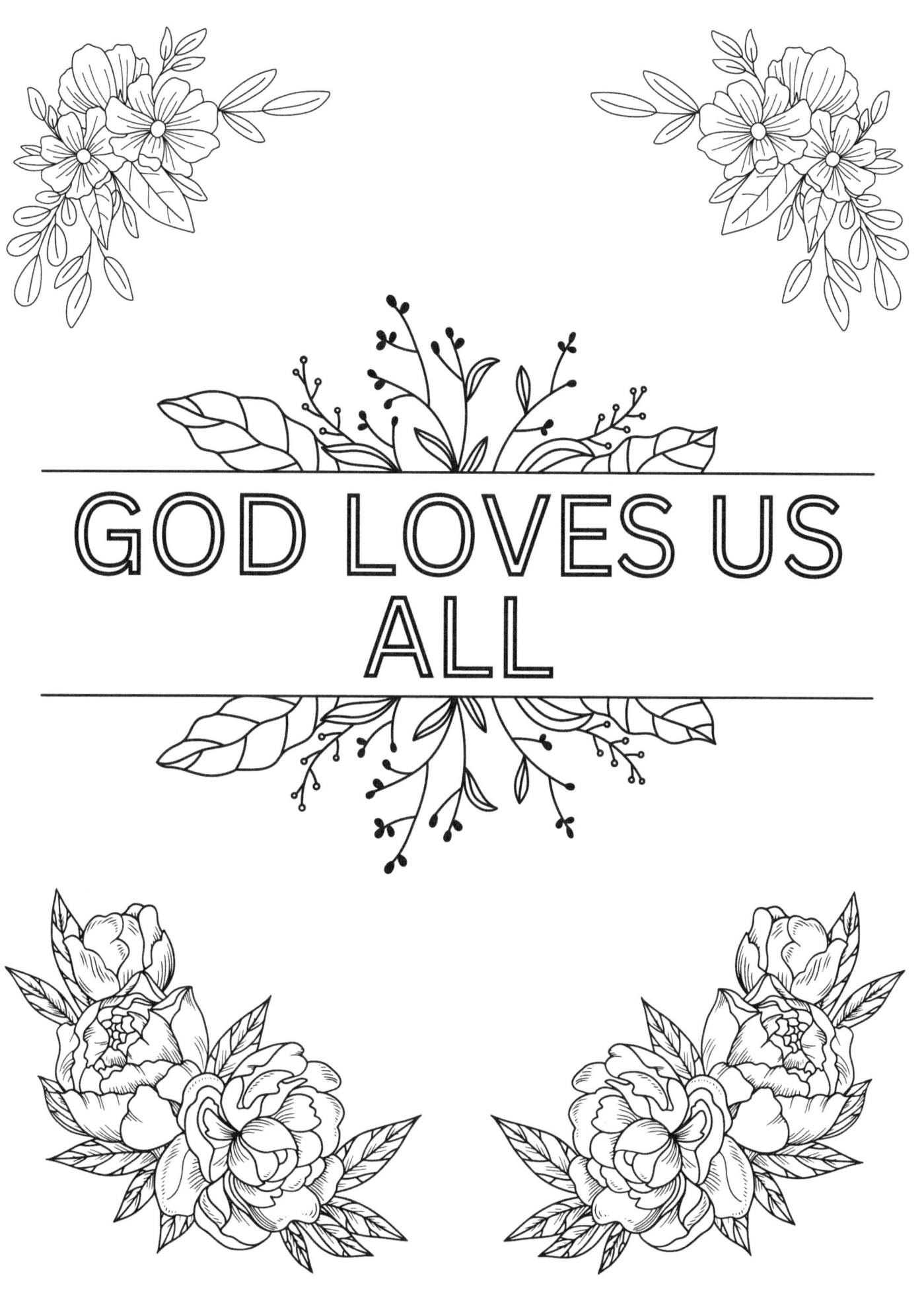

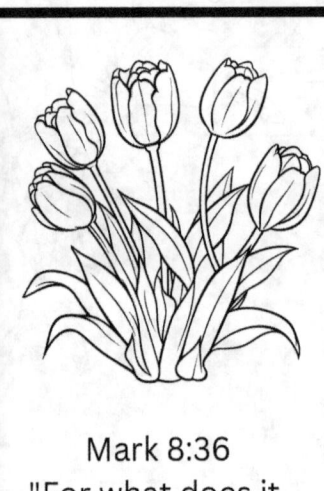
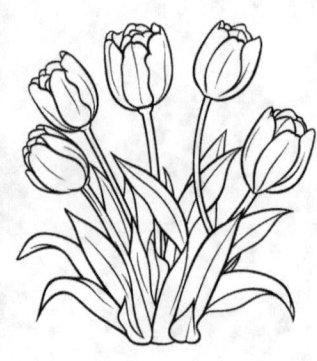
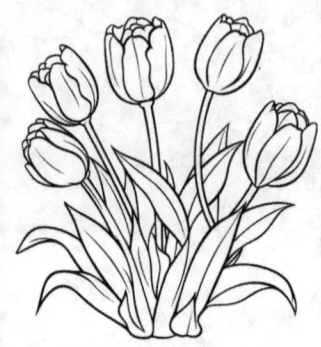

Mark 8:36
"For what does it profit a man to gain the whole world and forfeit his soul?"

Mark 8:36
"For what does it profit a man to gain the whole world and forfeit his soul?"

Mark 8:36
"For what does it profit a man to gain the whole world and forfeit his soul?"

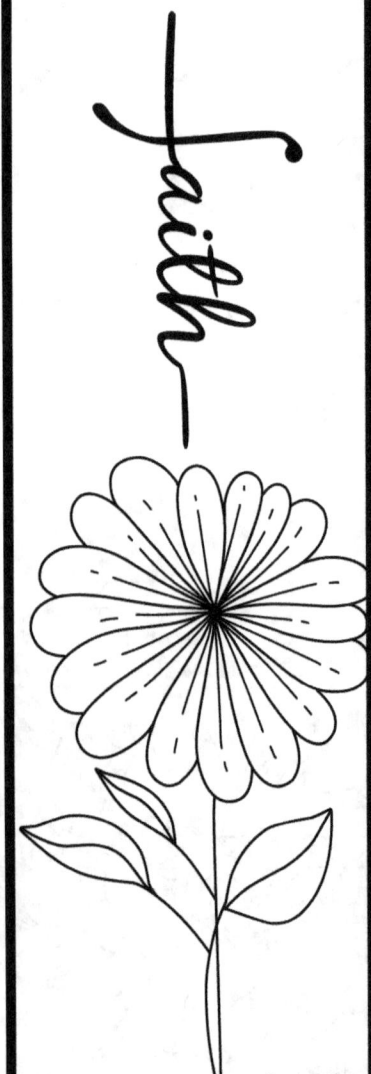
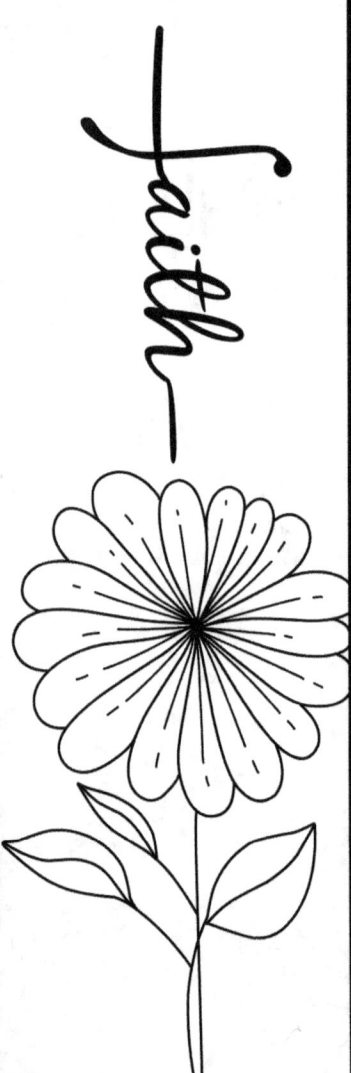
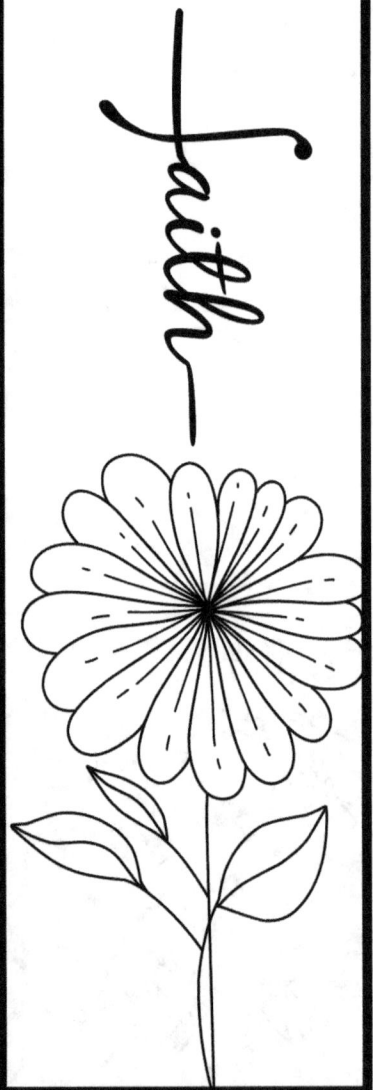

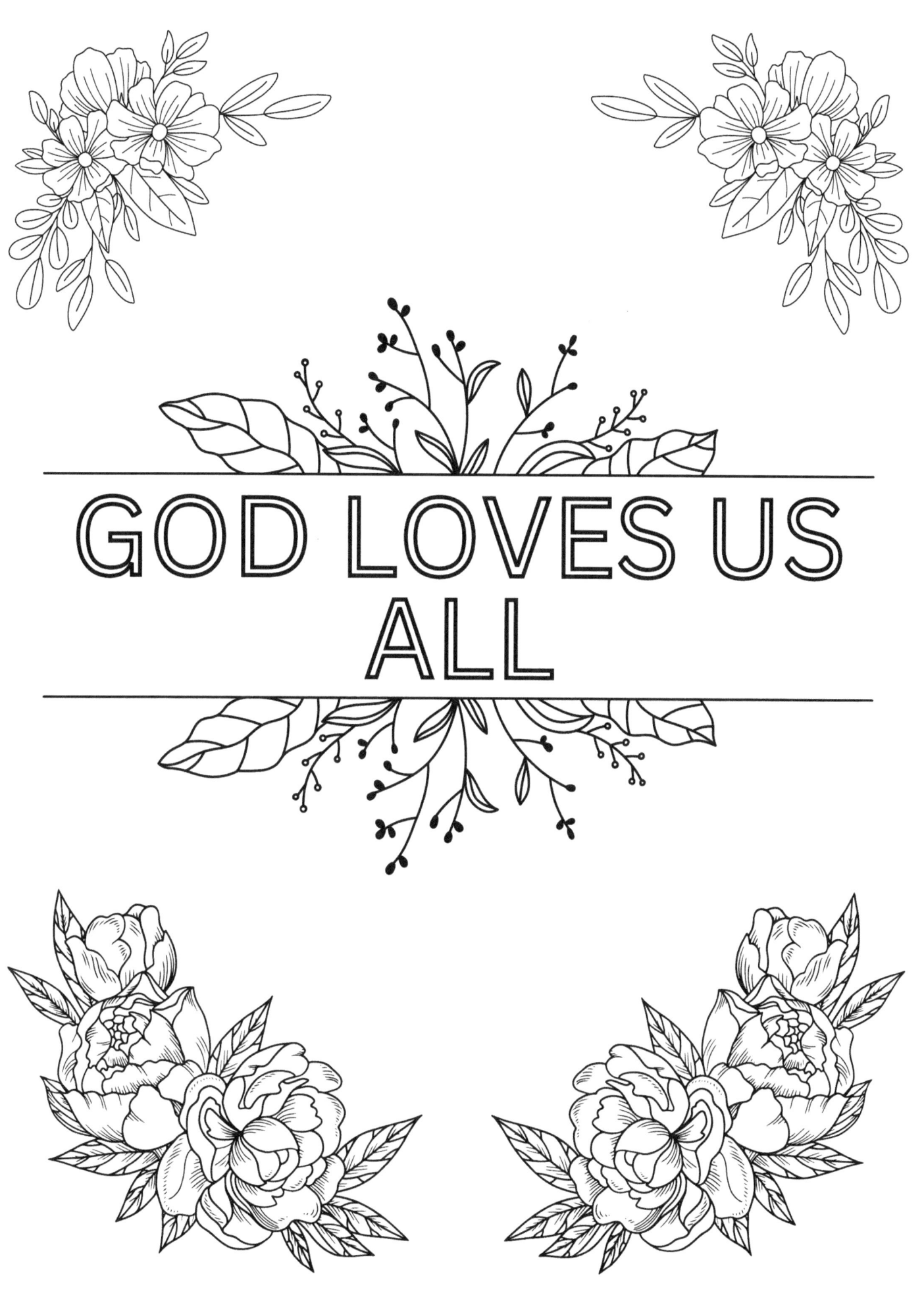

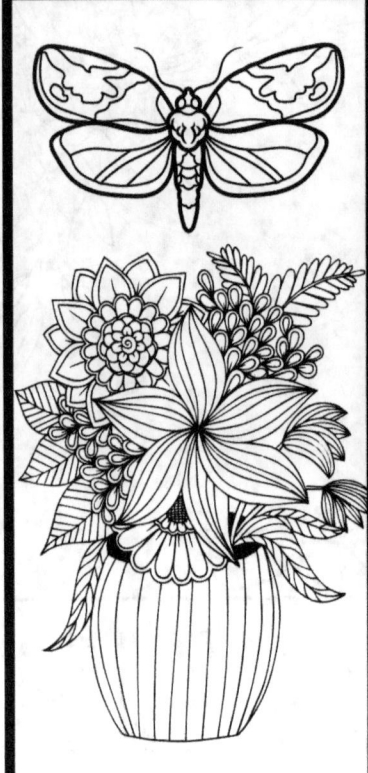
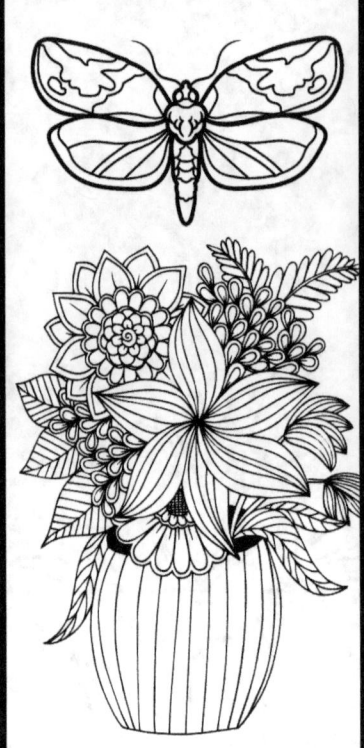
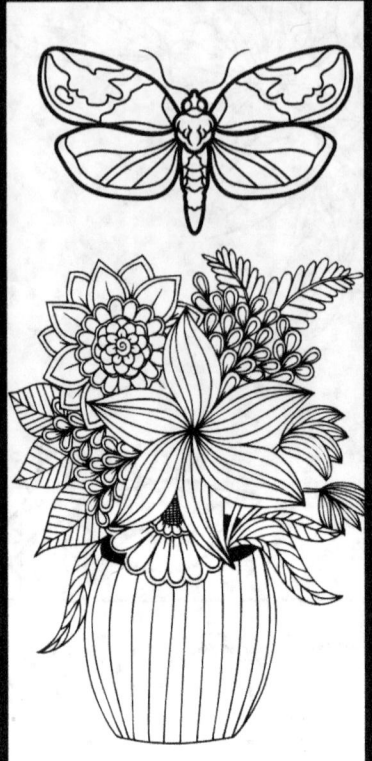

John 8:12
"I am the light of the world. Whoever follows me will not walk in darkness, but will have the light of life."

John 8:12
"I am the light of the world. Whoever follows me will not walk in darkness, but will have the light of life."

John 8:12
"I am the light of the world. Whoever follows me will not walk in darkness, but will have the light of life."

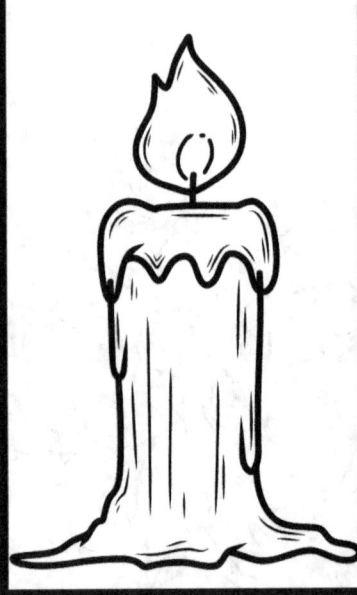
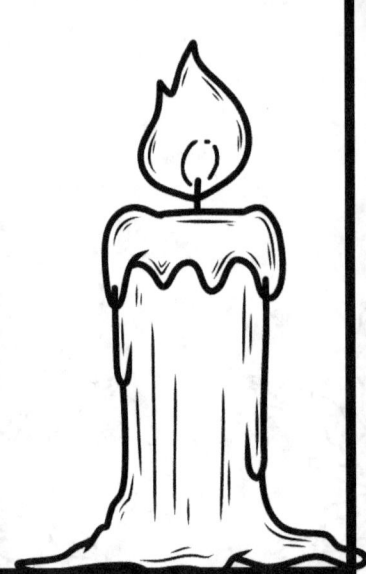
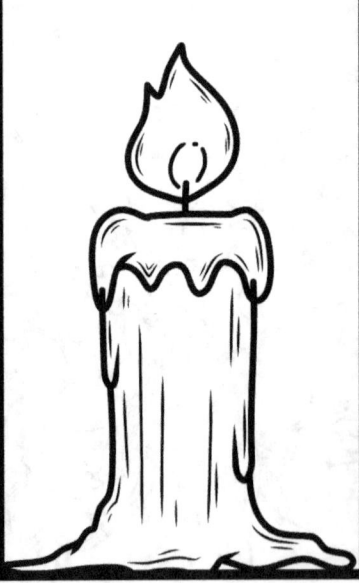

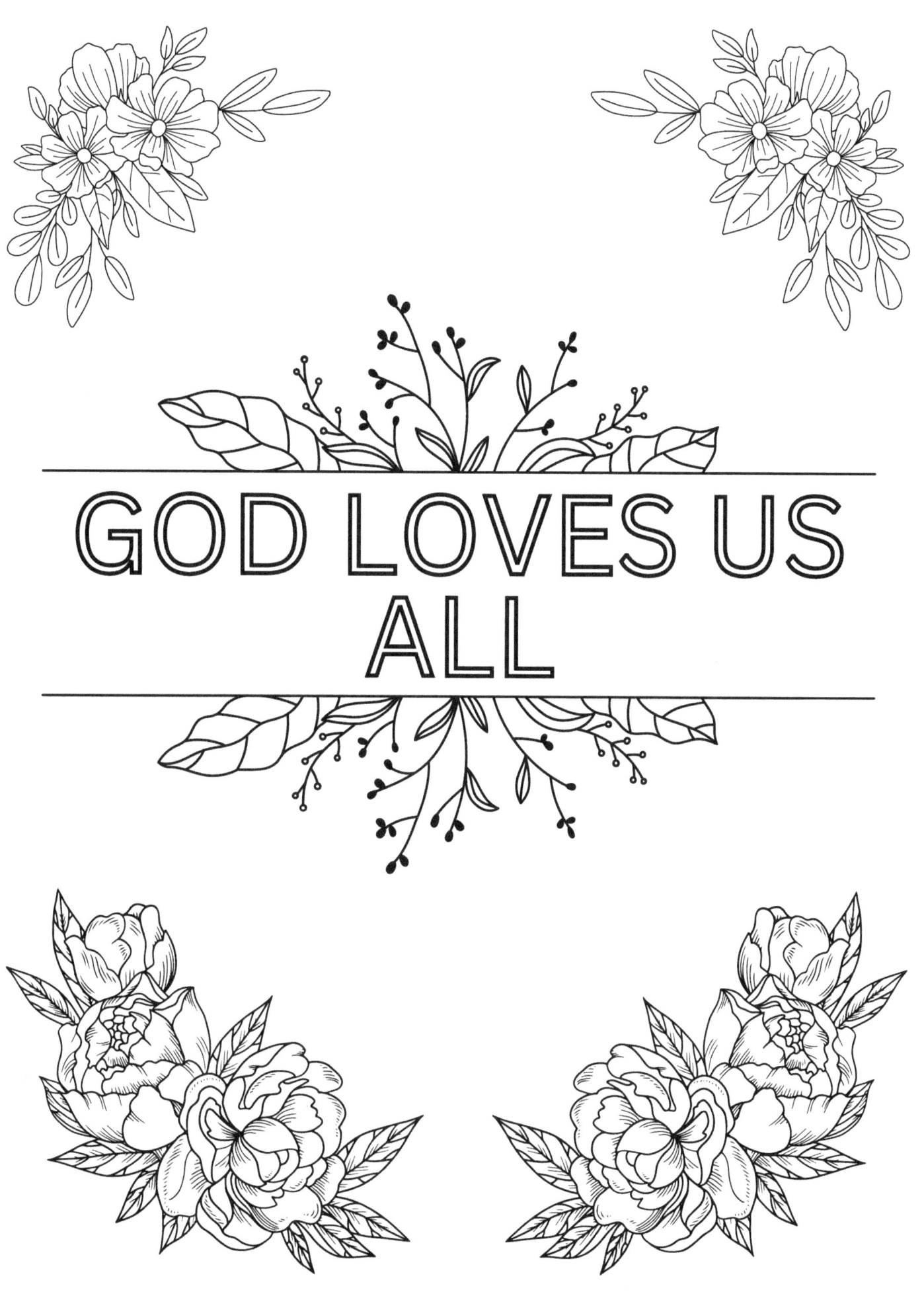

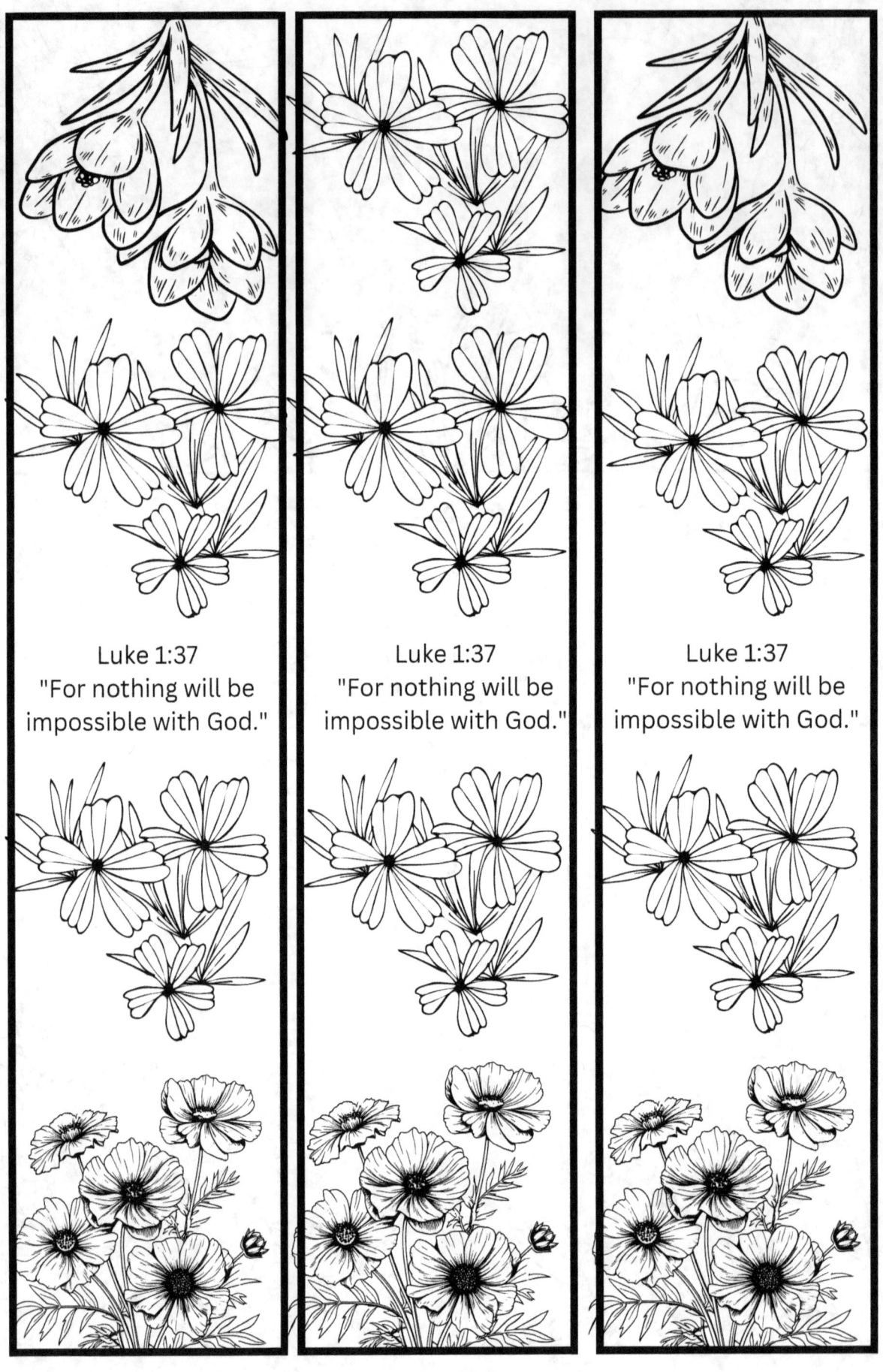

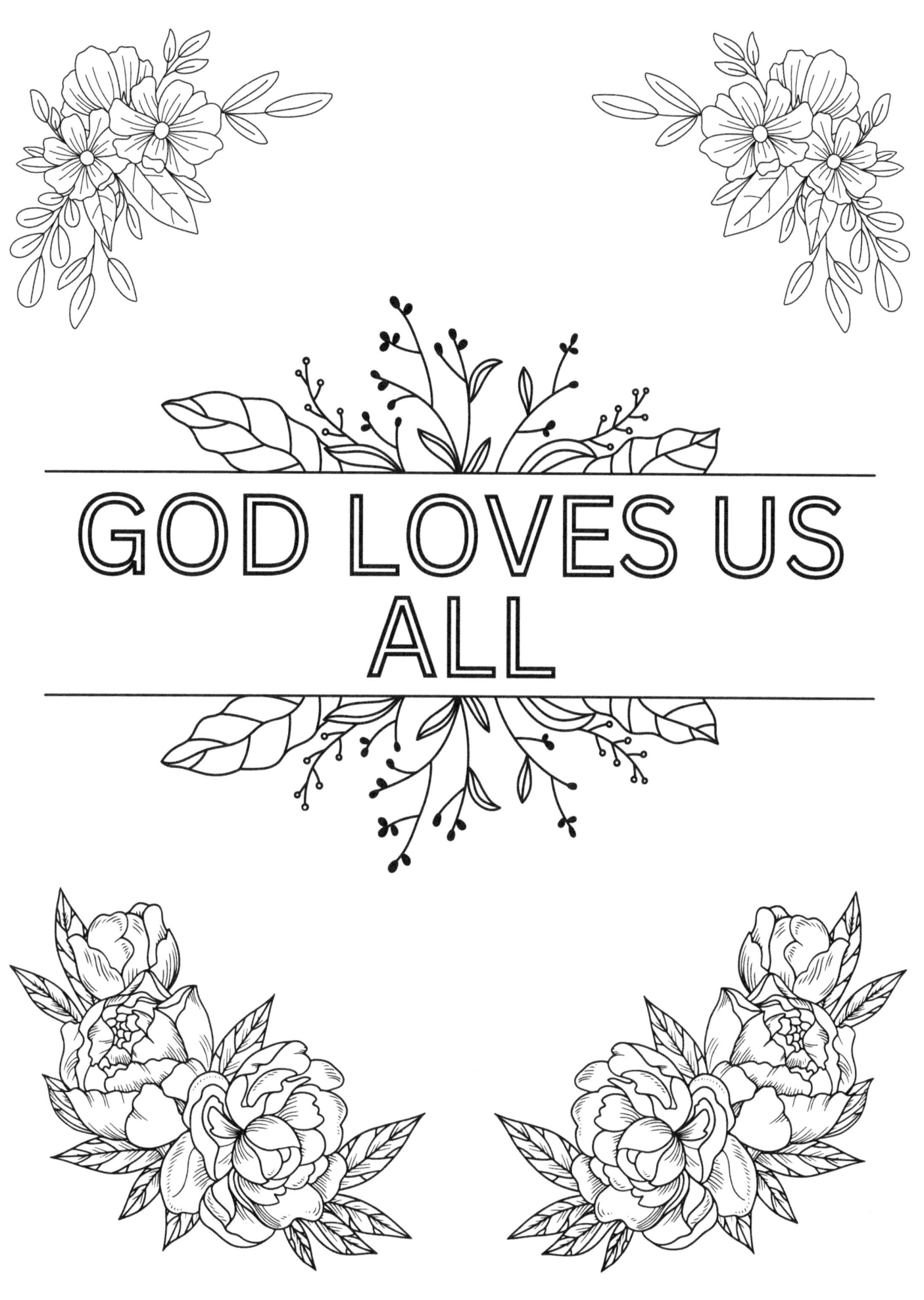

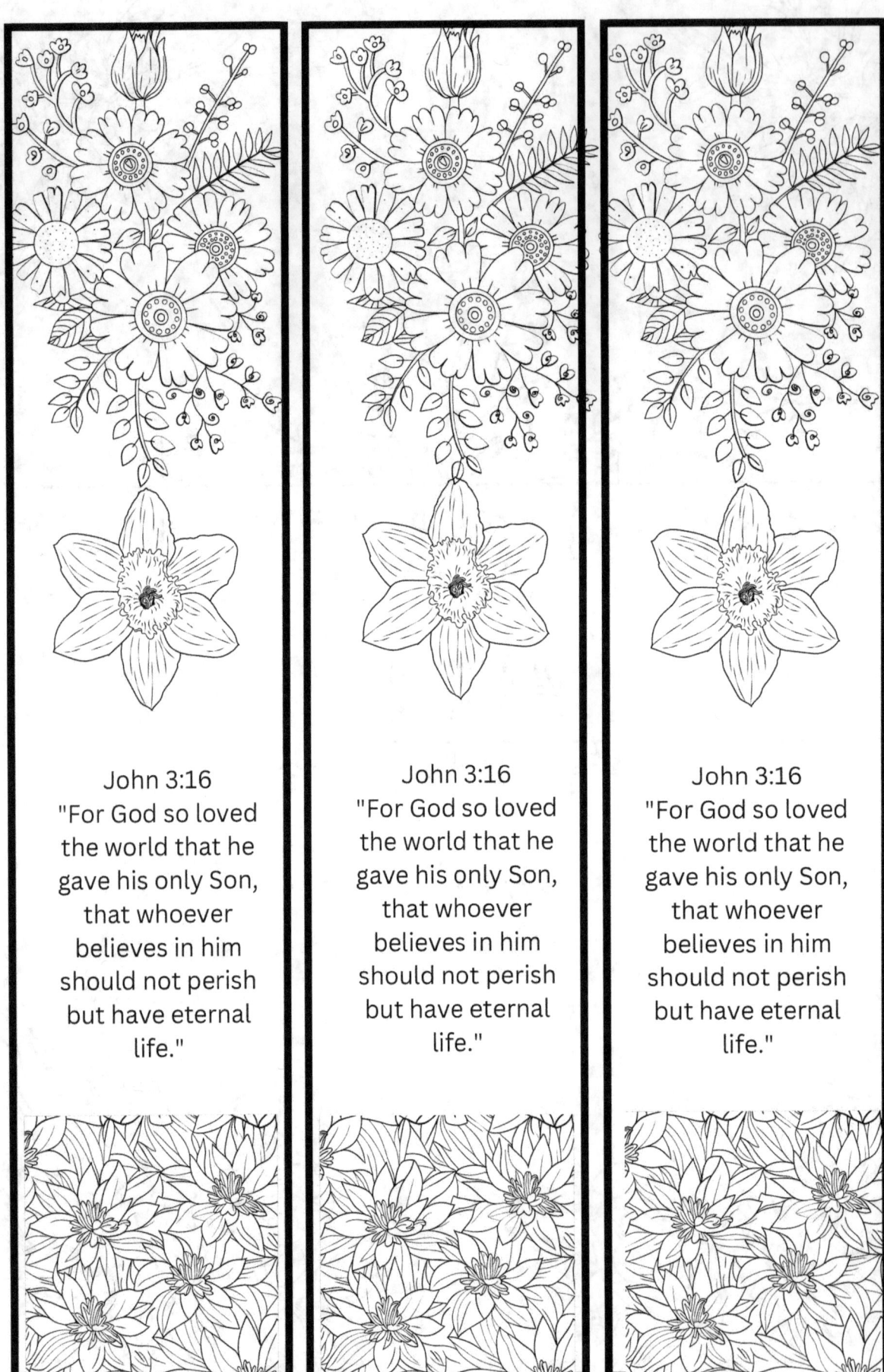

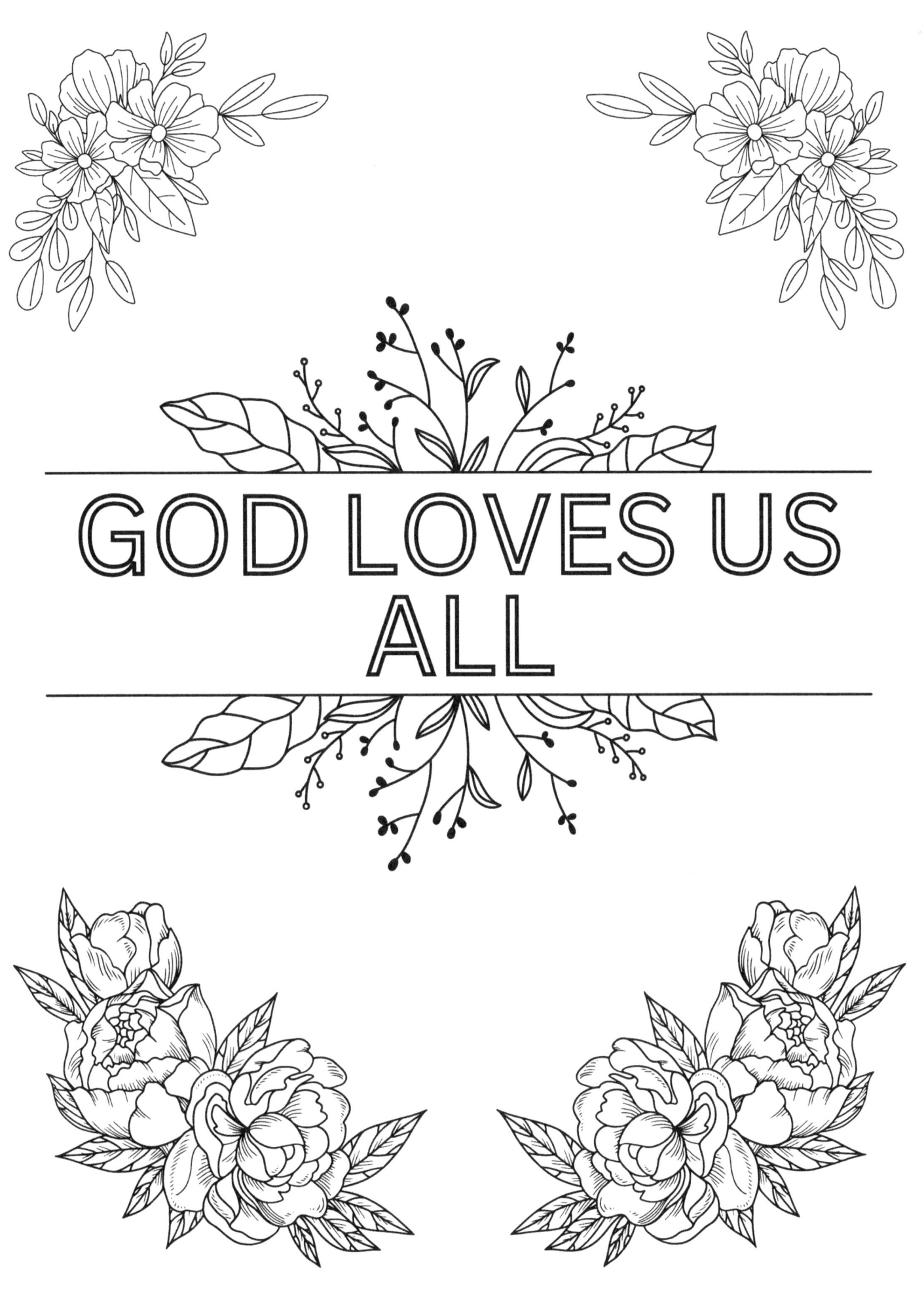

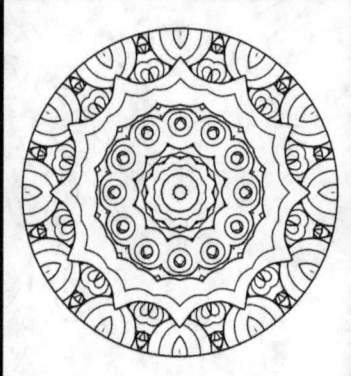 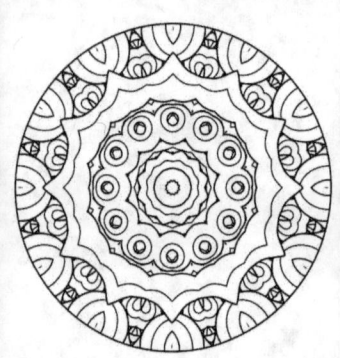 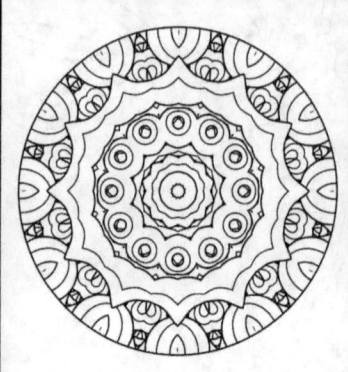

John 1:1
"In the beginning was the Word, and the Word was with God, and the Word was God."

John 1:1
"In the beginning was the Word, and the Word was with God, and the Word was God."

John 1:1
"In the beginning was the Word, and the Word was with God, and the Word was God."

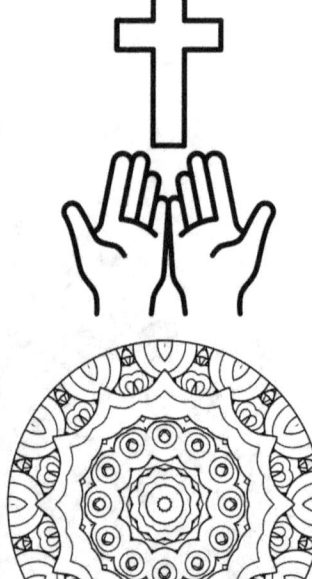 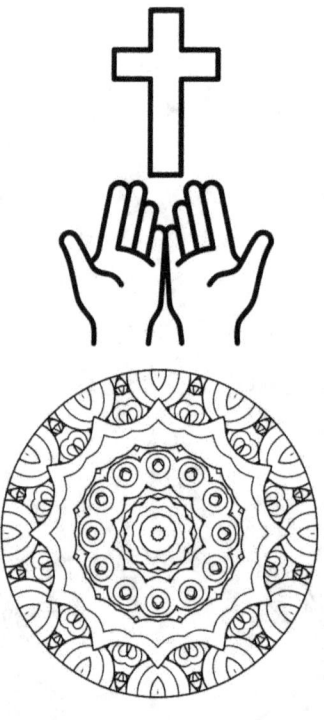 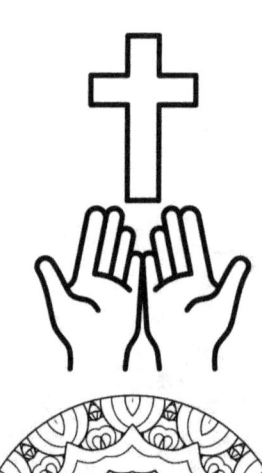

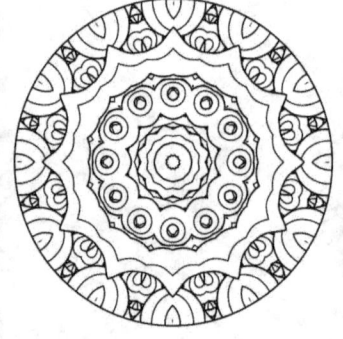

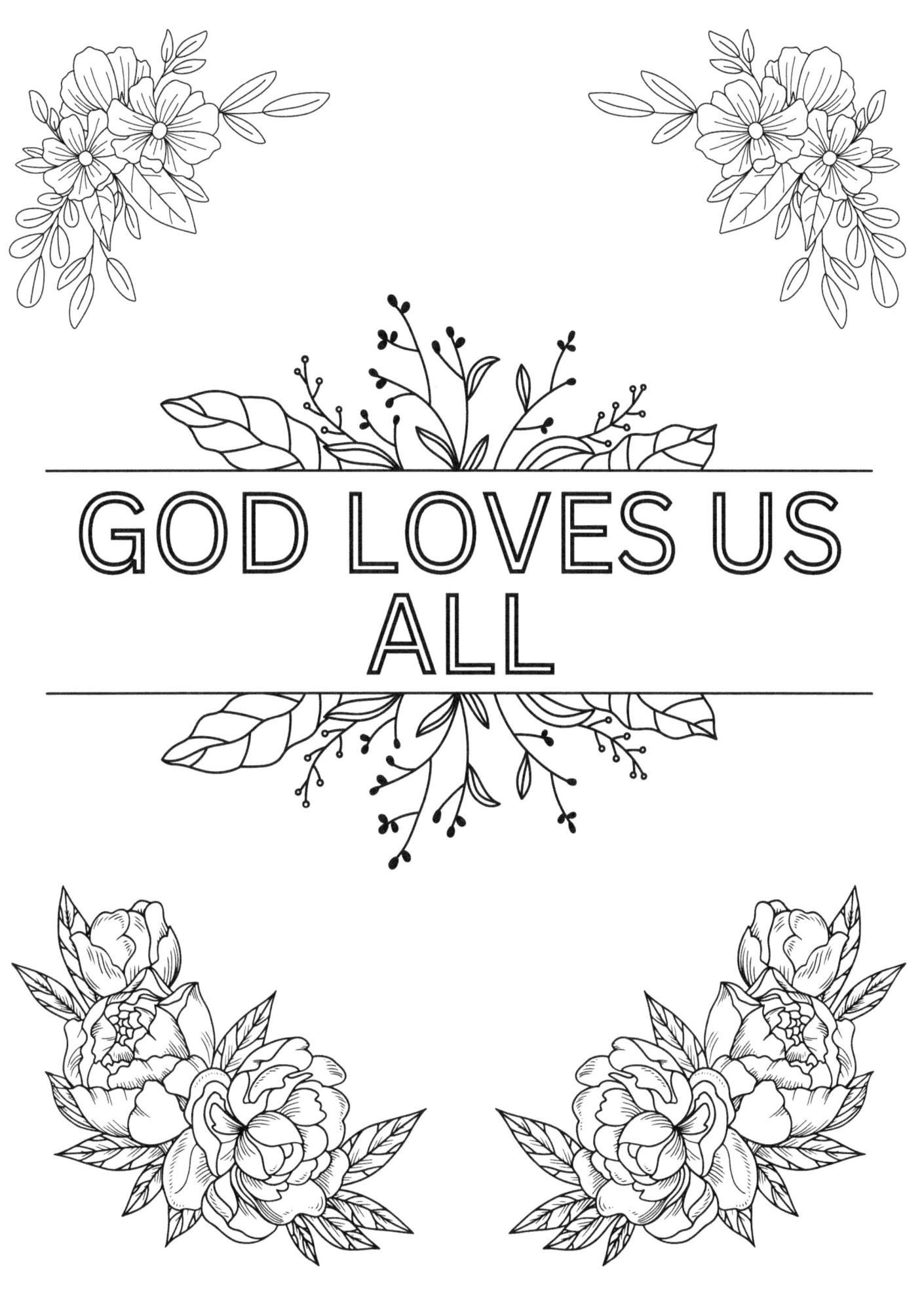

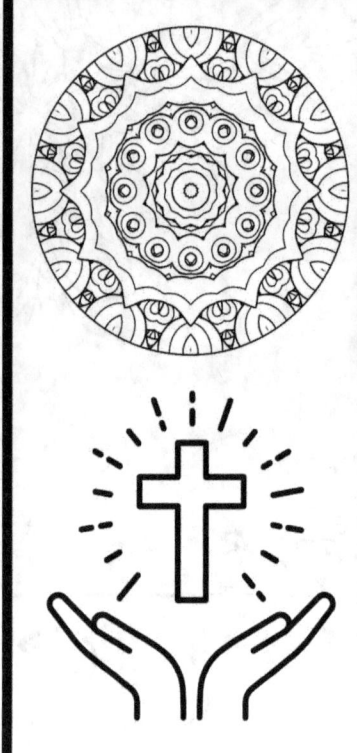
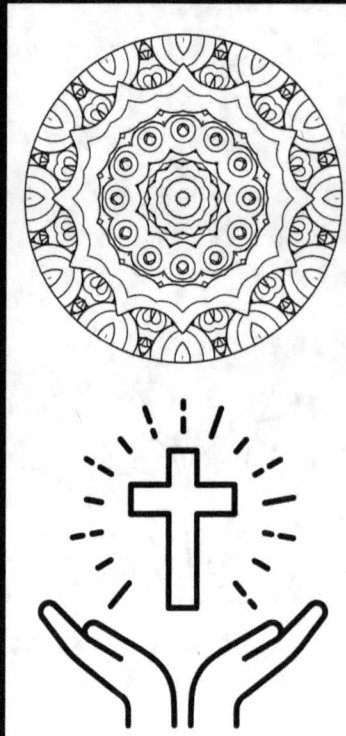
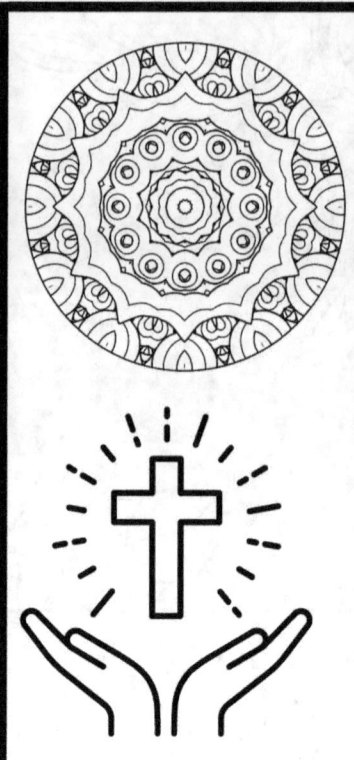

John 8:12 I am the light of the world. Whoever follows me will not walk in darkness, but will have the light of life."

John 8:12 I am the light of the world. Whoever follows me will not walk in darkness, but will have the light of life."

John 8:12 I am the light of the world. Whoever follows me will not walk in darkness, but will have the light of life."

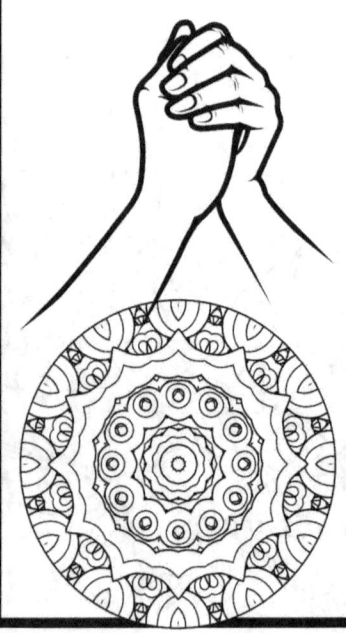
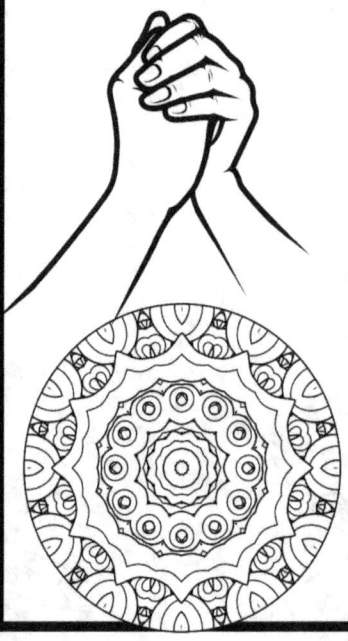
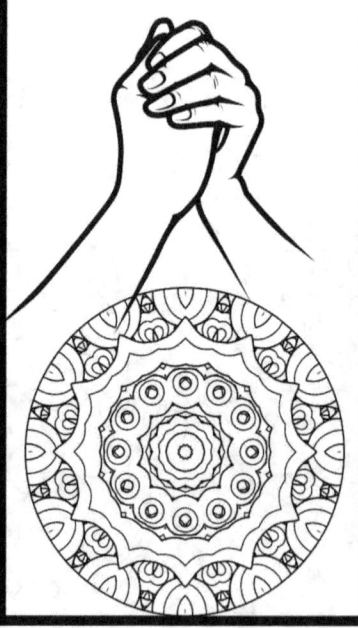

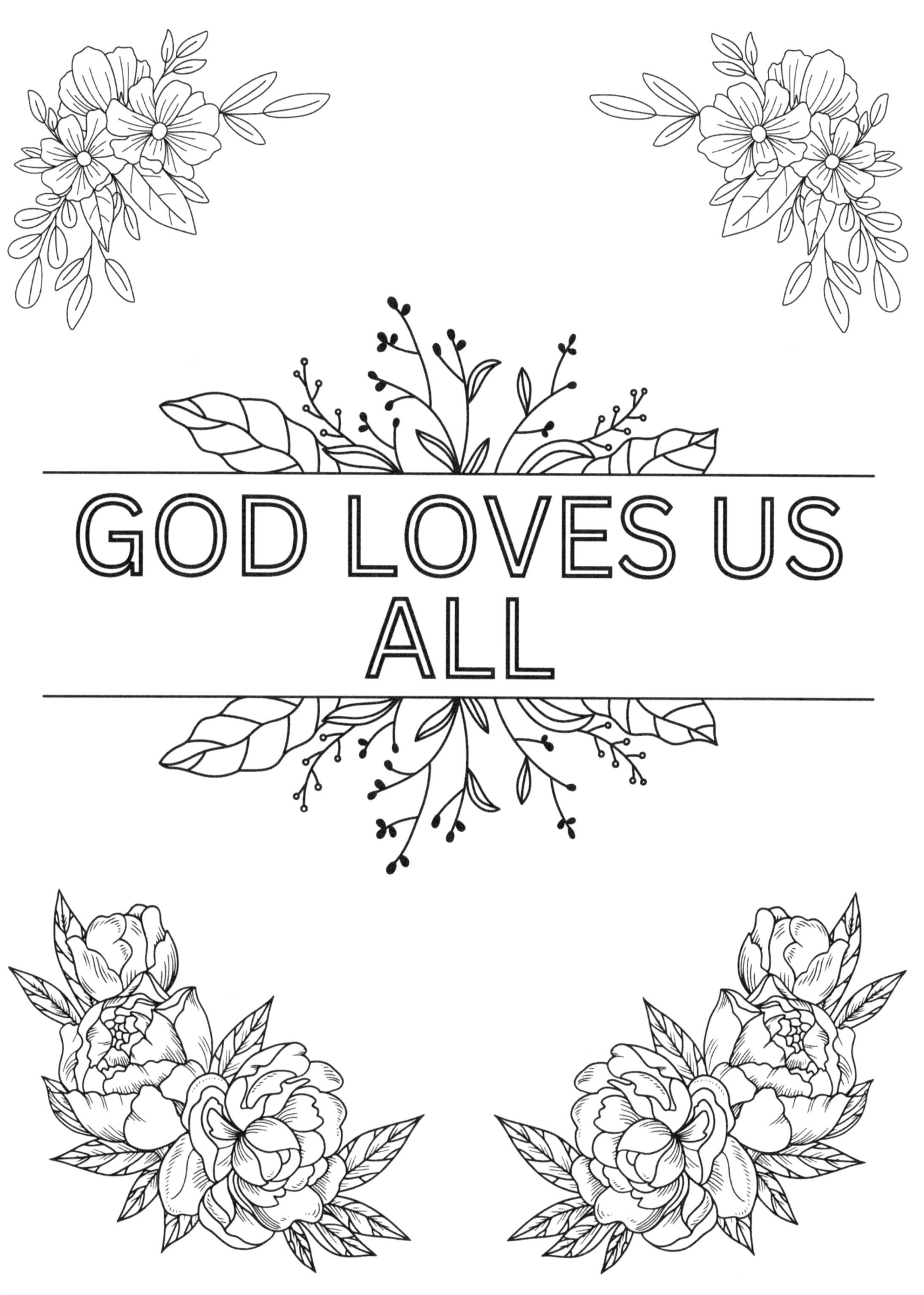

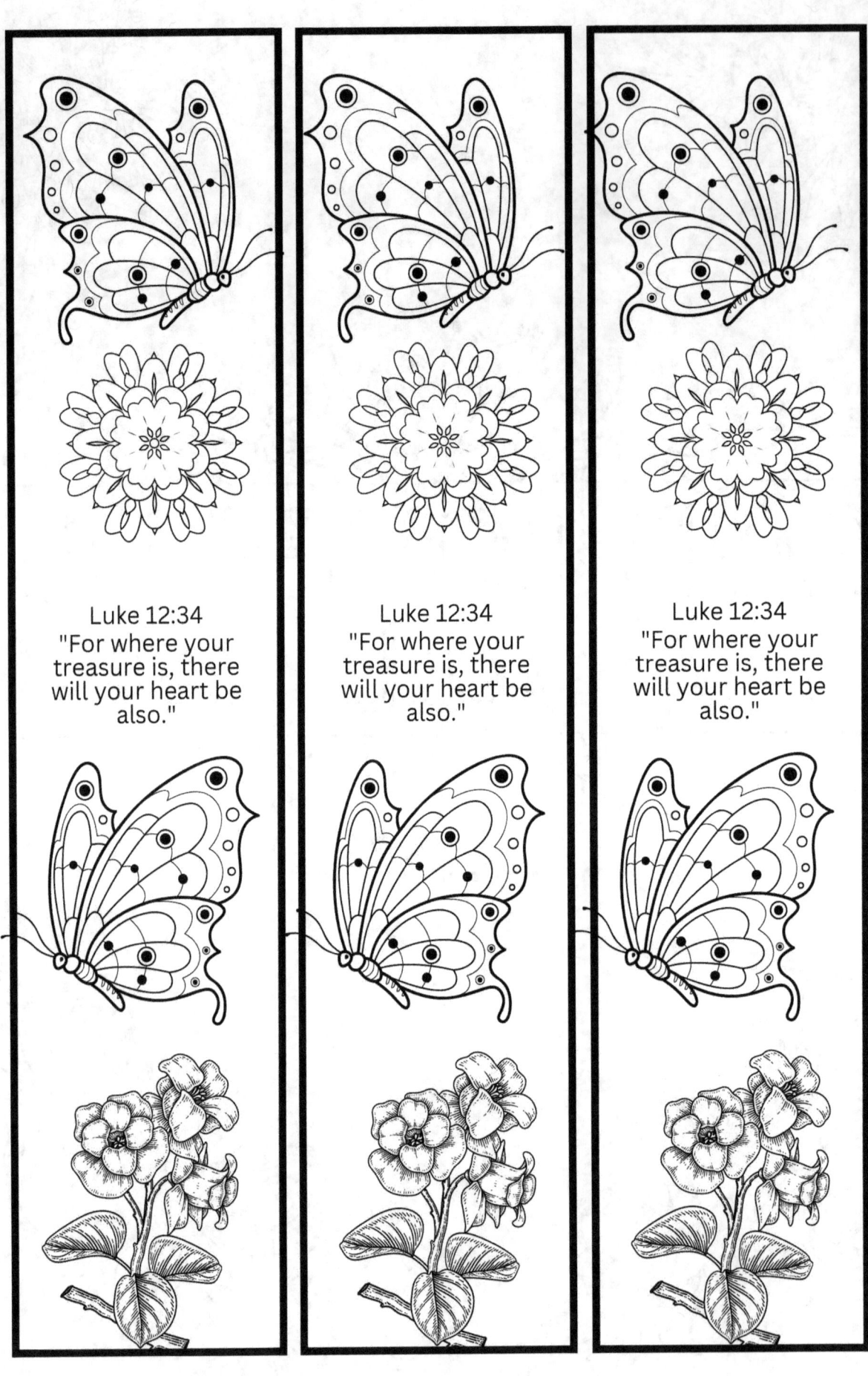

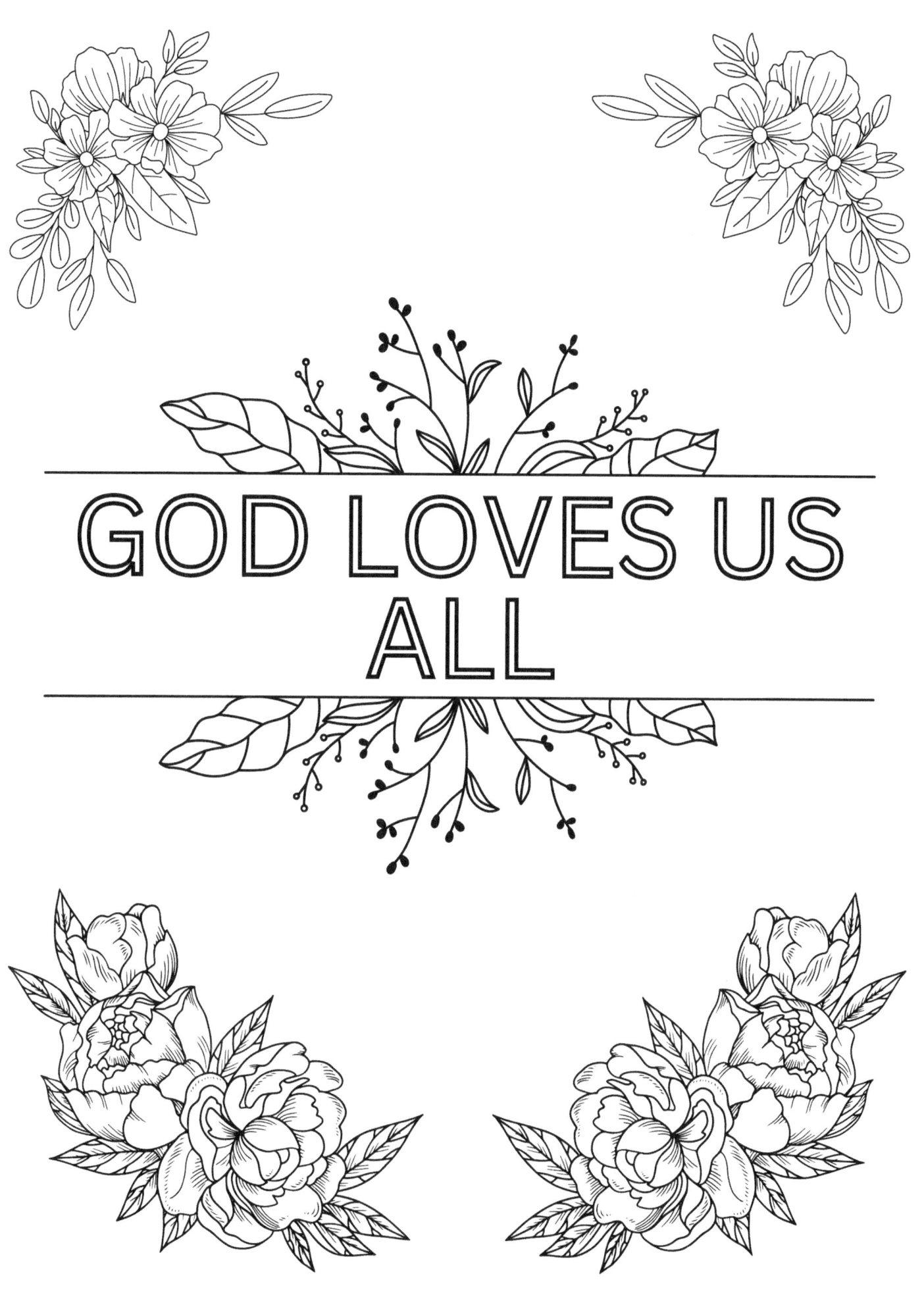

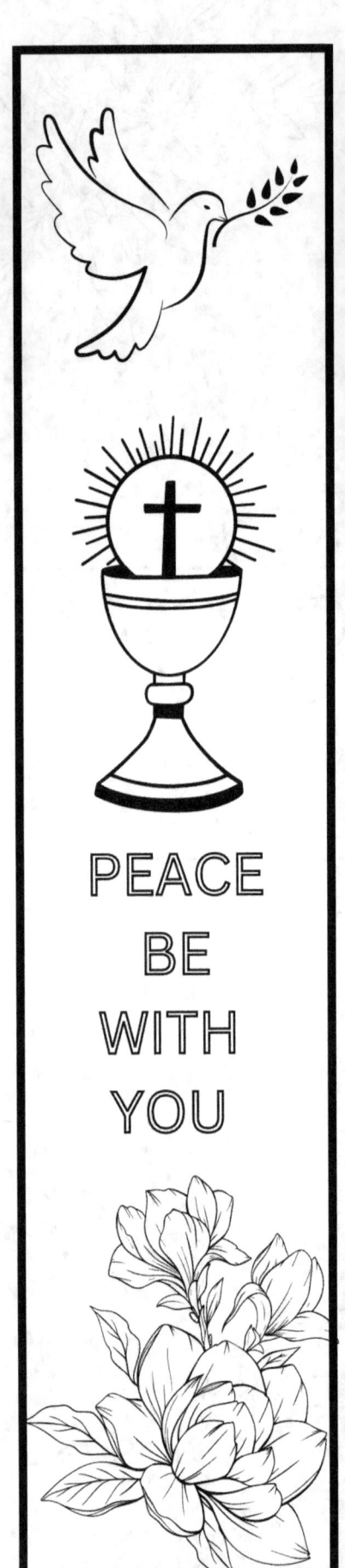
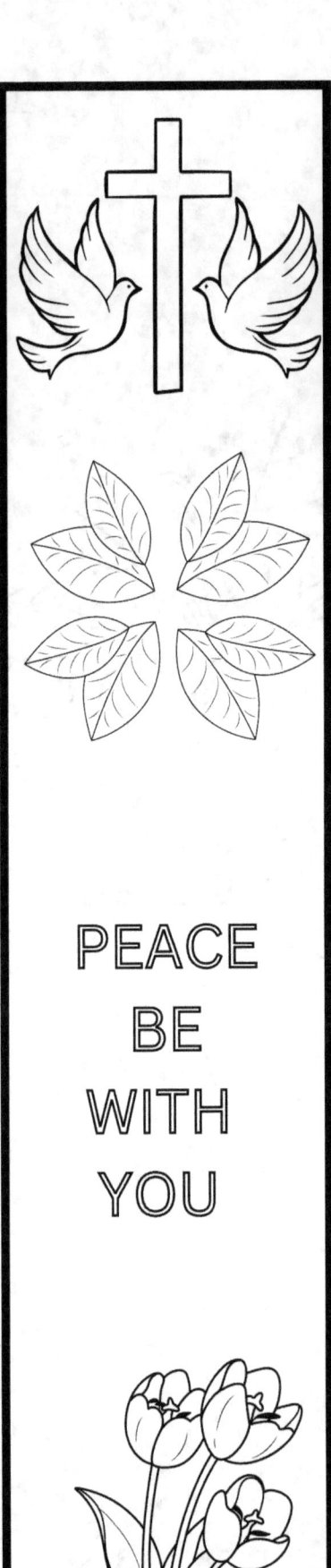
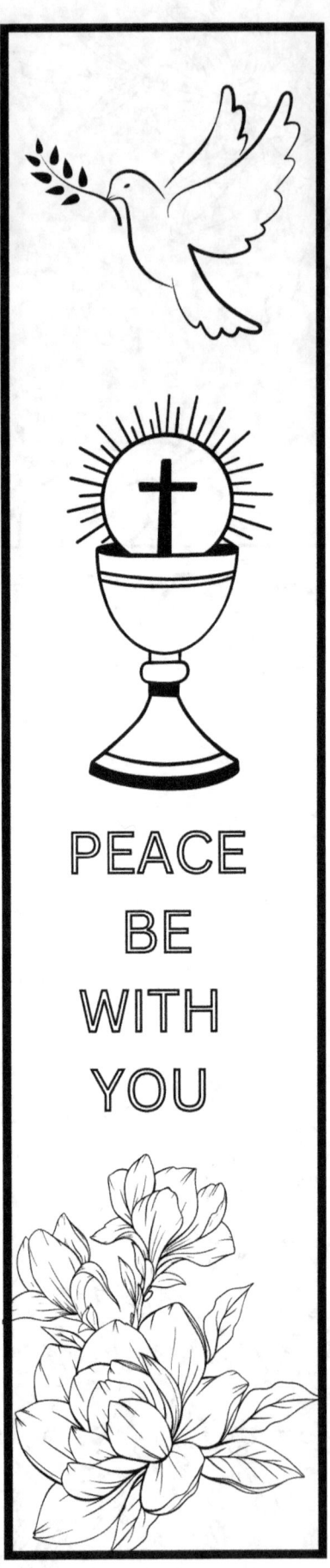

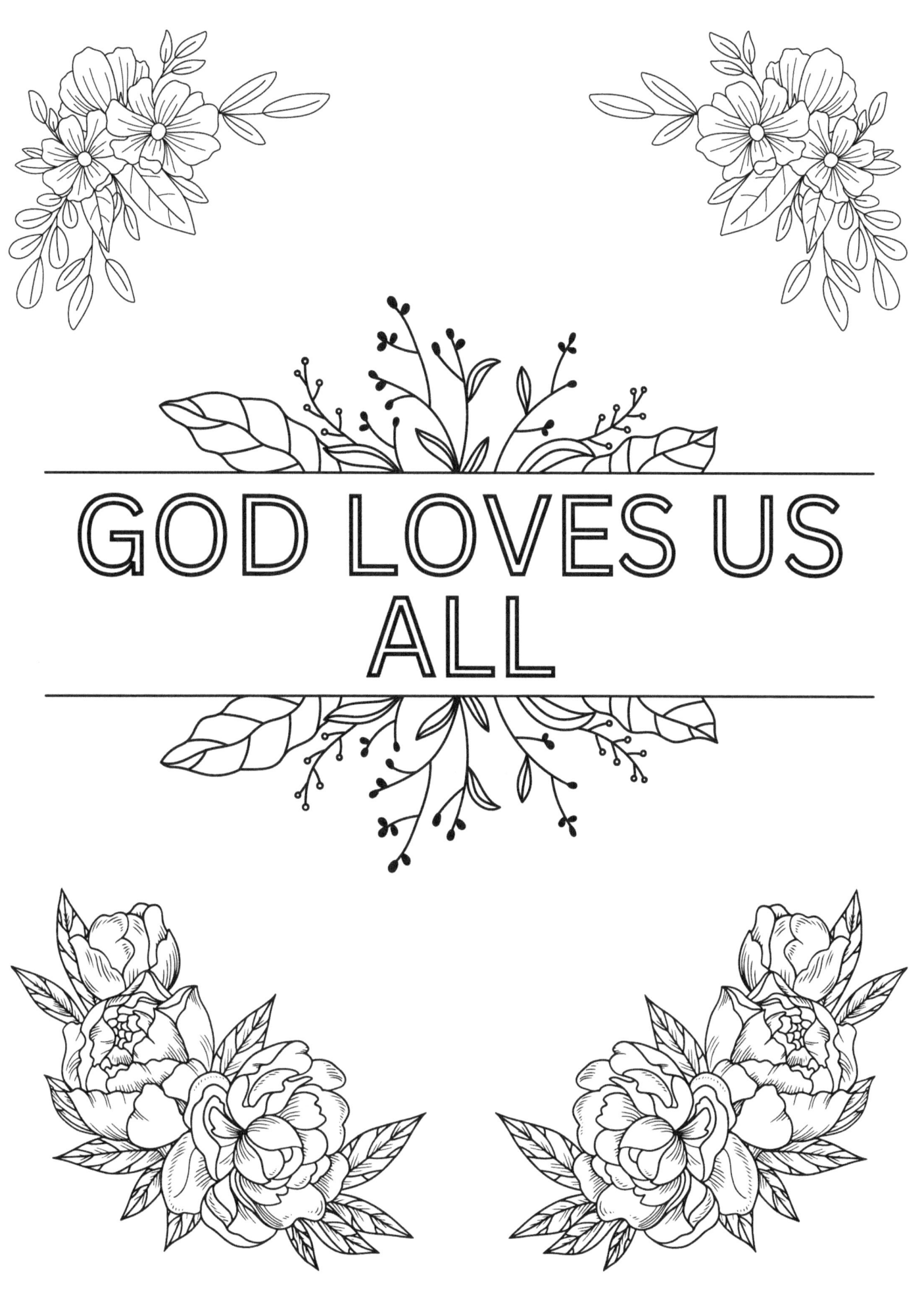

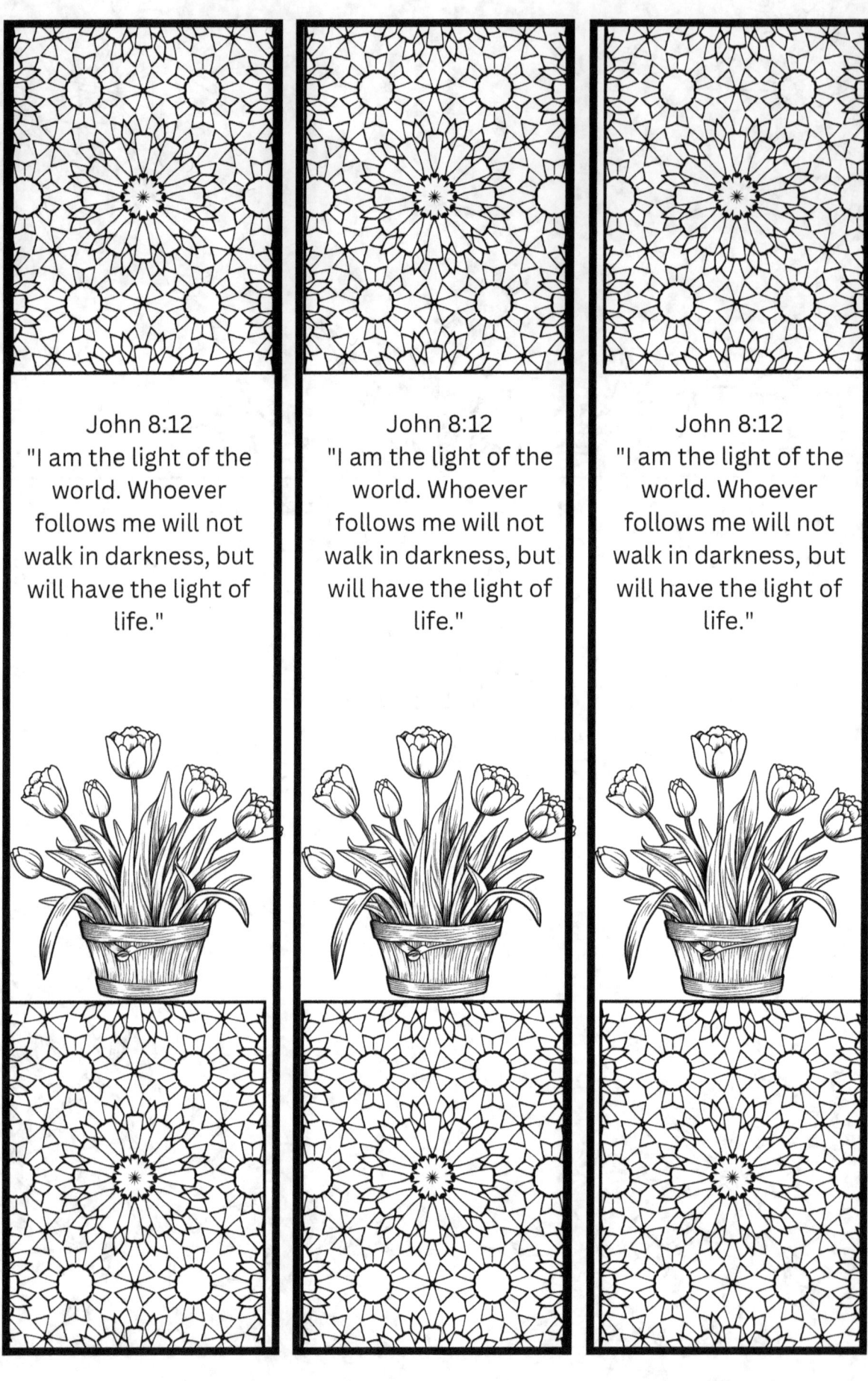

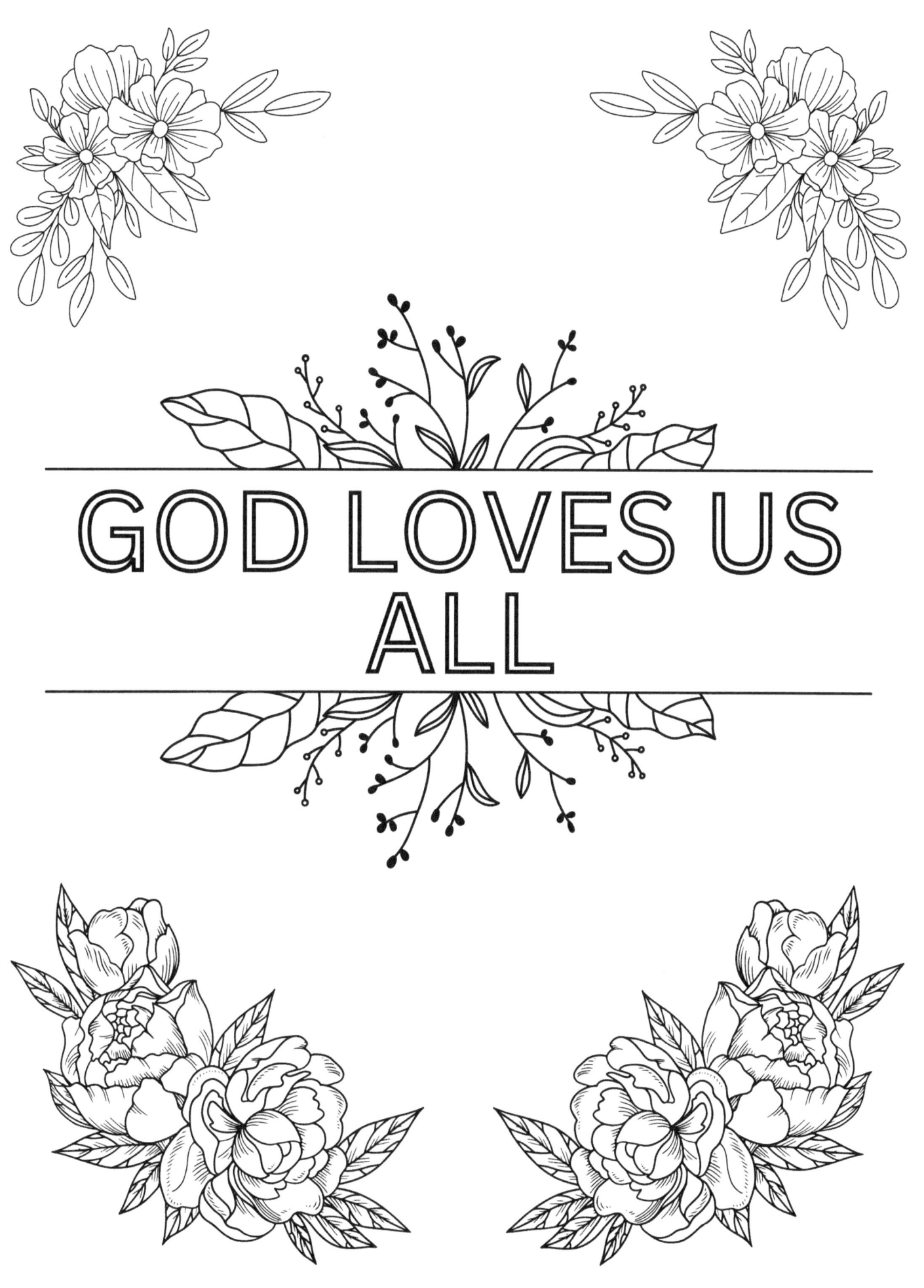

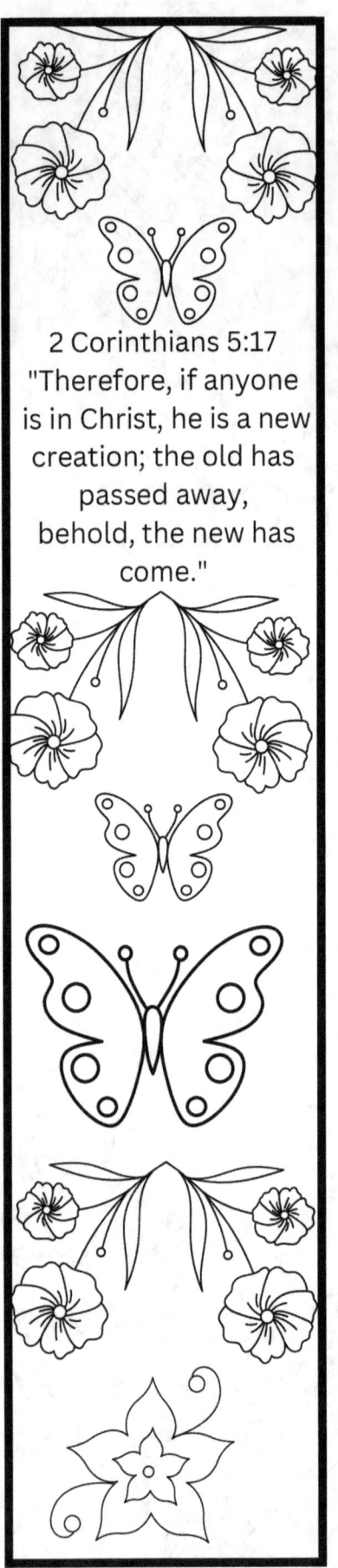
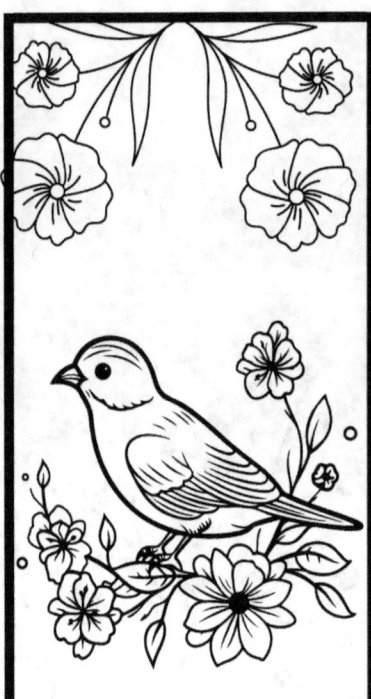
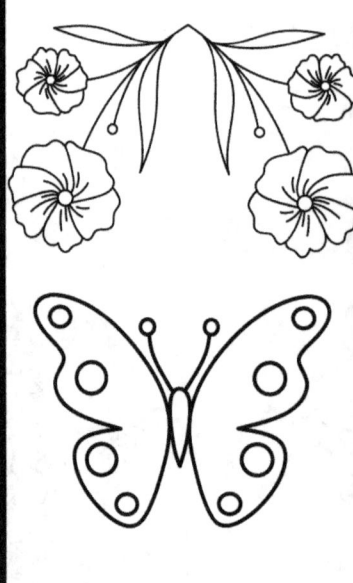
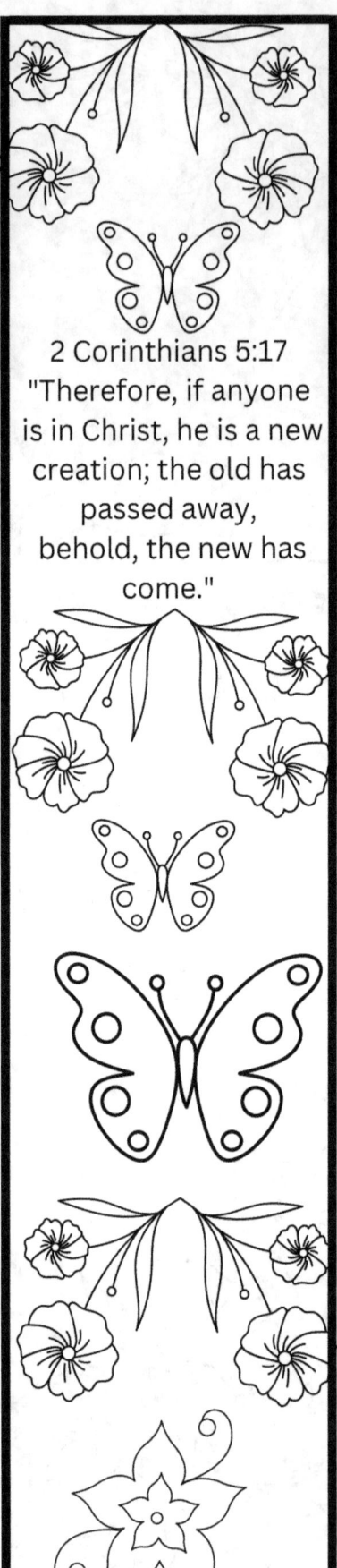

2 Corinthians 5:17 "Therefore, if anyone is in Christ, he is a new creation; the old has passed away, behold, the new has come."

2 Corinthians 5:17 "Therefore, if anyone is in Christ, he is a new creation; the old has passed away, behold, the new has come."

2 Corinthians 5:17 "Therefore, if anyone is in Christ, he is a new creation; the old has passed away, behold, the new has come."

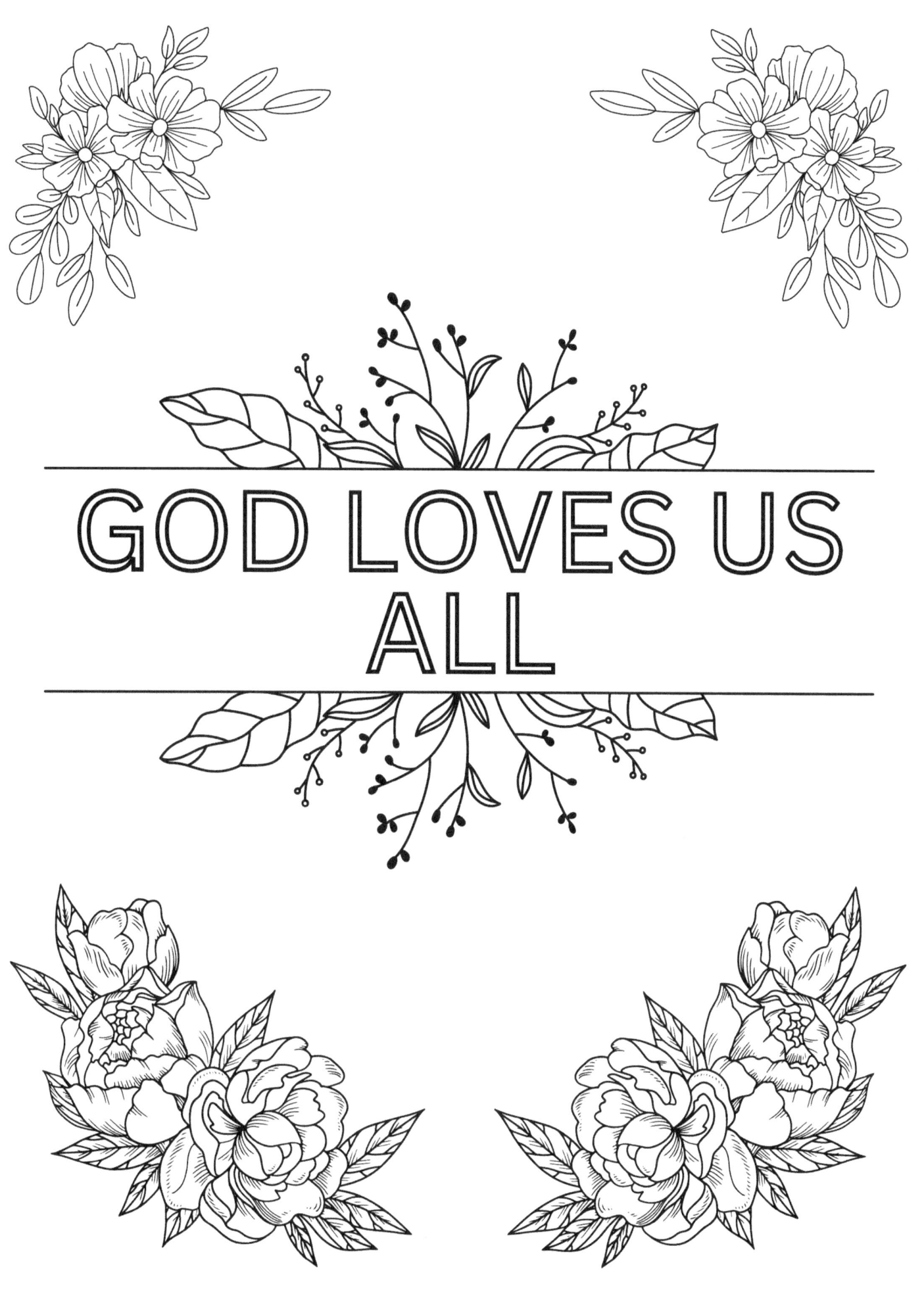

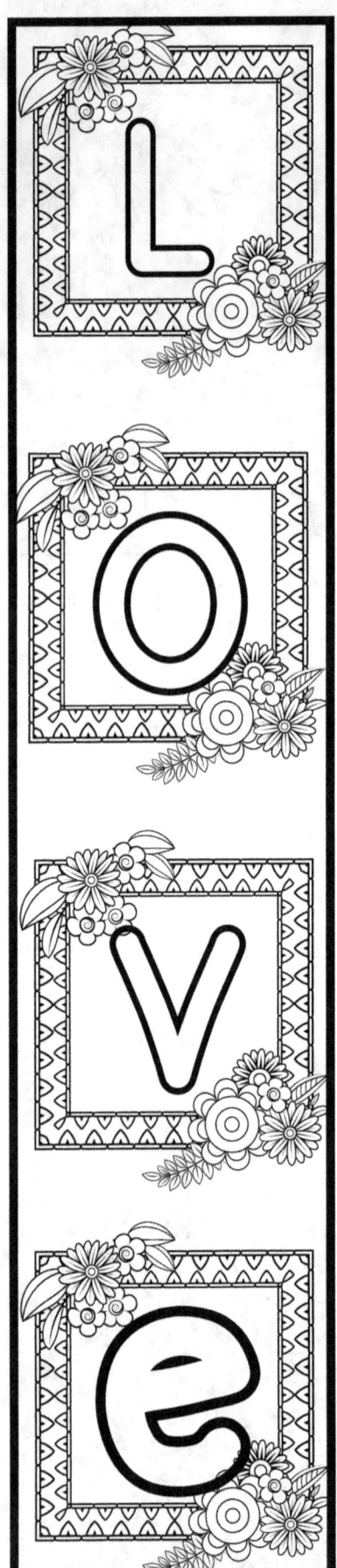
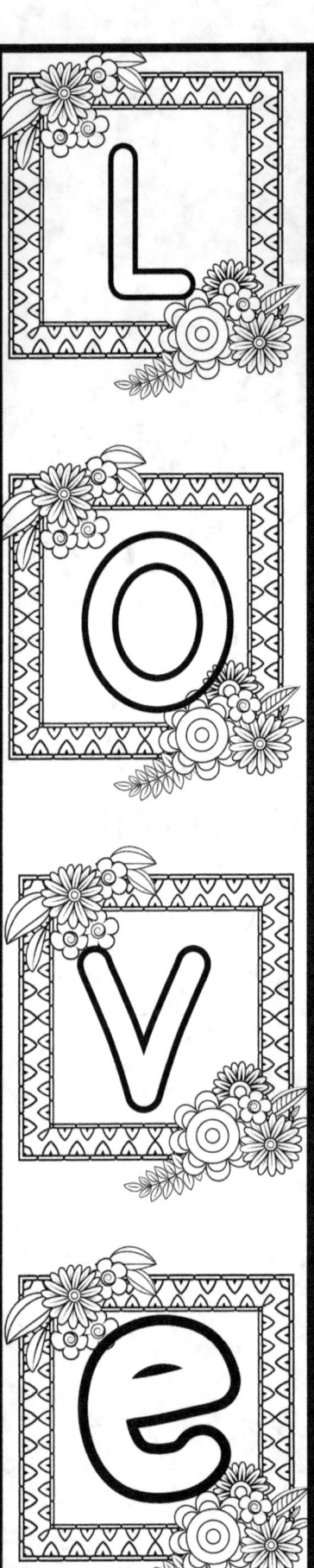
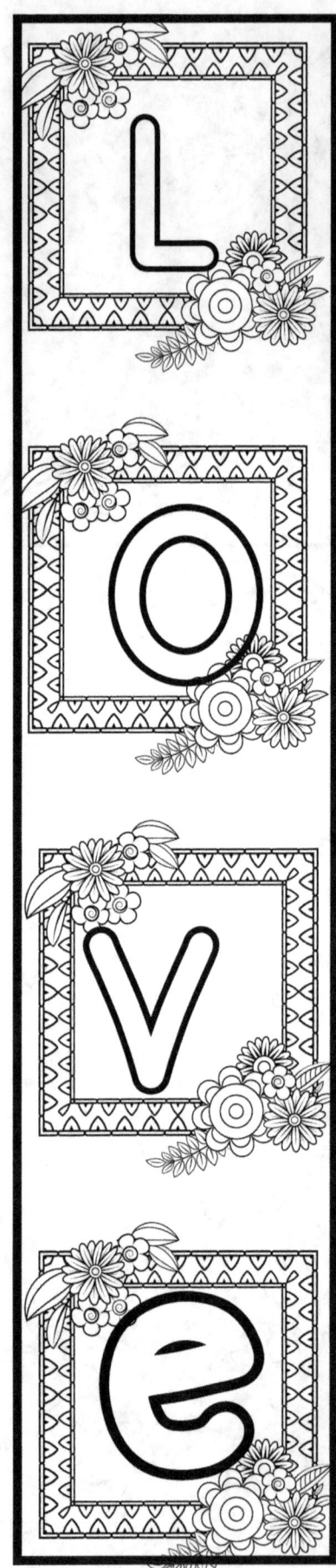

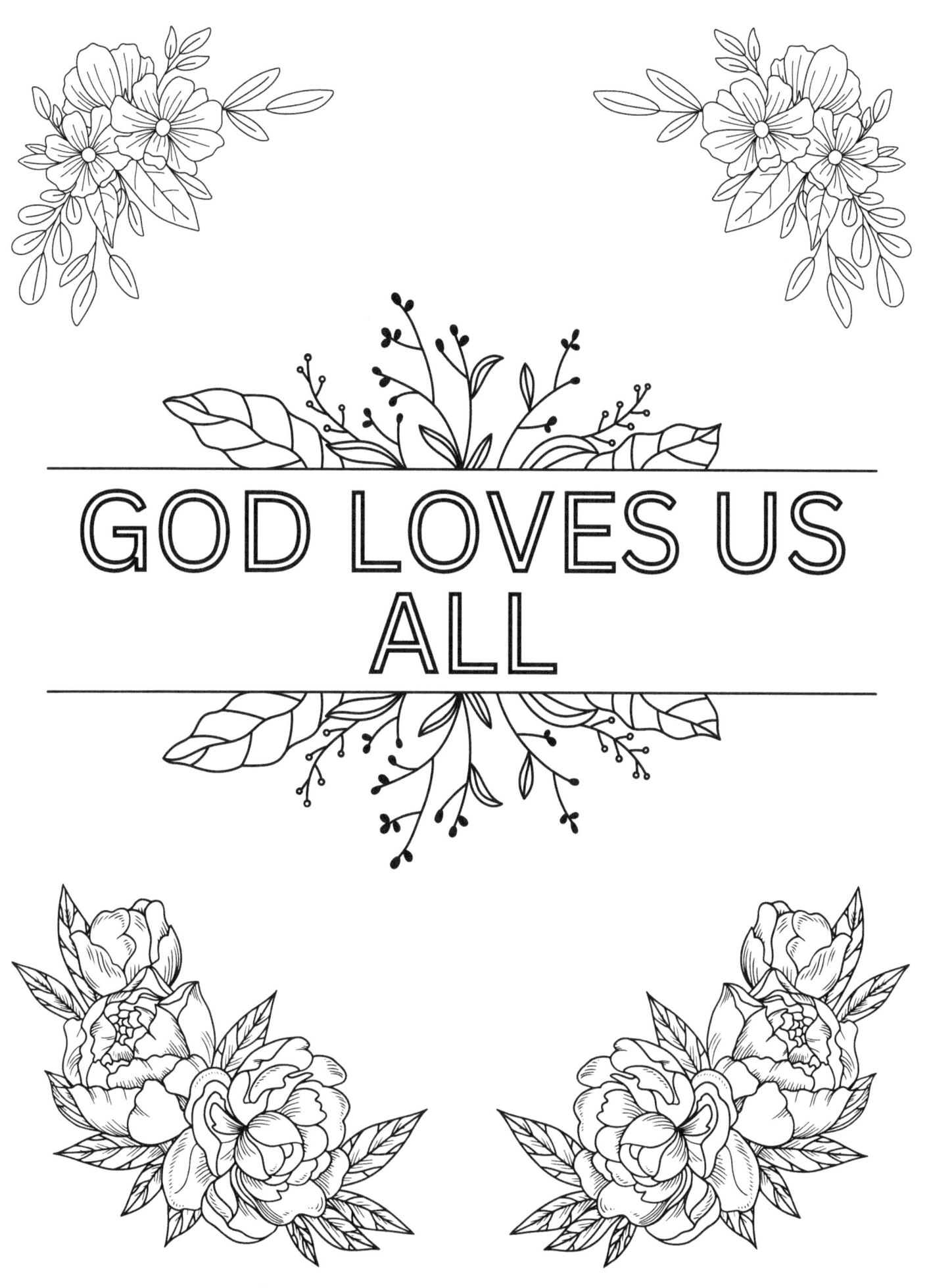

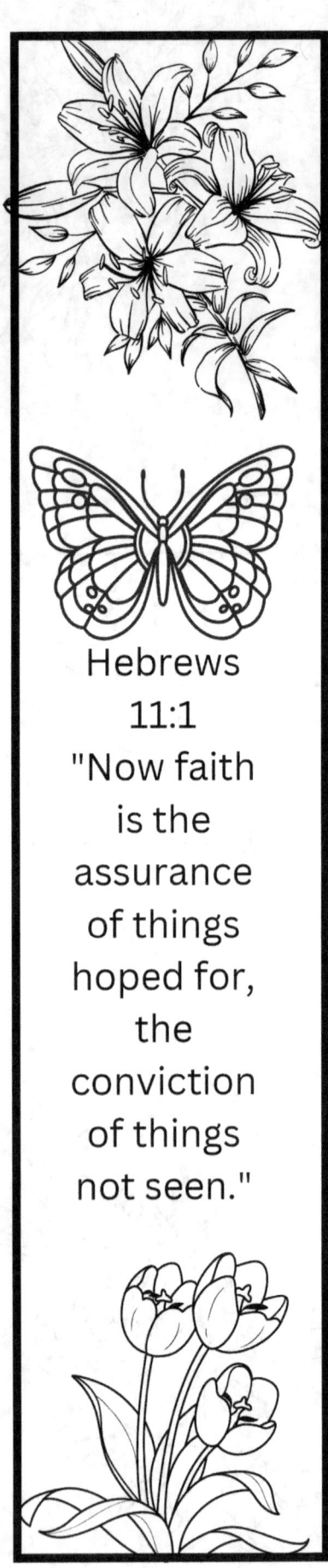
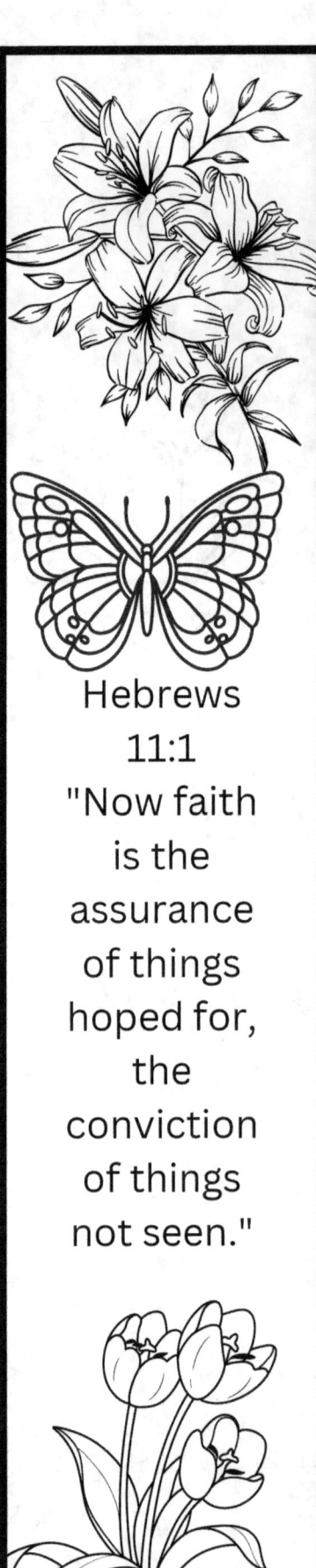
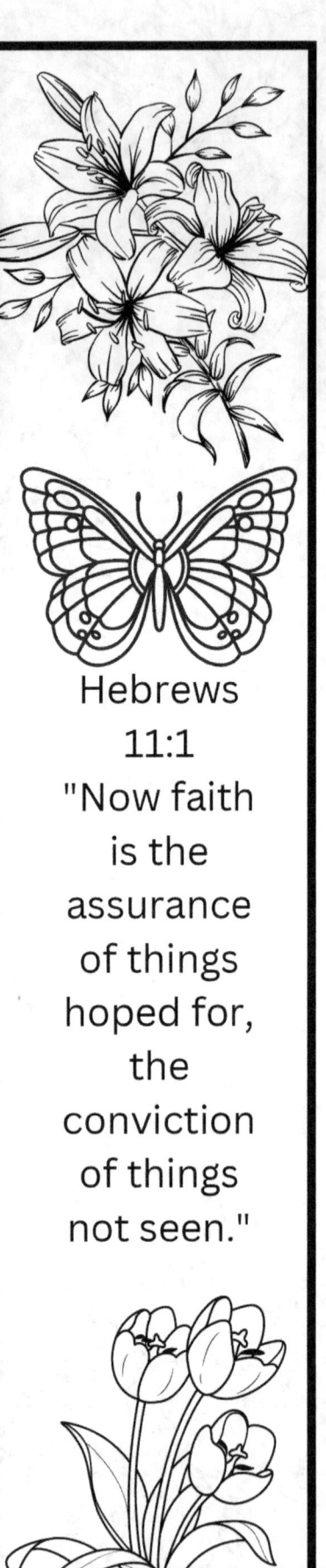

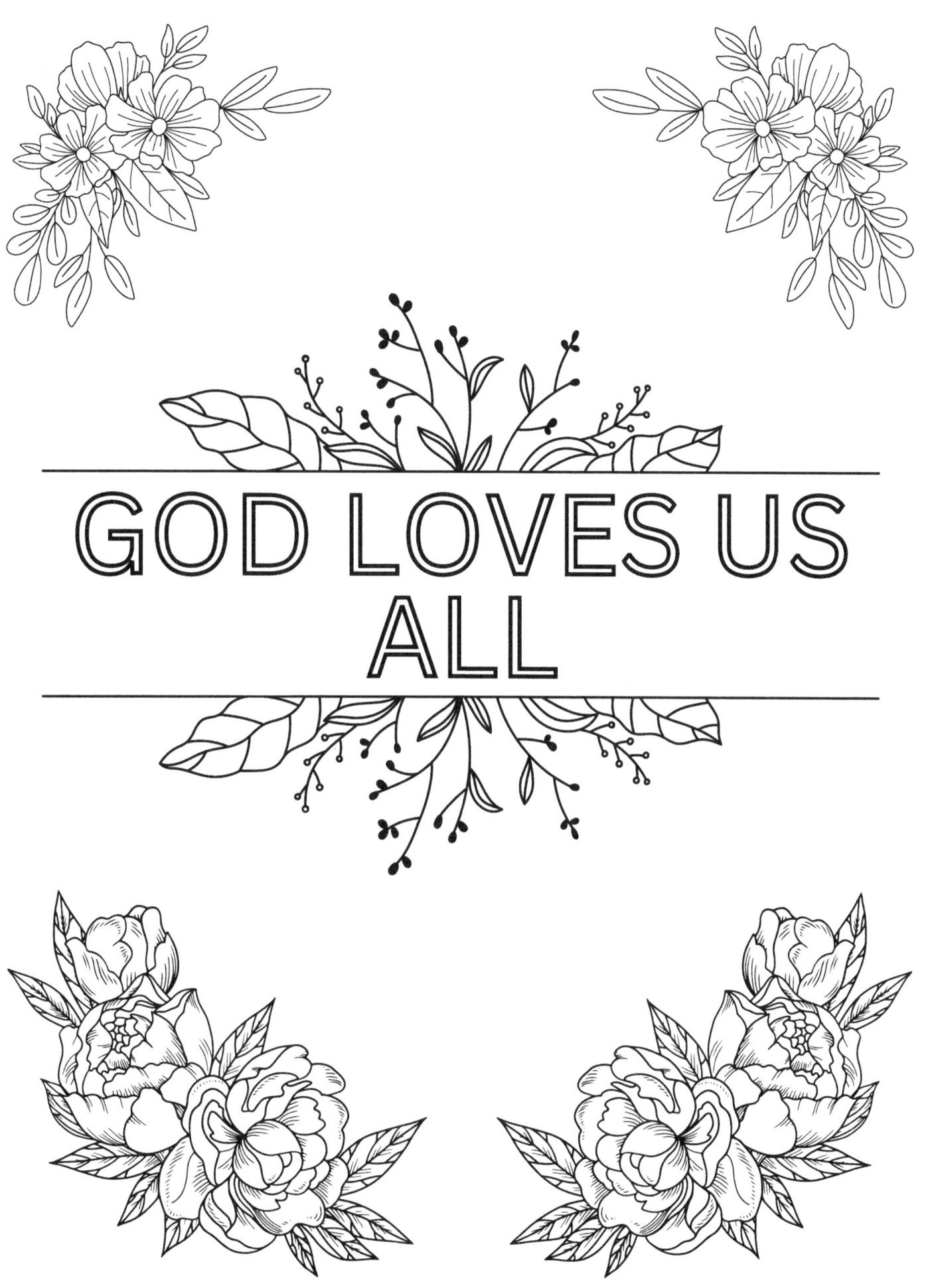

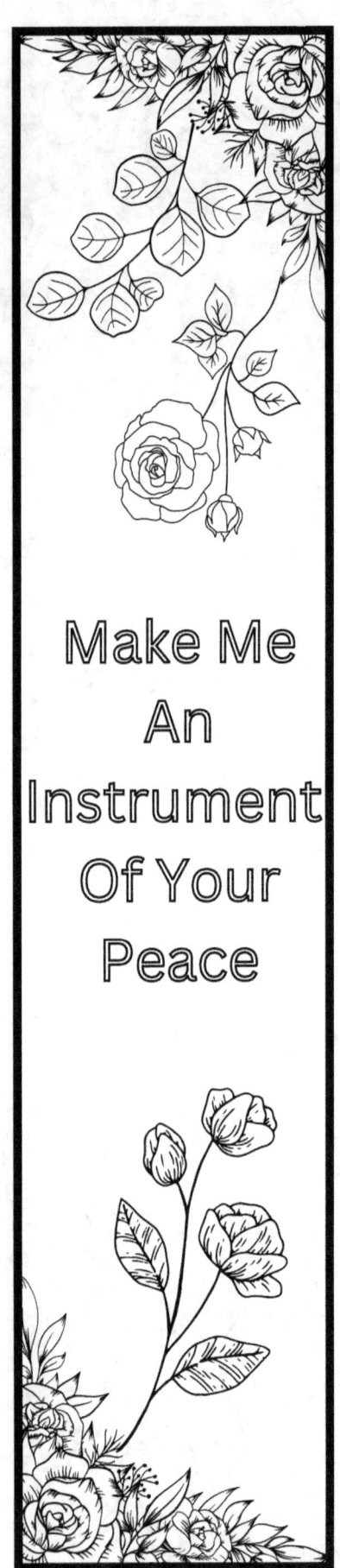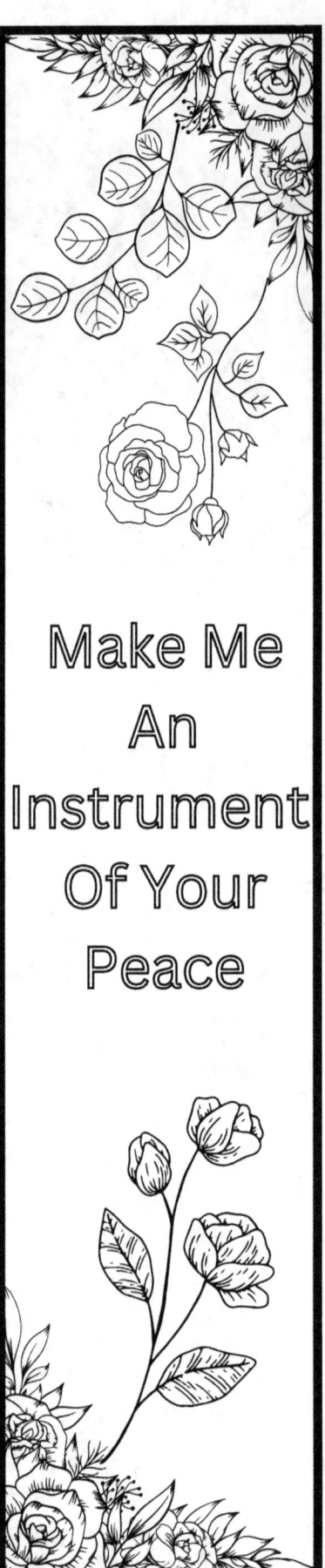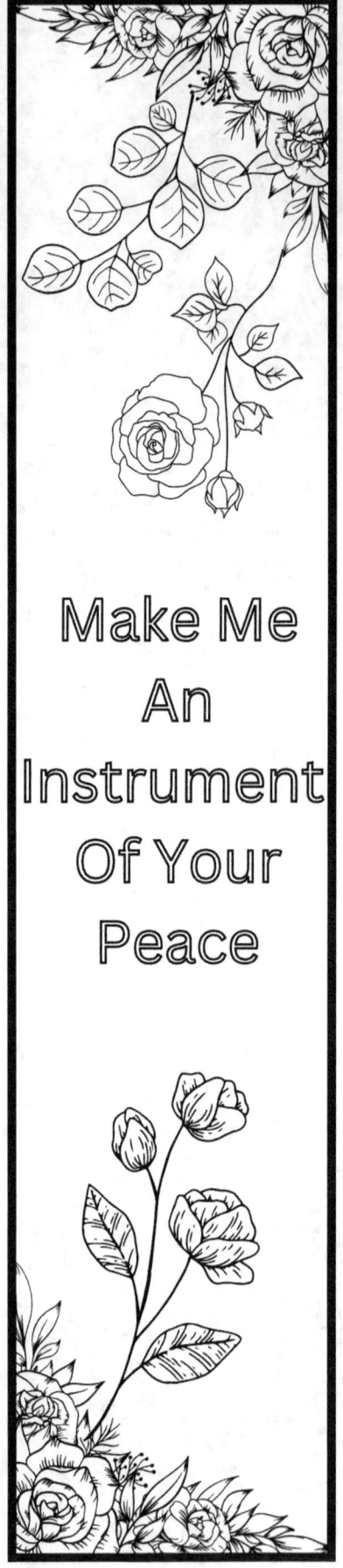

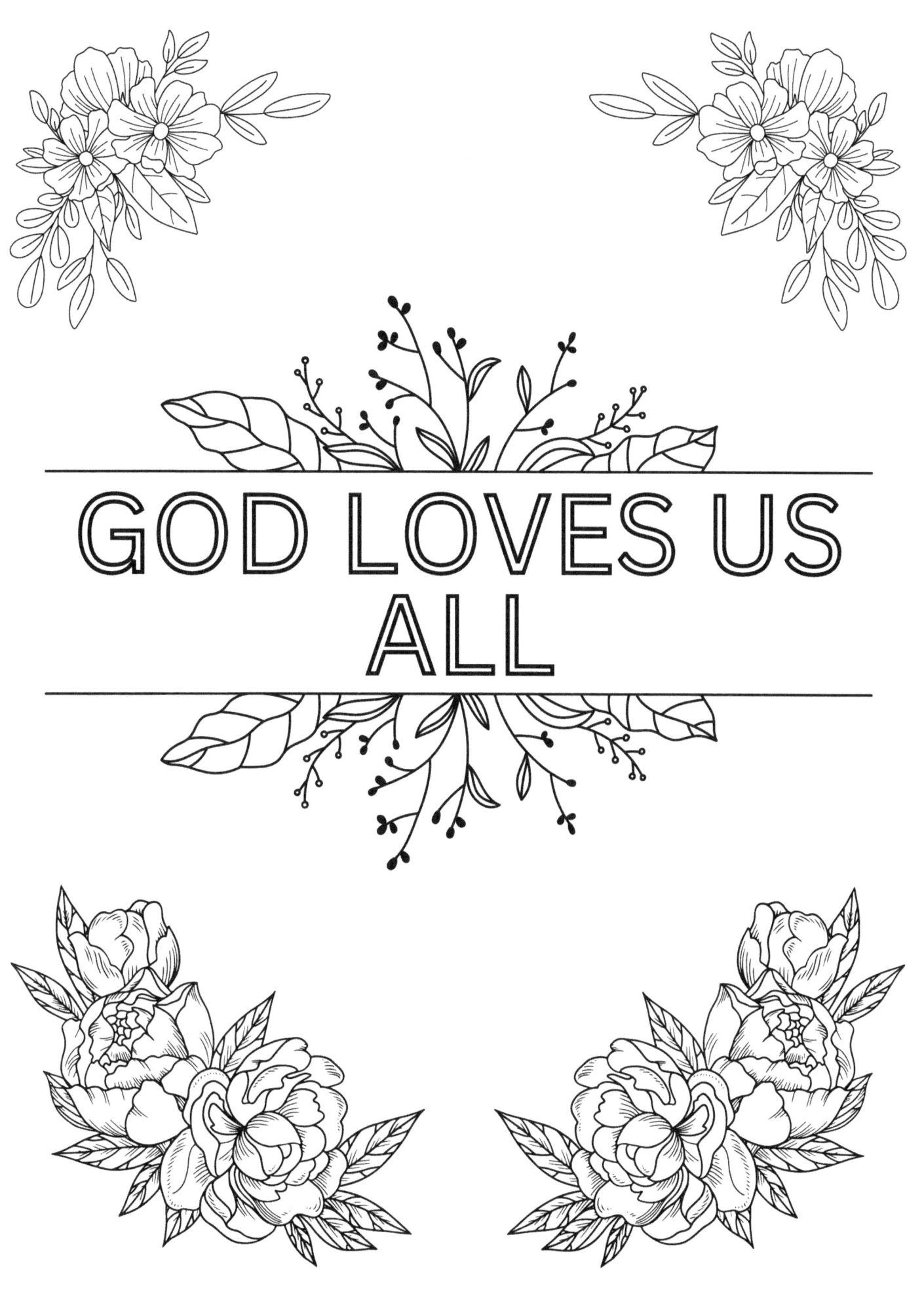

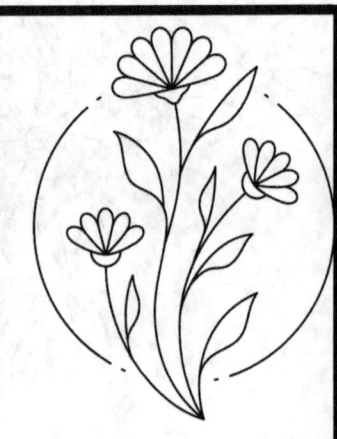
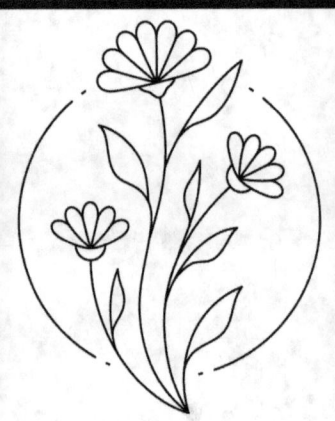
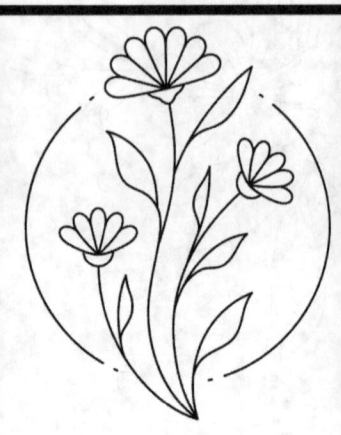

Romans 8:28
"And we know that in all things God works for the good of those who love him, who have been called according to his purpose."

Romans 8:28
"And we know that in all things God works for the good of those who love him, who have been called according to his purpose."

Romans 8:28
"And we know that in all things God works for the good of those who love him, who have been called according to his purpose."

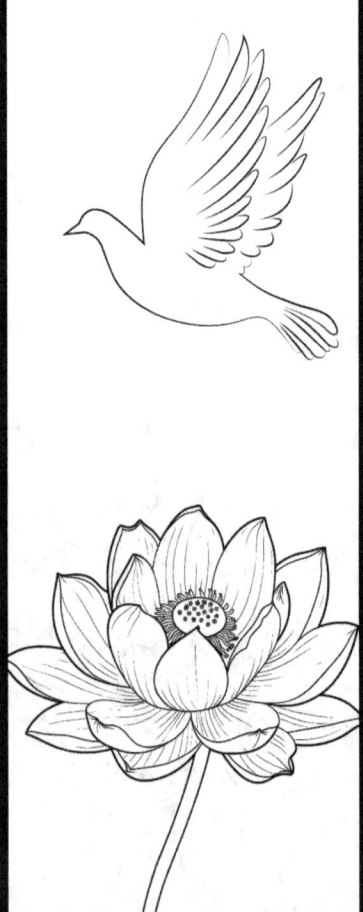
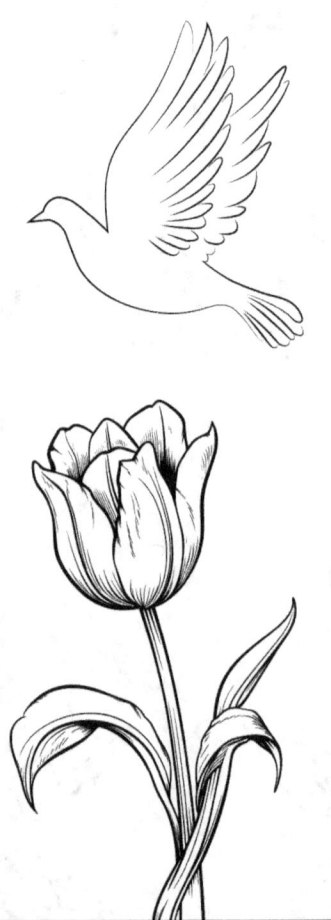
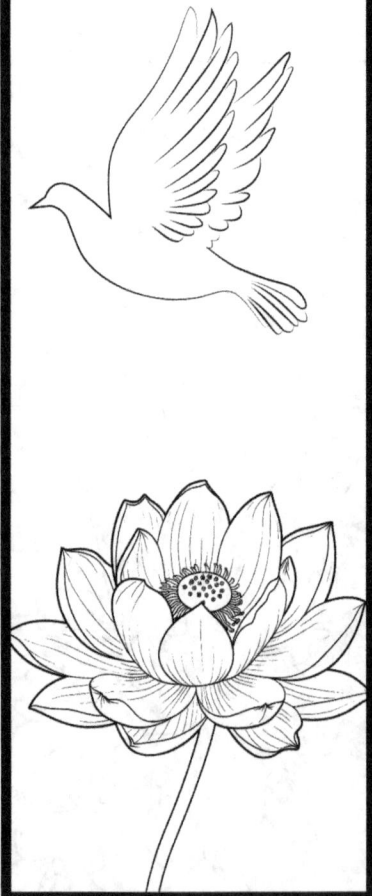

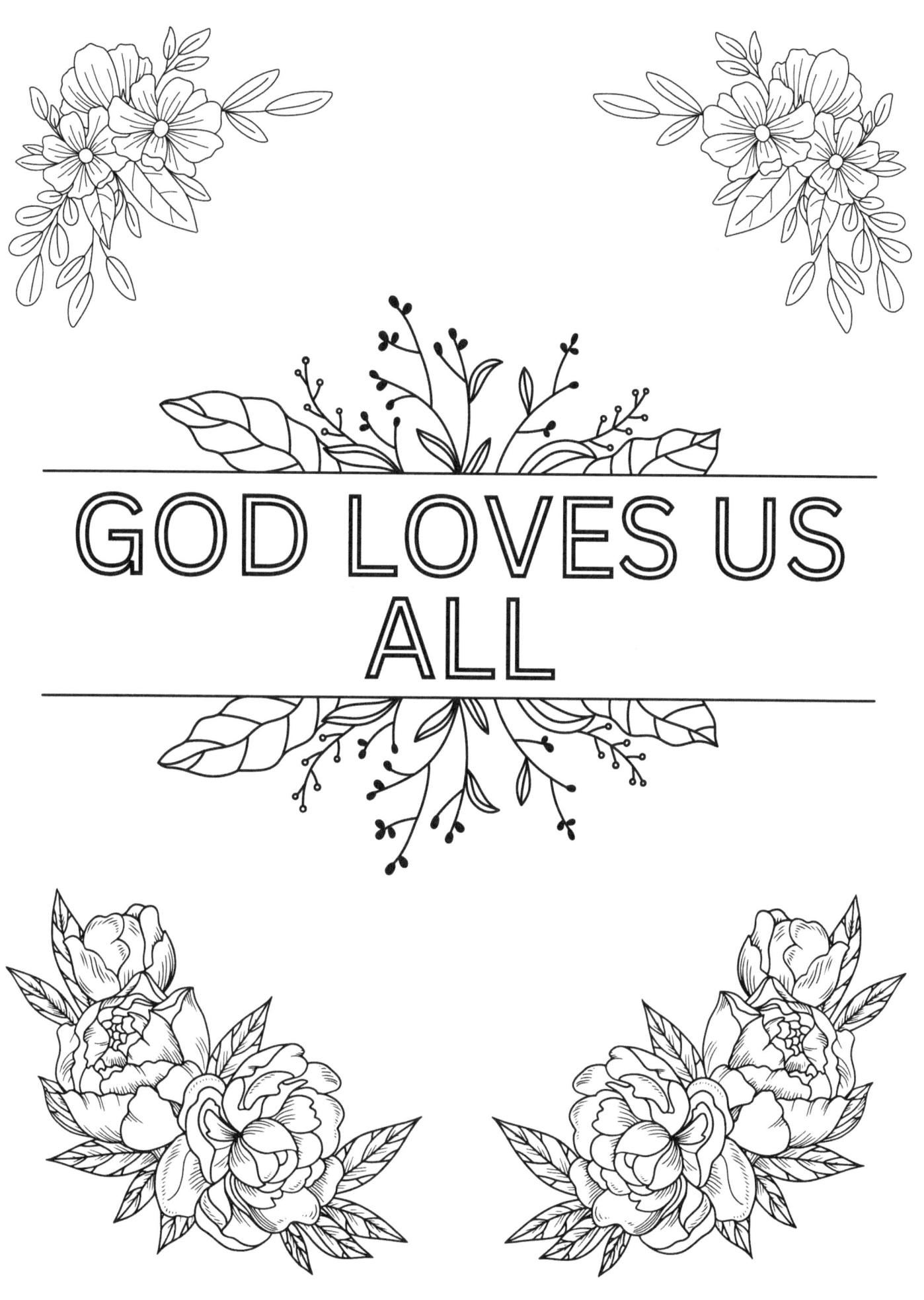

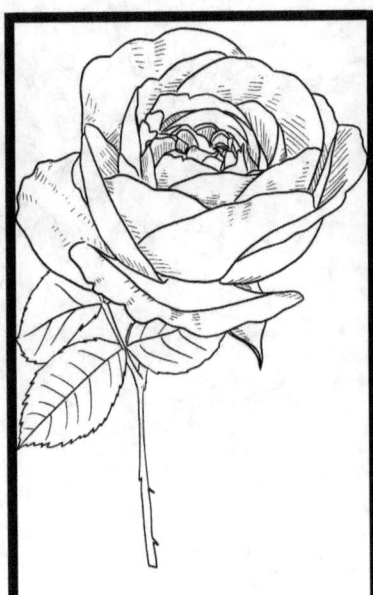 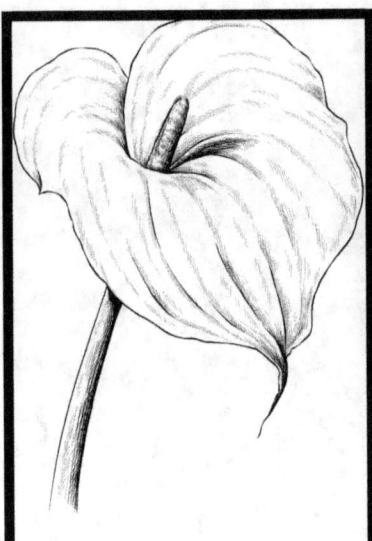 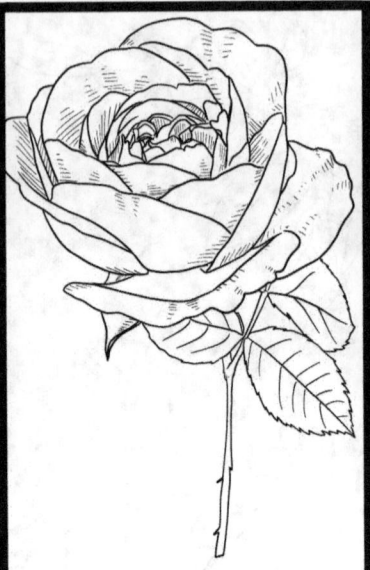

1 Corinthians 13:4-5 "Love is patient and kind; love does not envy or boast; it is not arrogant or rude."

1 Corinthians 13:4-5 "Love is patient and kind; love does not envy or boast; it is not arrogant or rude."

1 Corinthians 13:4-5 "Love is patient and kind; love does not envy or boast; it is not arrogant or rude."

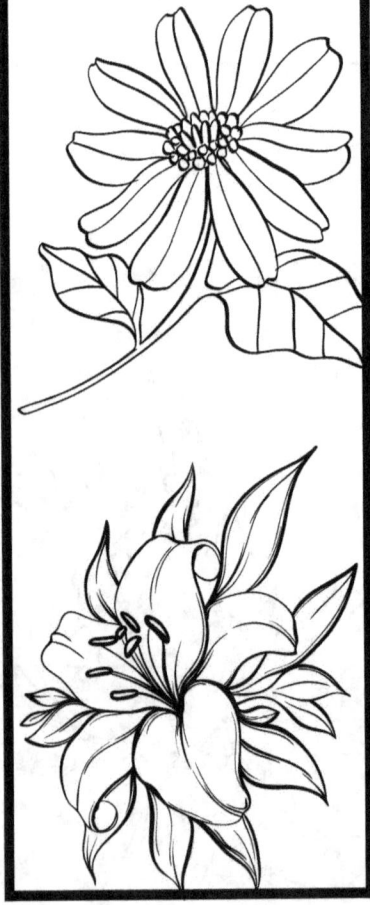 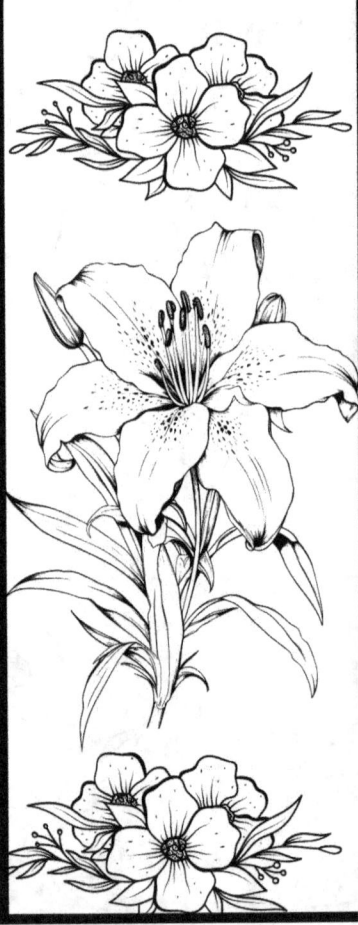 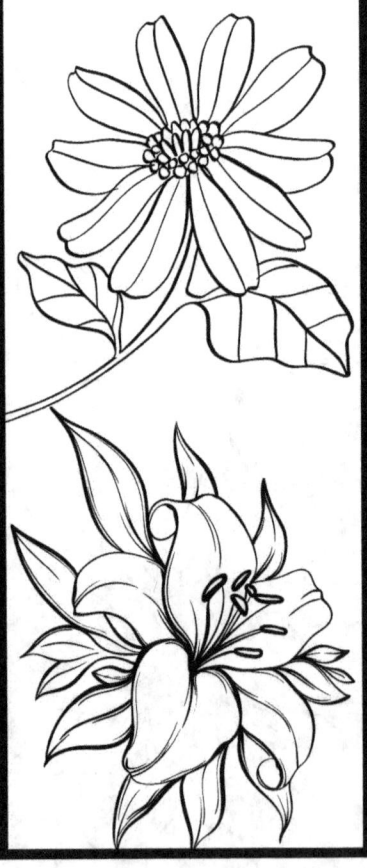

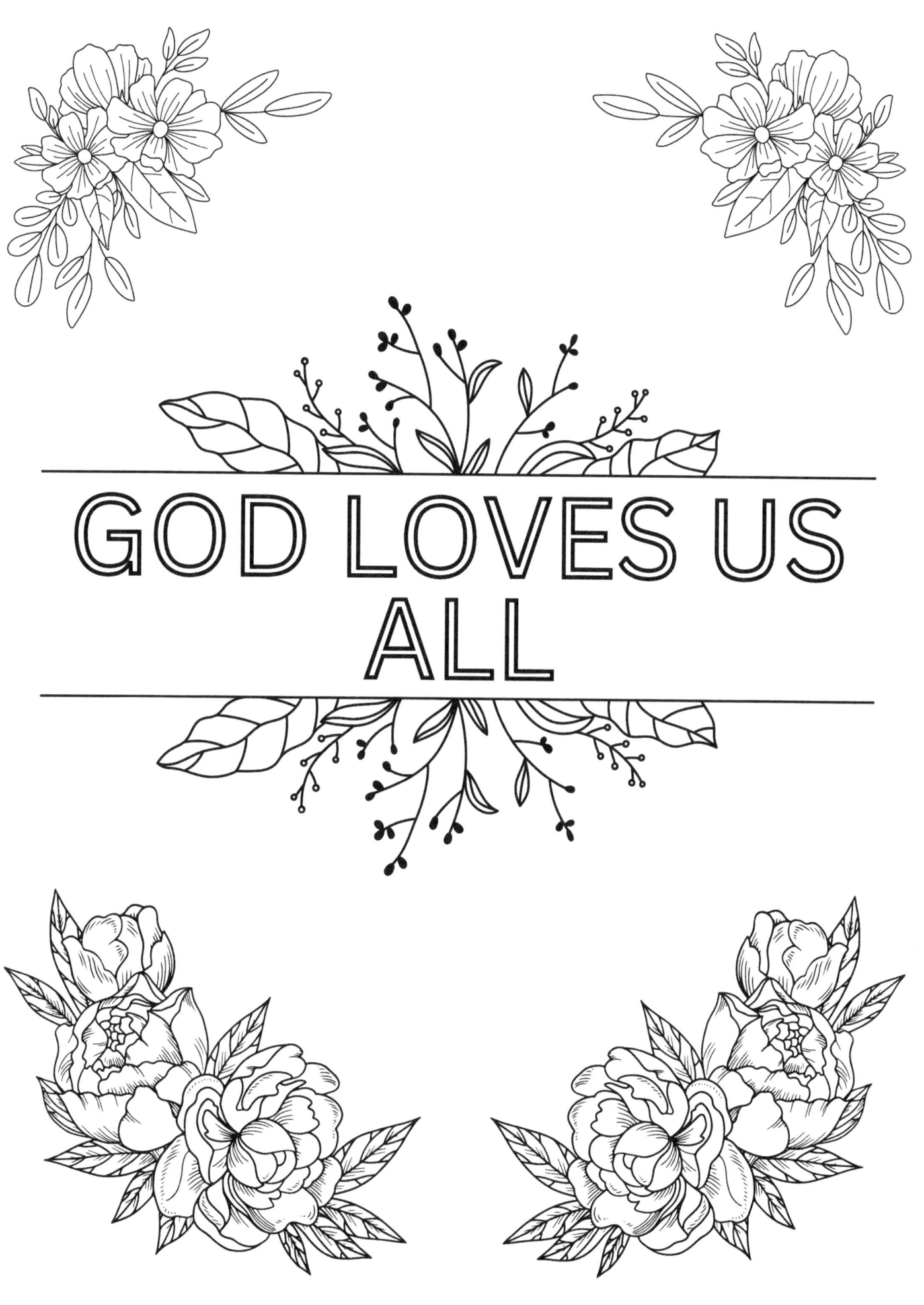

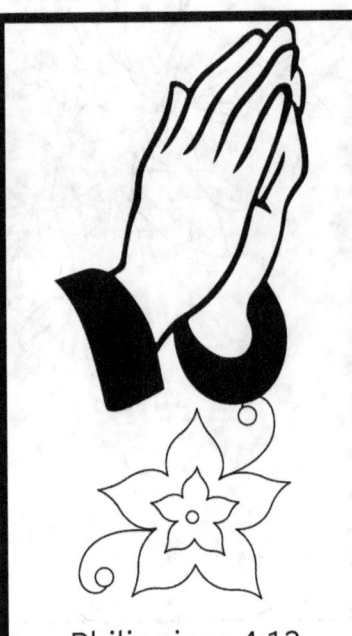
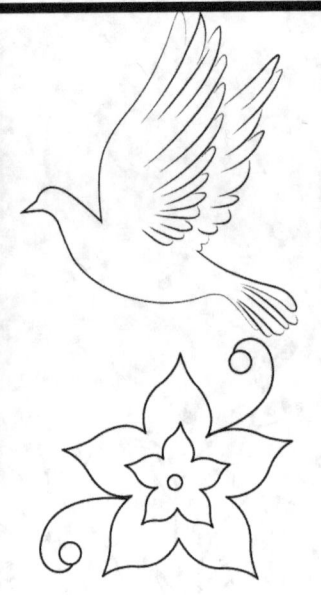
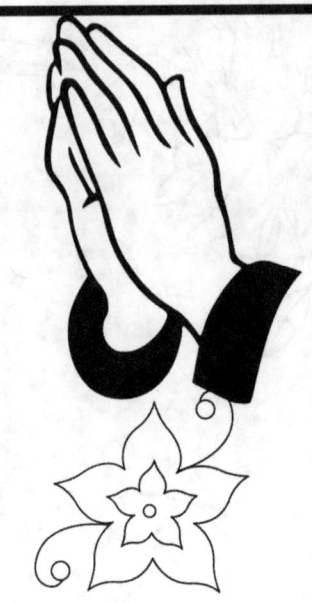

Philippians 4:13
"I can do all things through Christ who strengthens me."

Philippians 4:13
"I can do all things through Christ who strengthens me."

Philippians 4:13
"I can do all things through Christ who strengthens me."

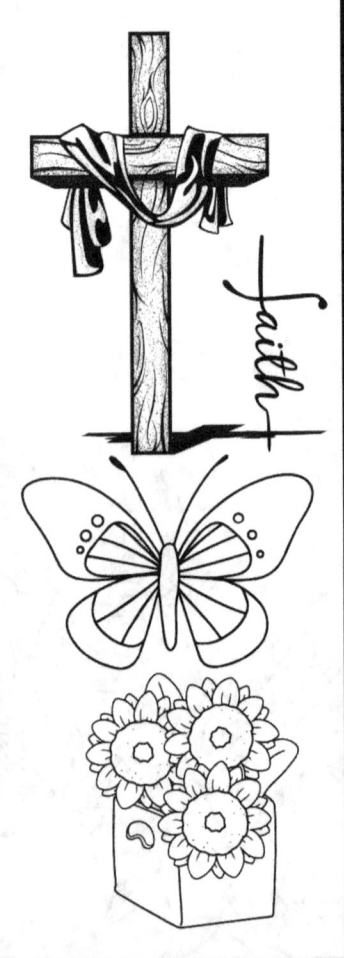
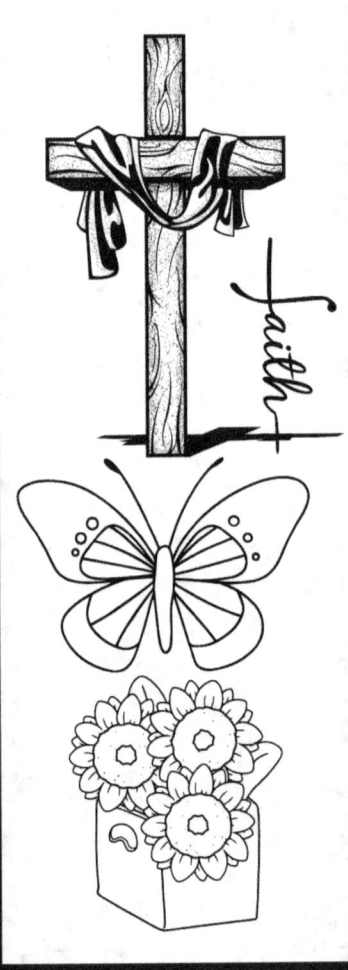
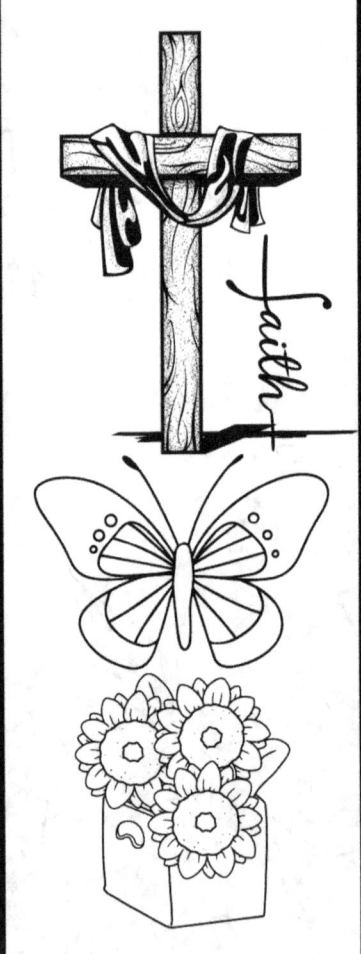

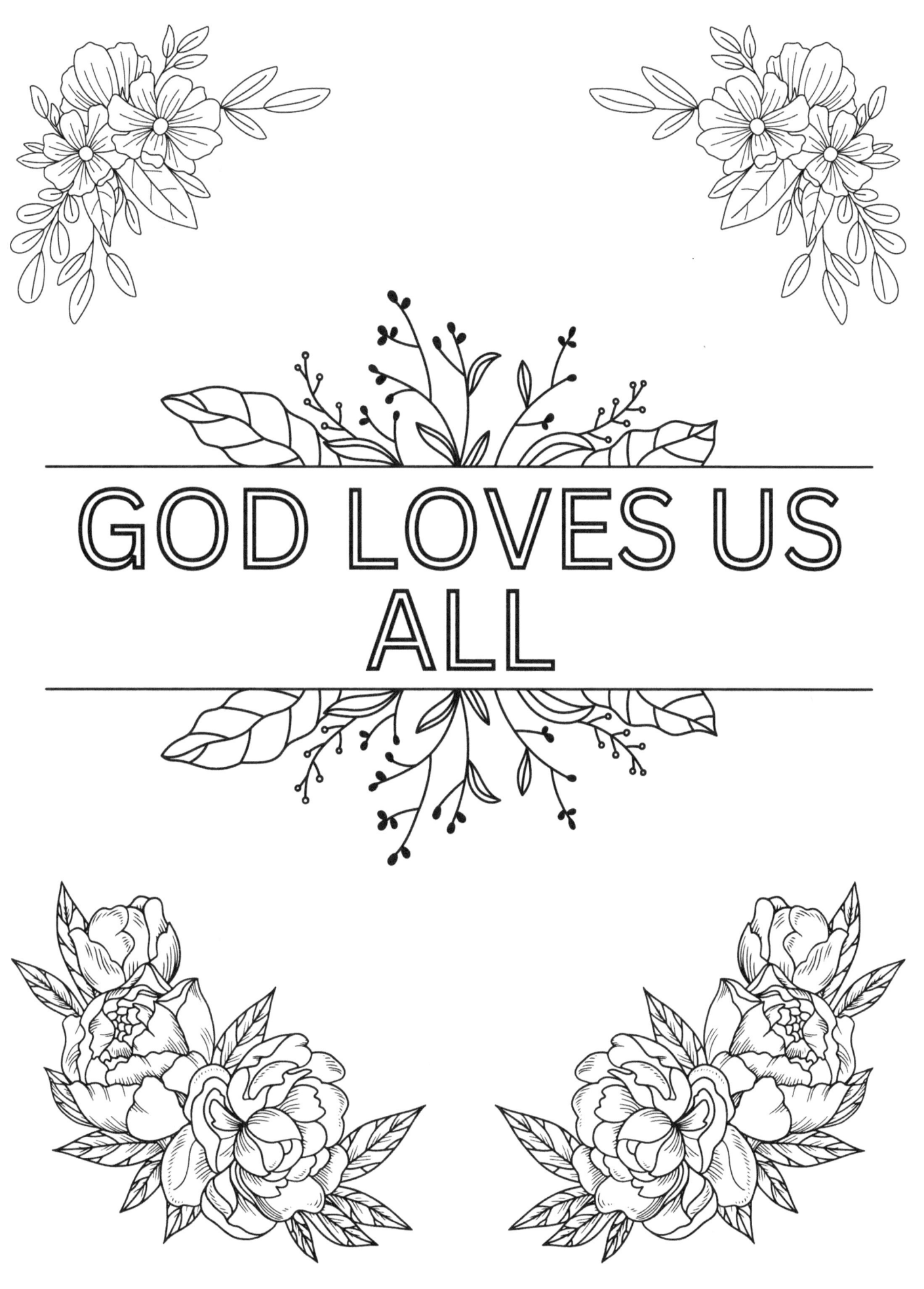

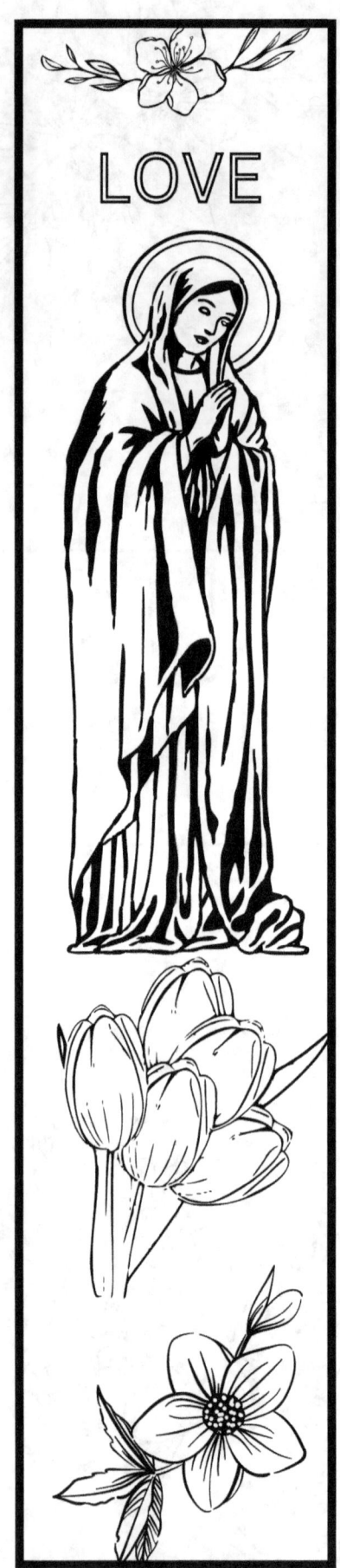
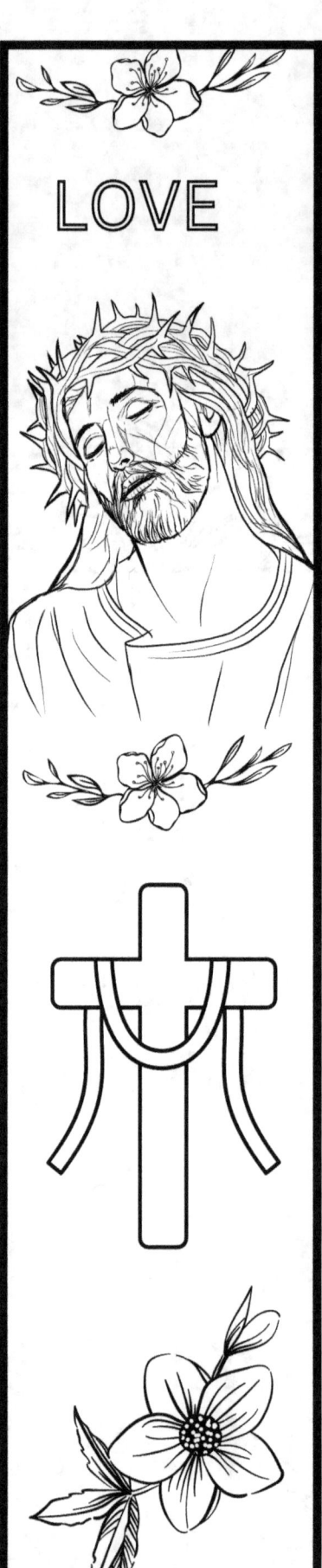
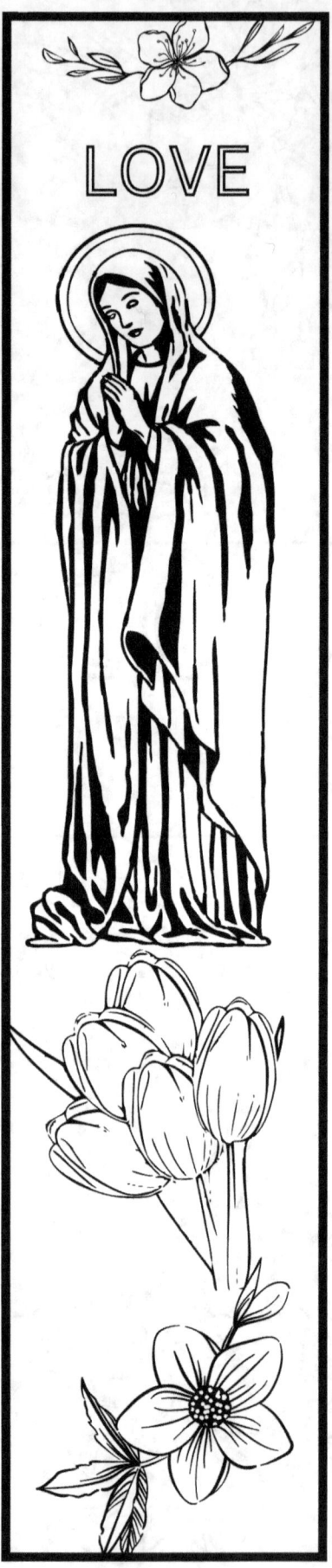

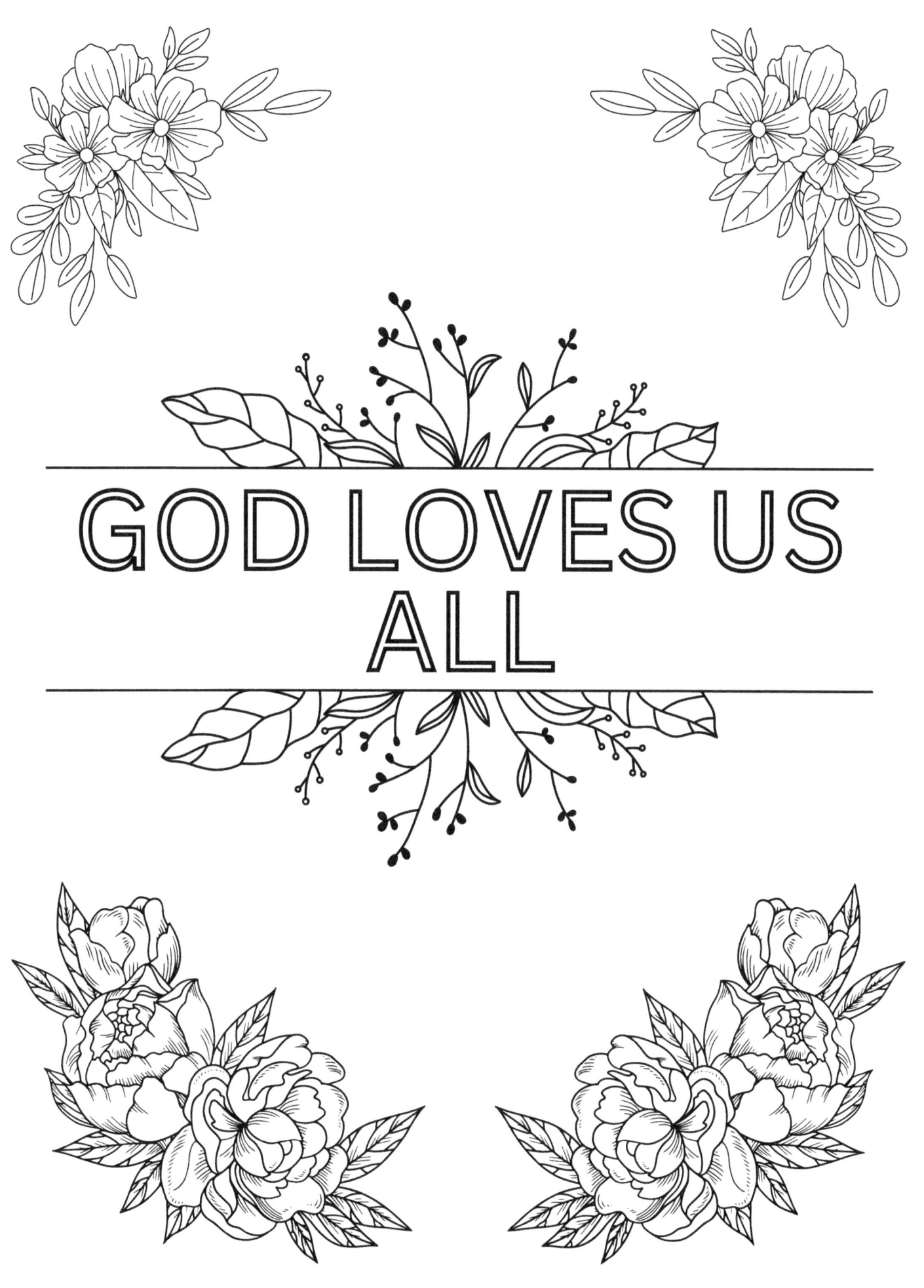

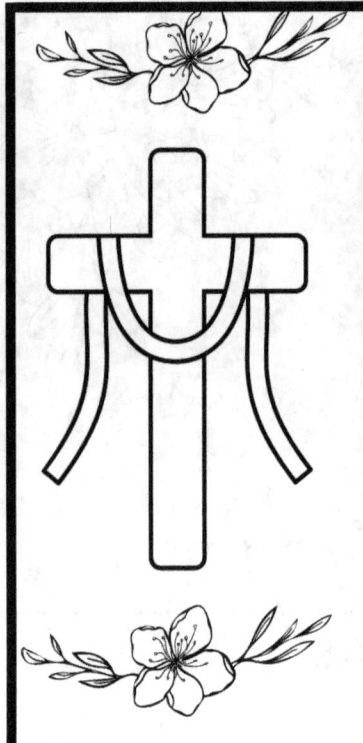
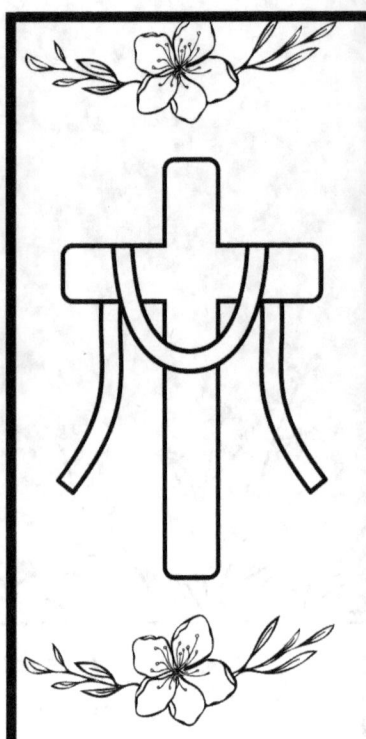
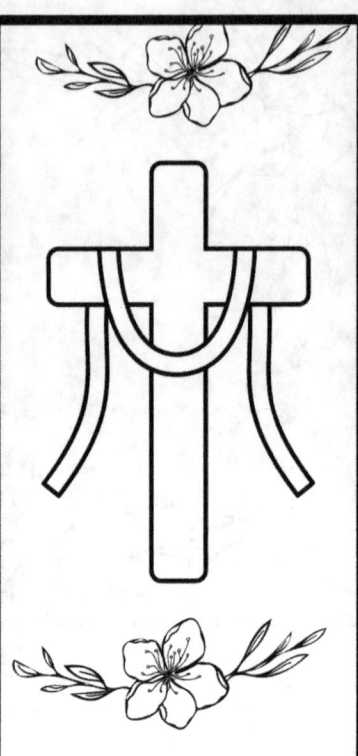

Joshua 1:9 "Have I not commanded you? Be strong and courageous. Do not be frightened, and do not be dismayed, for the Lord your God is with you wherever you go."

Joshua 1:9 "Have I not commanded you? Be strong and courageous. Do not be frightened, and do not be dismayed, for the Lord your God is with you wherever you go."

Joshua 1:9 "Have I not commanded you? Be strong and courageous. Do not be frightened, and do not be dismayed, for the Lord your God is with you wherever you go."

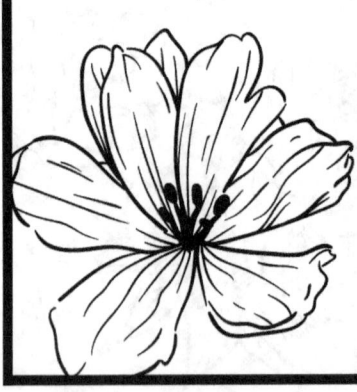
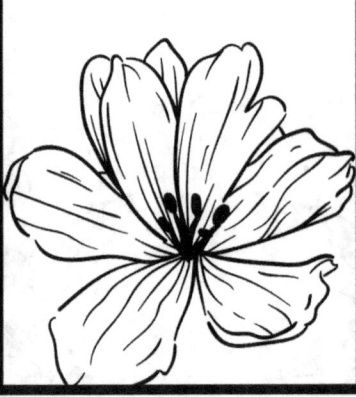
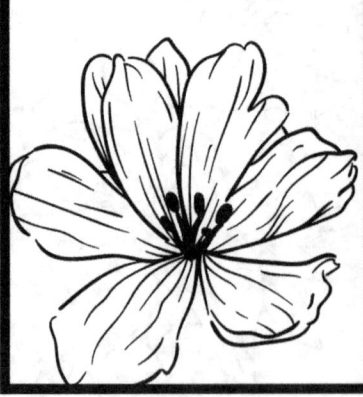

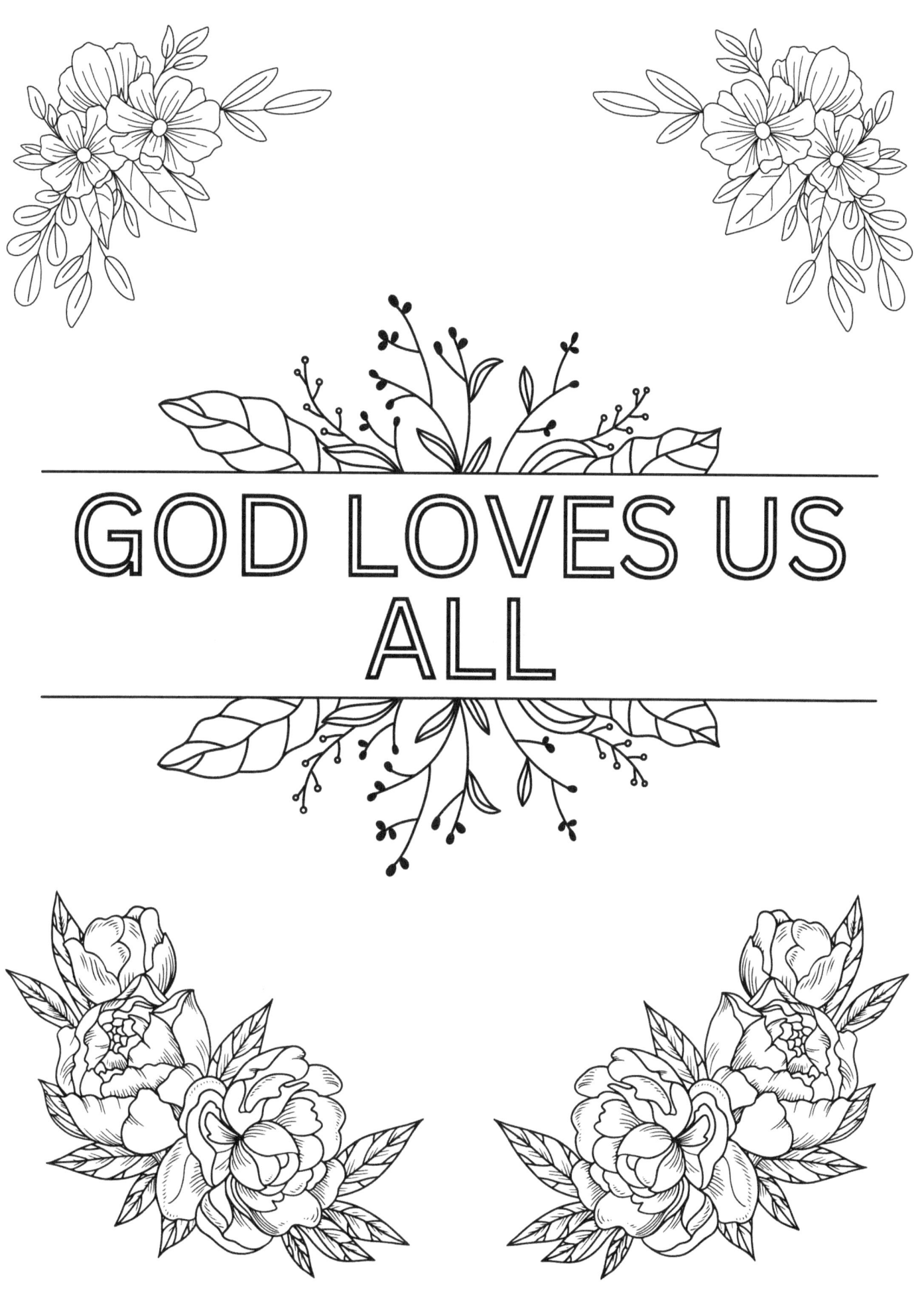

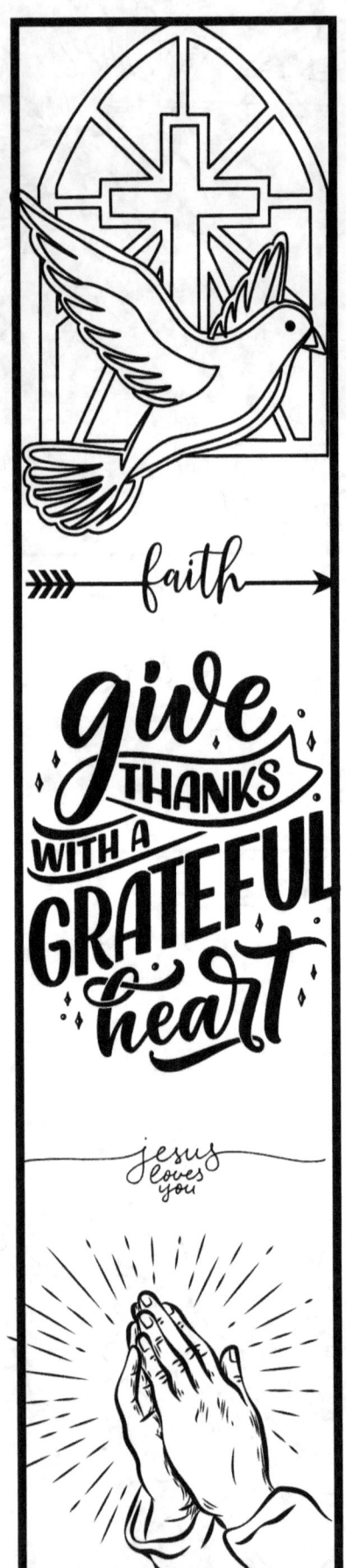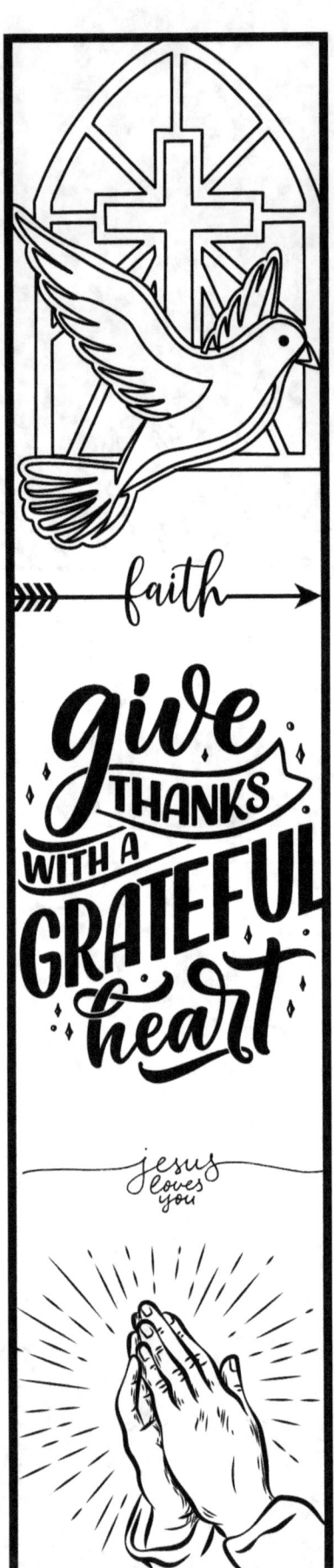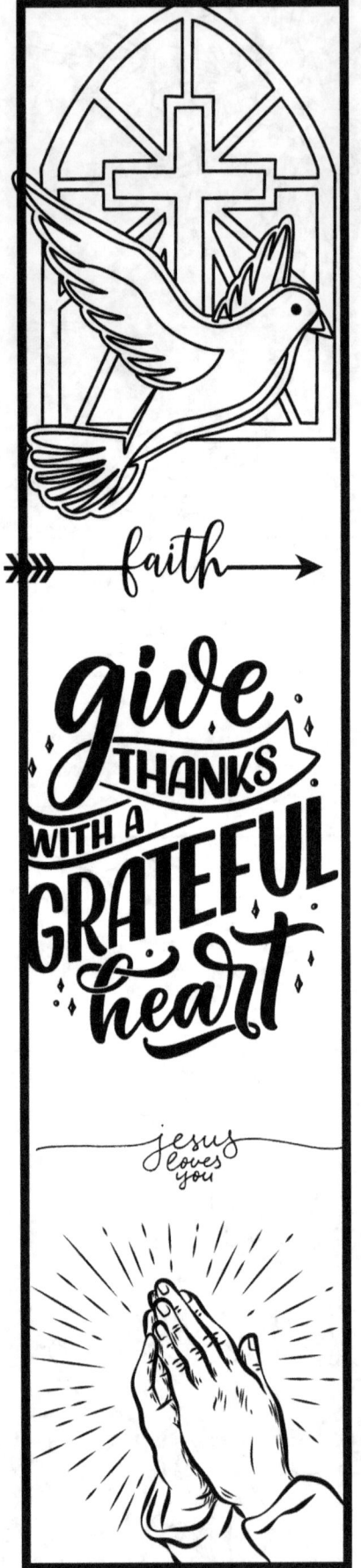

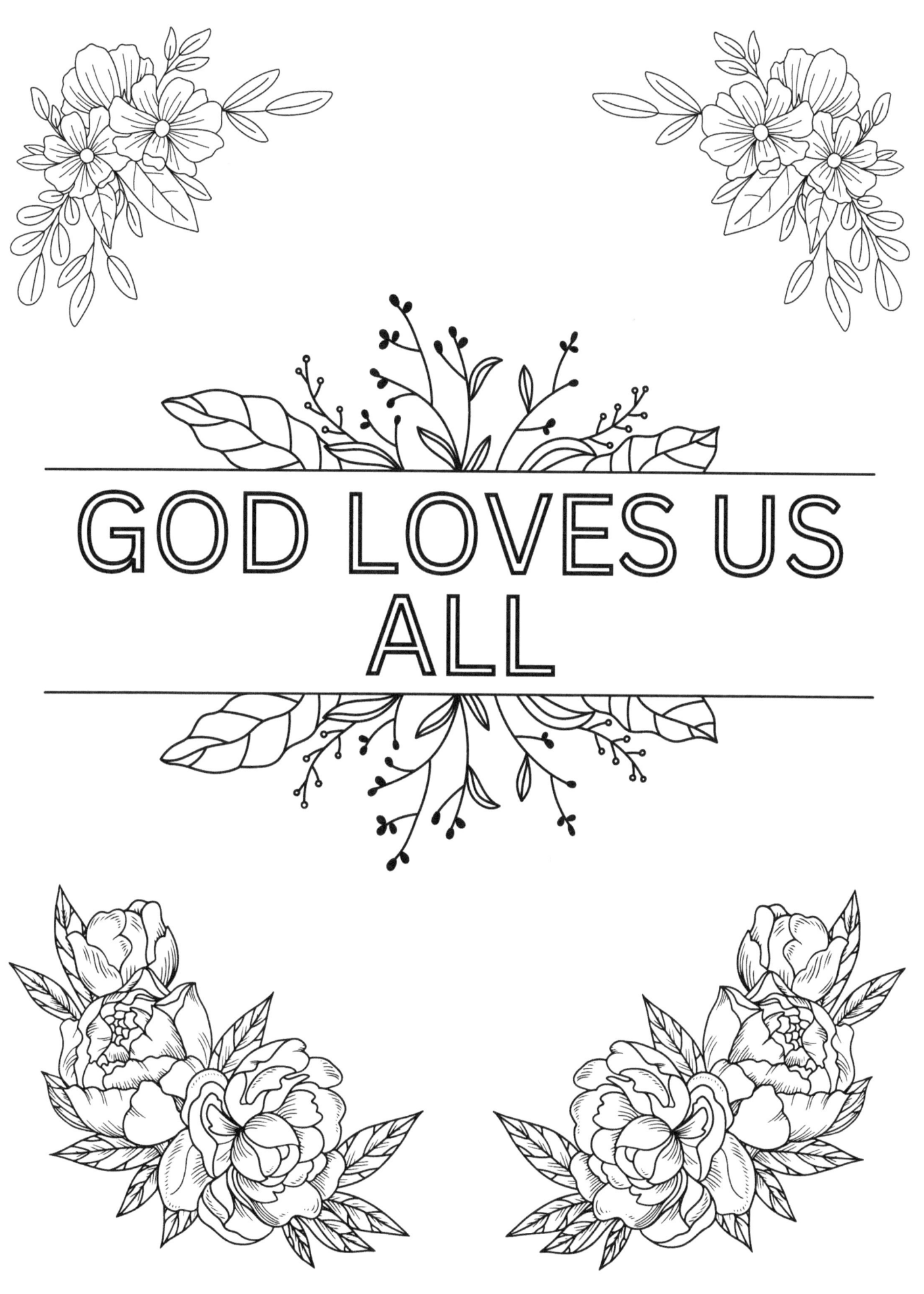

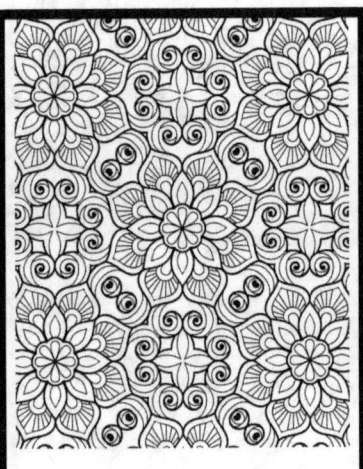 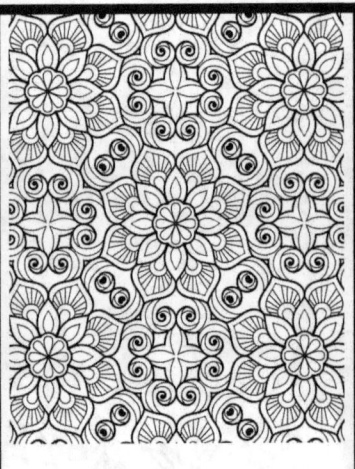 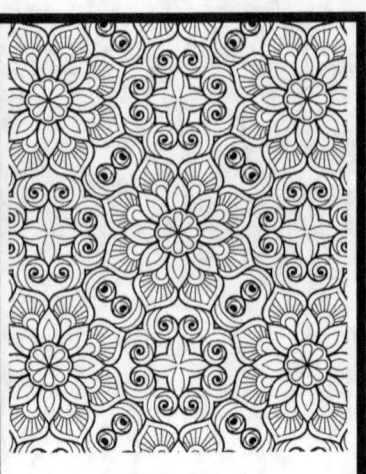

Psalm 27:1
"The Lord is my light and my salvation; whom shall I fear? The Lord is the stronghold of my life; of whom shall I be afraid?"

Psalm 27:1
"The Lord is my light and my salvation; whom shall I fear? The Lord is the stronghold of my life; of whom shall I be afraid?"

Psalm 27:1
"The Lord is my light and my salvation; whom shall I fear? The Lord is the stronghold of my life; of whom shall I be afraid?"

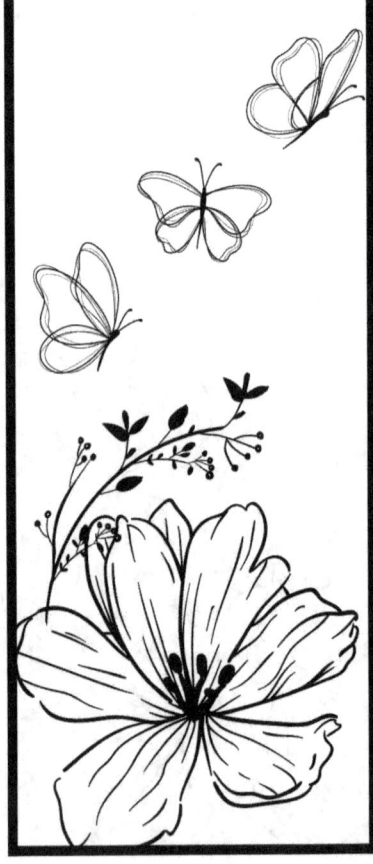 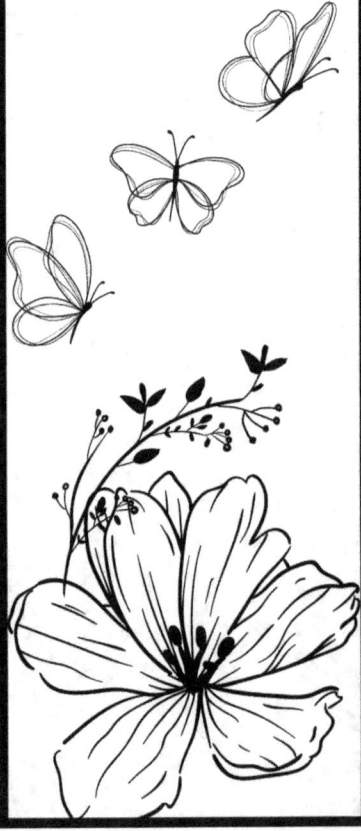 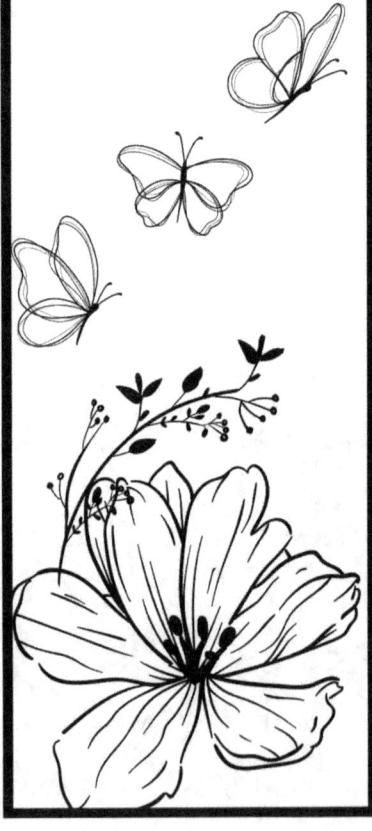

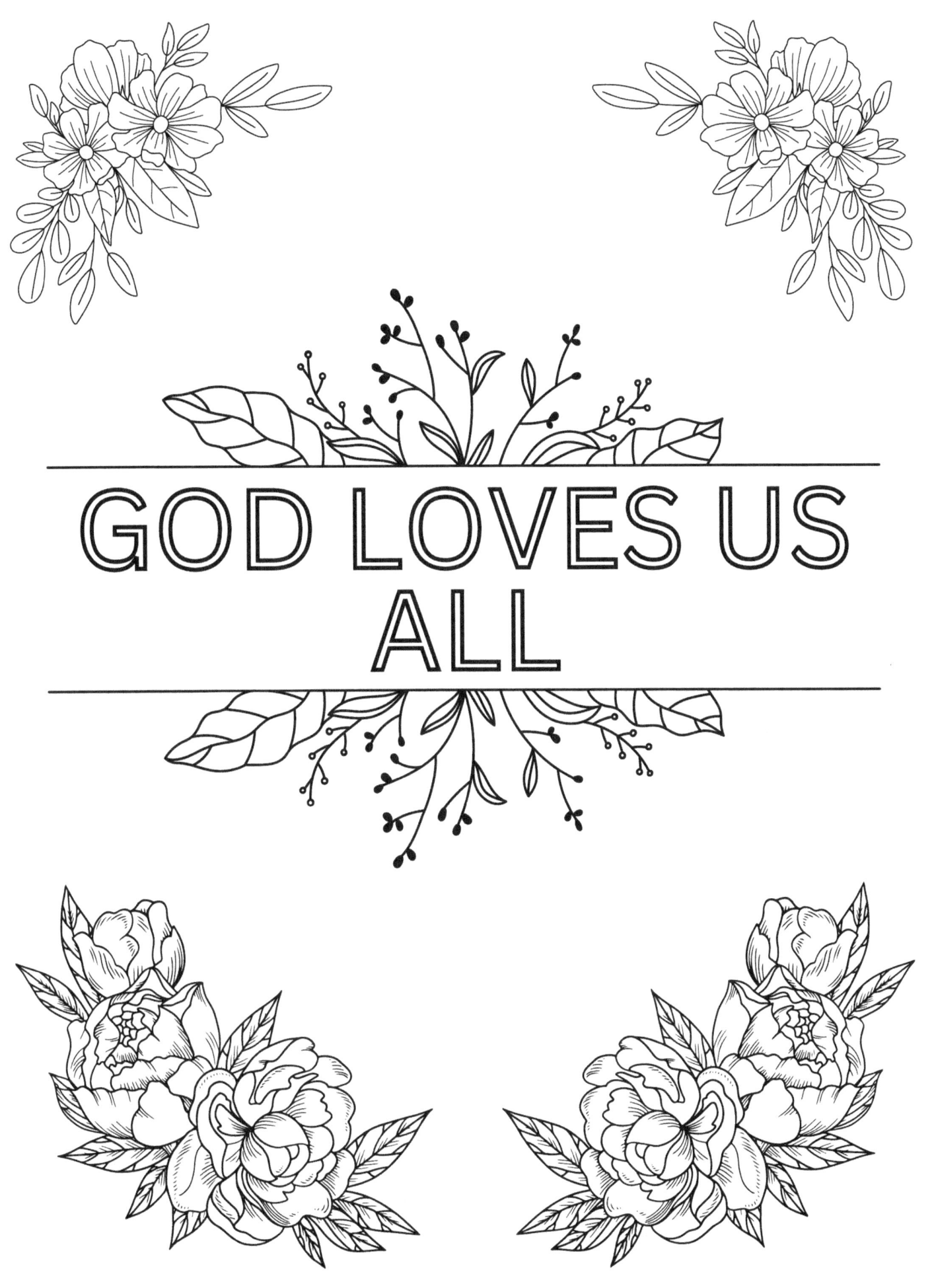

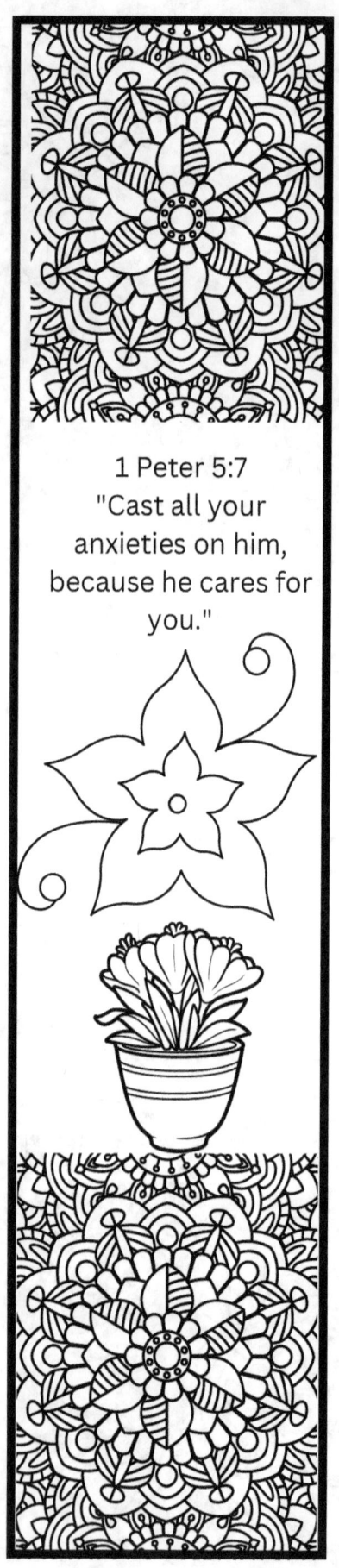#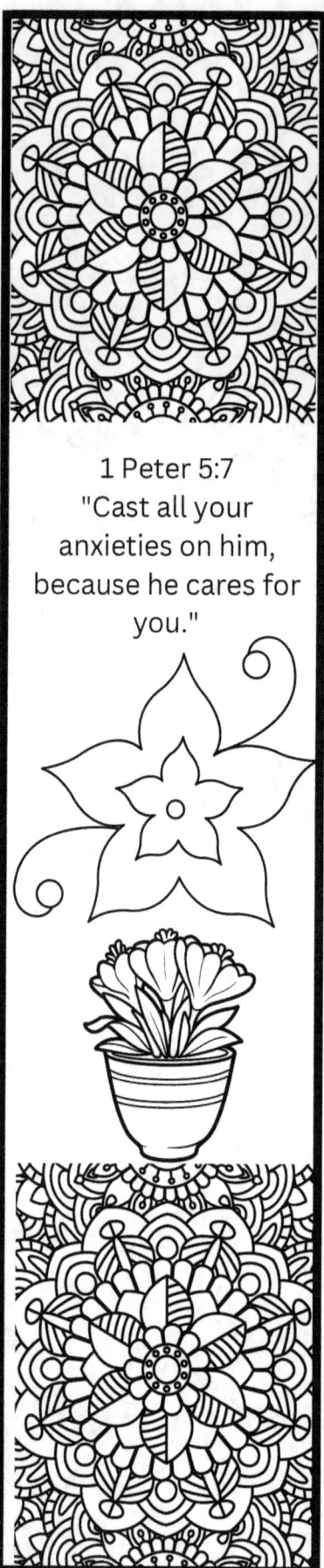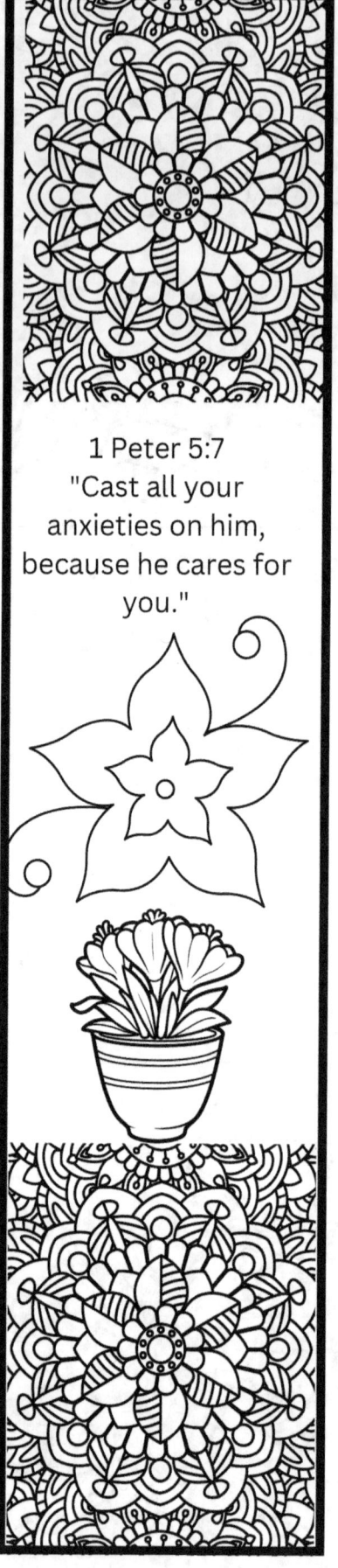

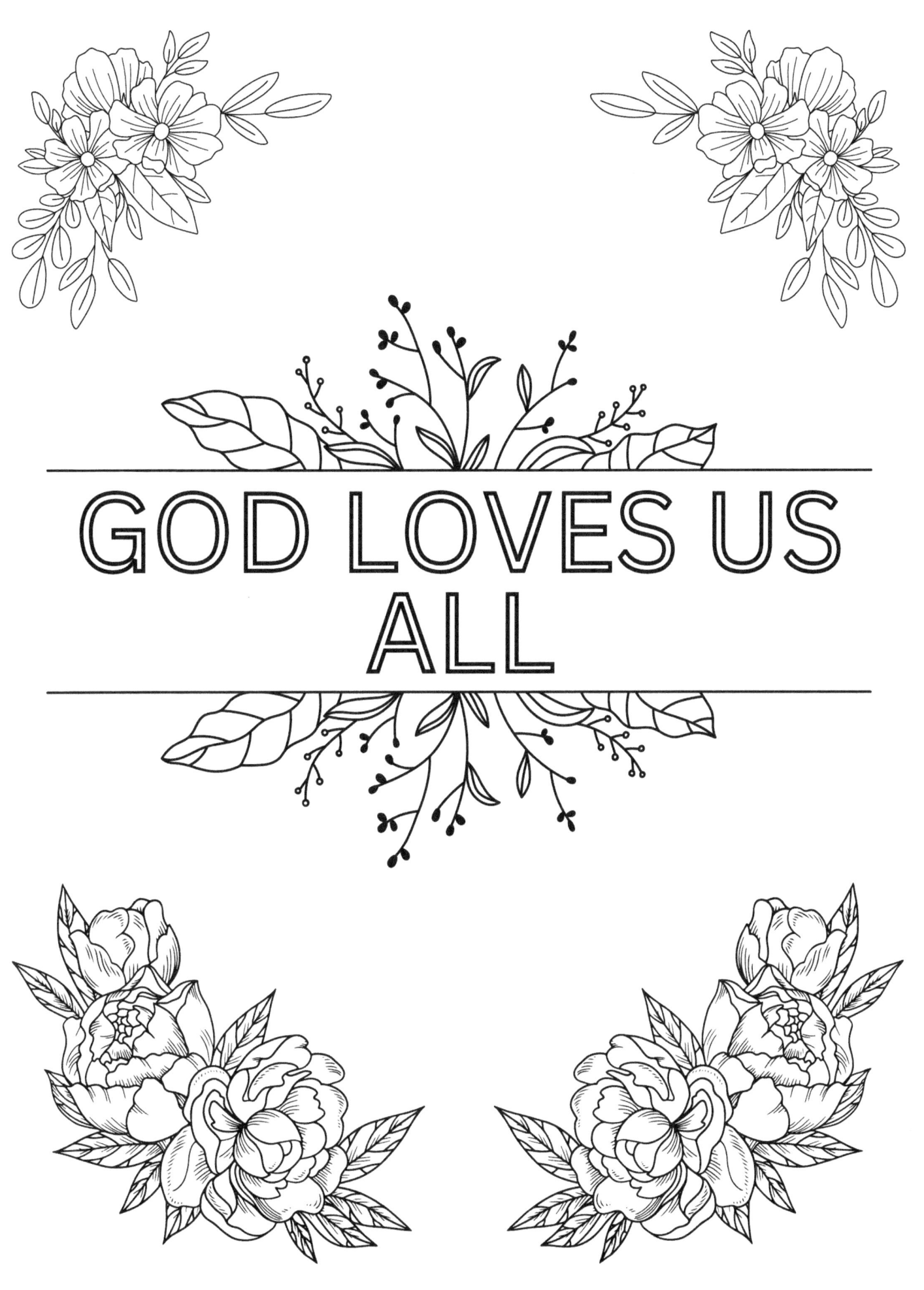

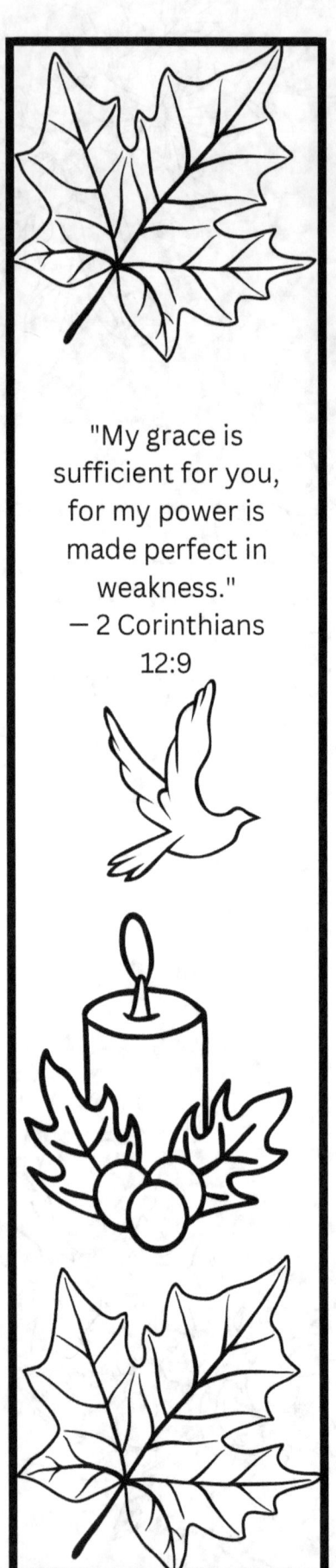
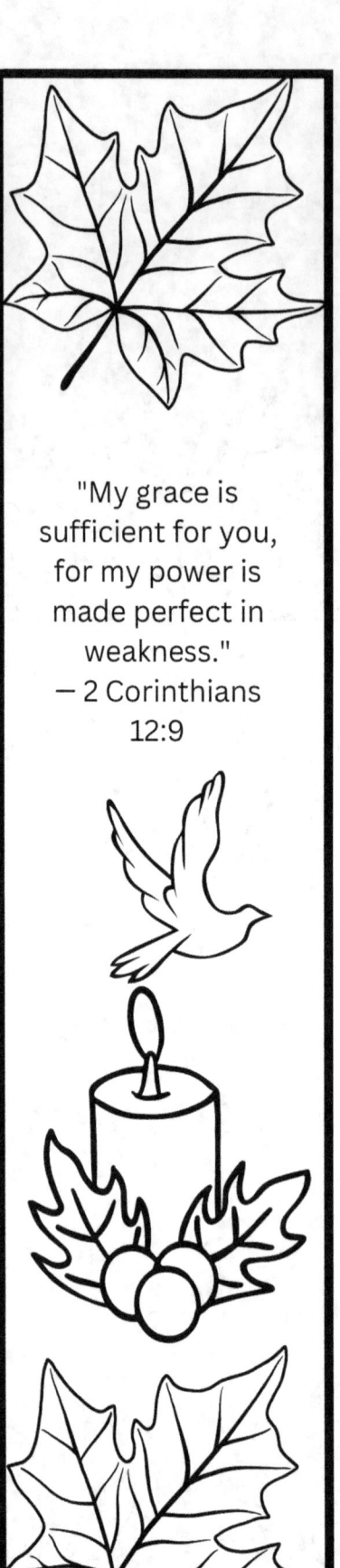
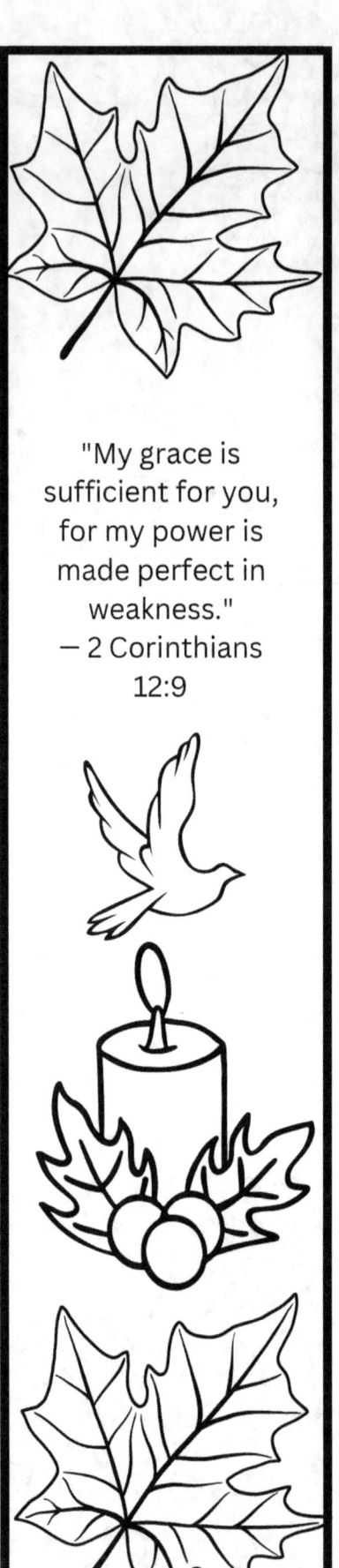

"My grace is sufficient for you, for my power is made perfect in weakness."
— 2 Corinthians 12:9

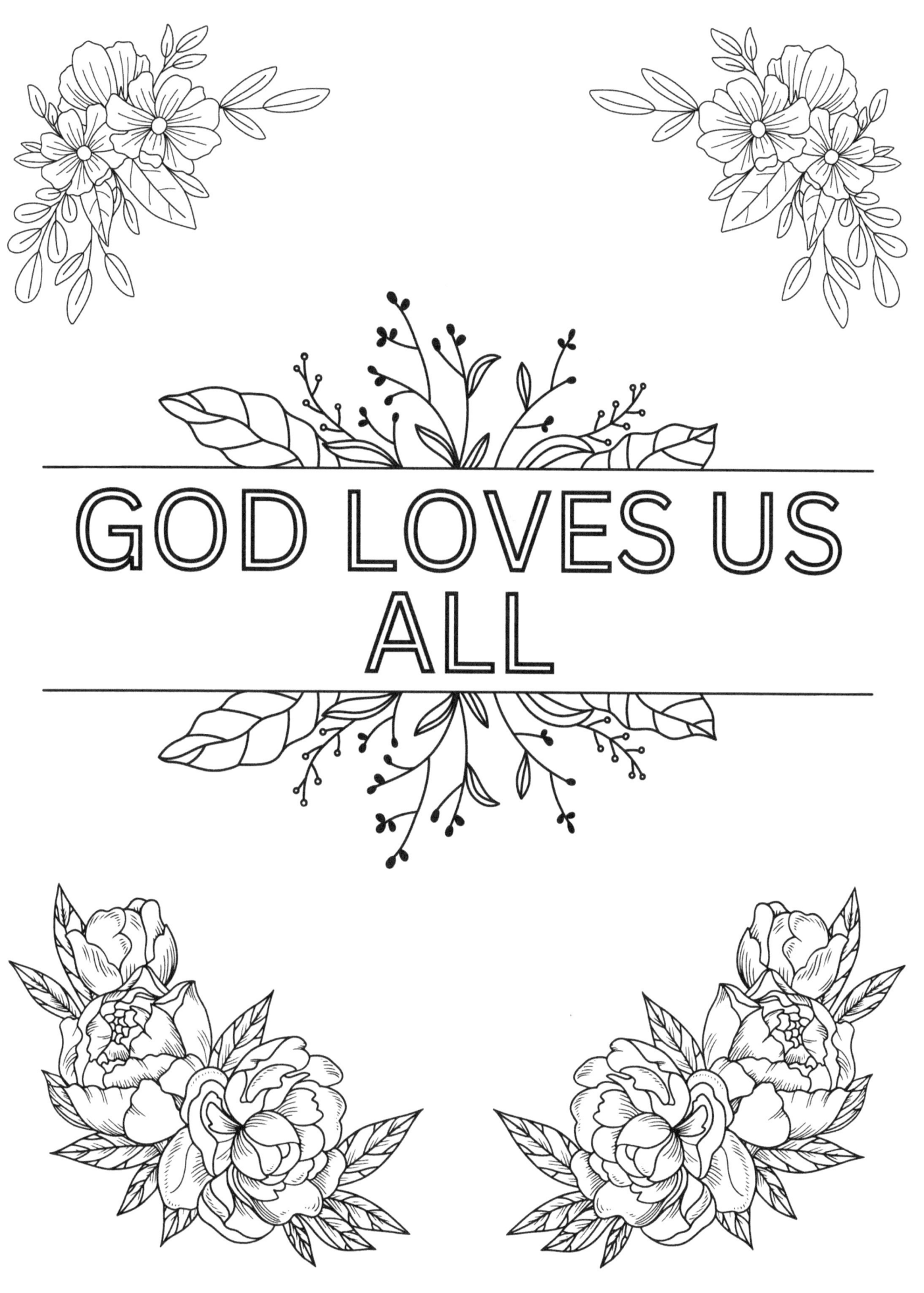

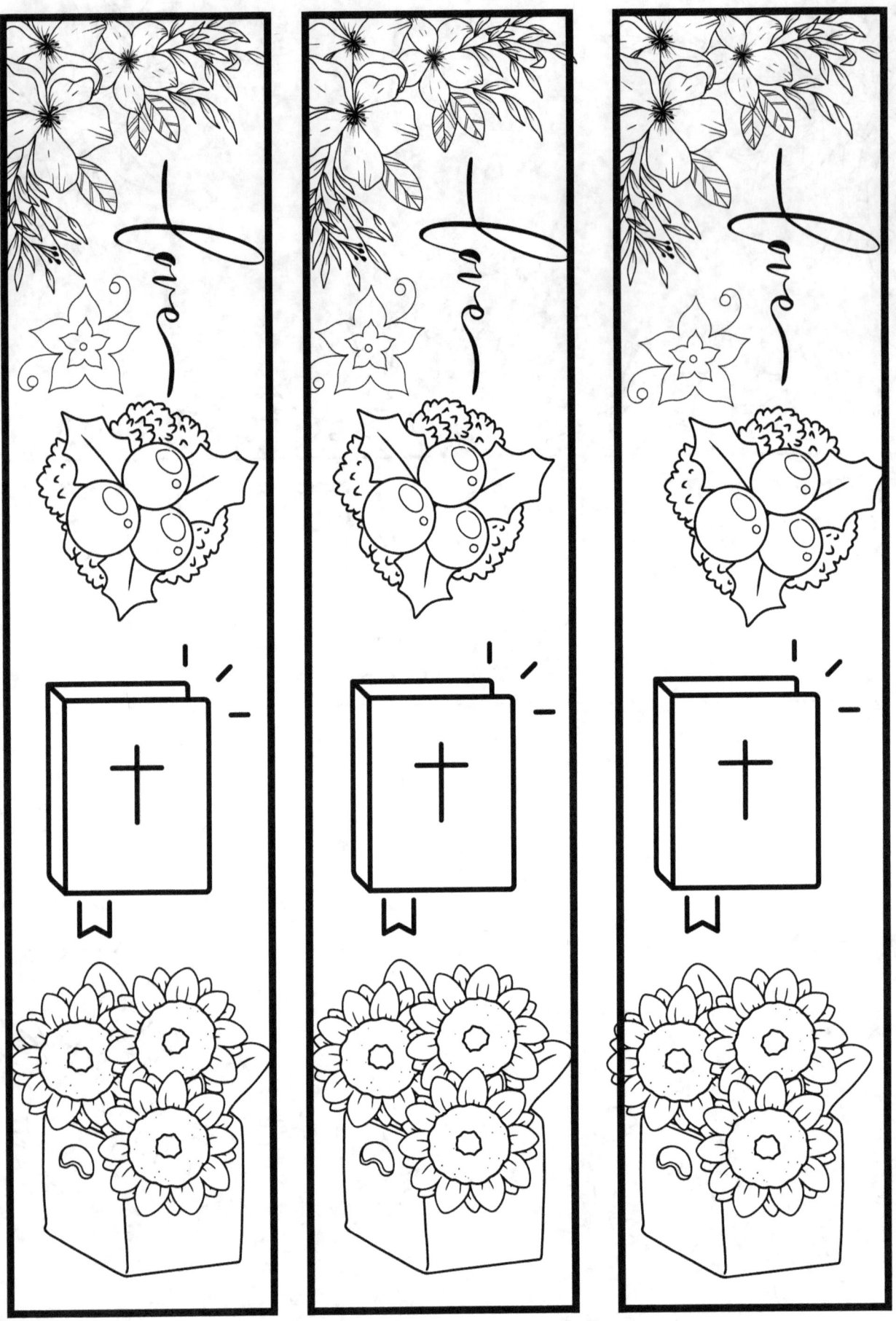

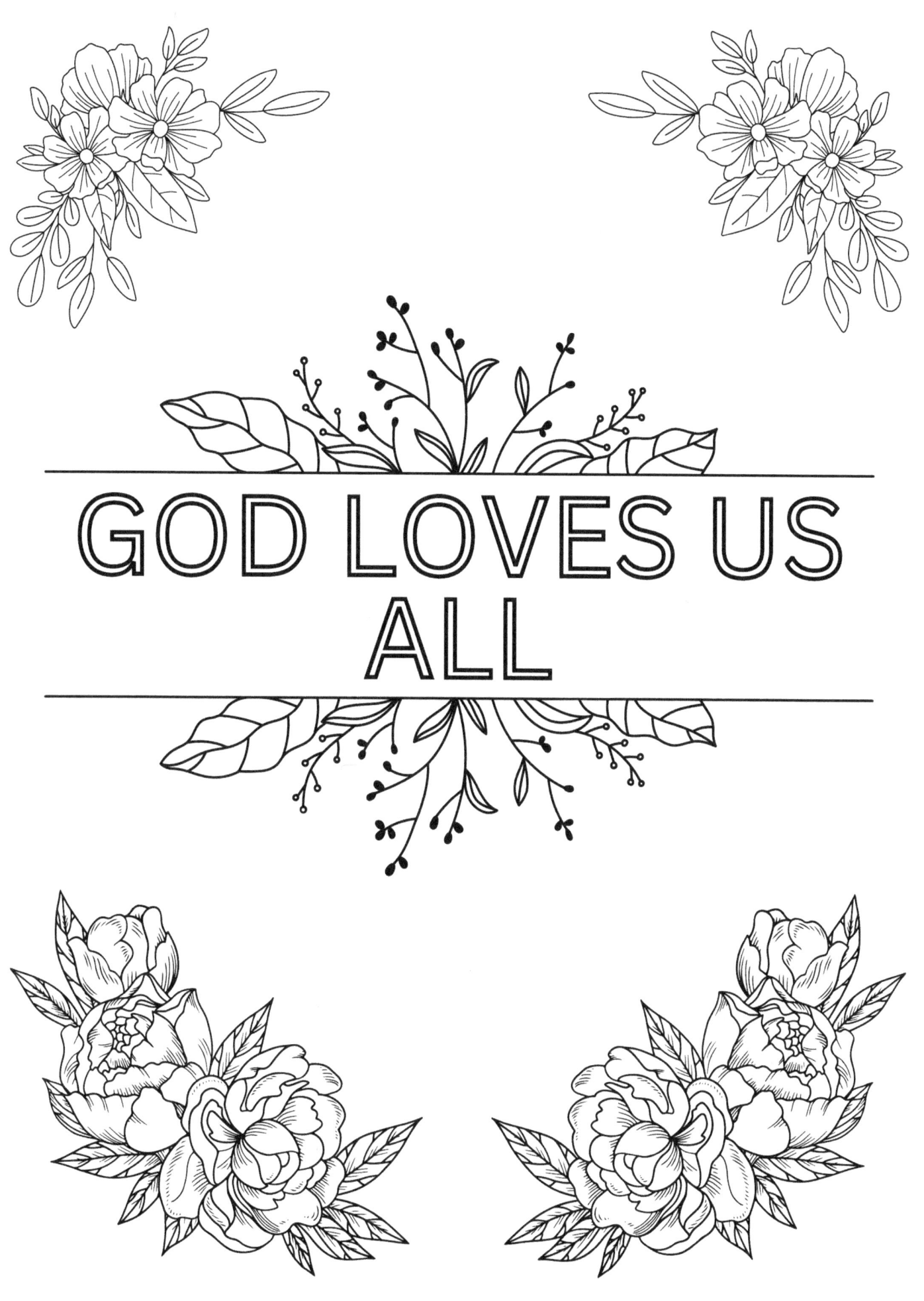

Philippians 4:6-7 (NIV):
"Do not be anxious about anything, but in every situation, by prayer and petition, with thanksgiving, present your requests to God. And the peace of God, which transcends all understanding, will guard your hearts and your minds in Christ Jesus."

Philippians 4:6-7 (NIV):
"Do not be anxious about anything, but in every situation, by prayer and petition, with thanksgiving, present your requests to God. And the peace of God, which transcends all understanding, will guard your hearts and your minds in Christ Jesus."

Philippians 4:6-7 (NIV):
"Do not be anxious about anything, but in every situation, by prayer and petition, with thanksgiving, present your requests to God. And the peace of God, which transcends all understanding, will guard your hearts and your minds in Christ Jesus."

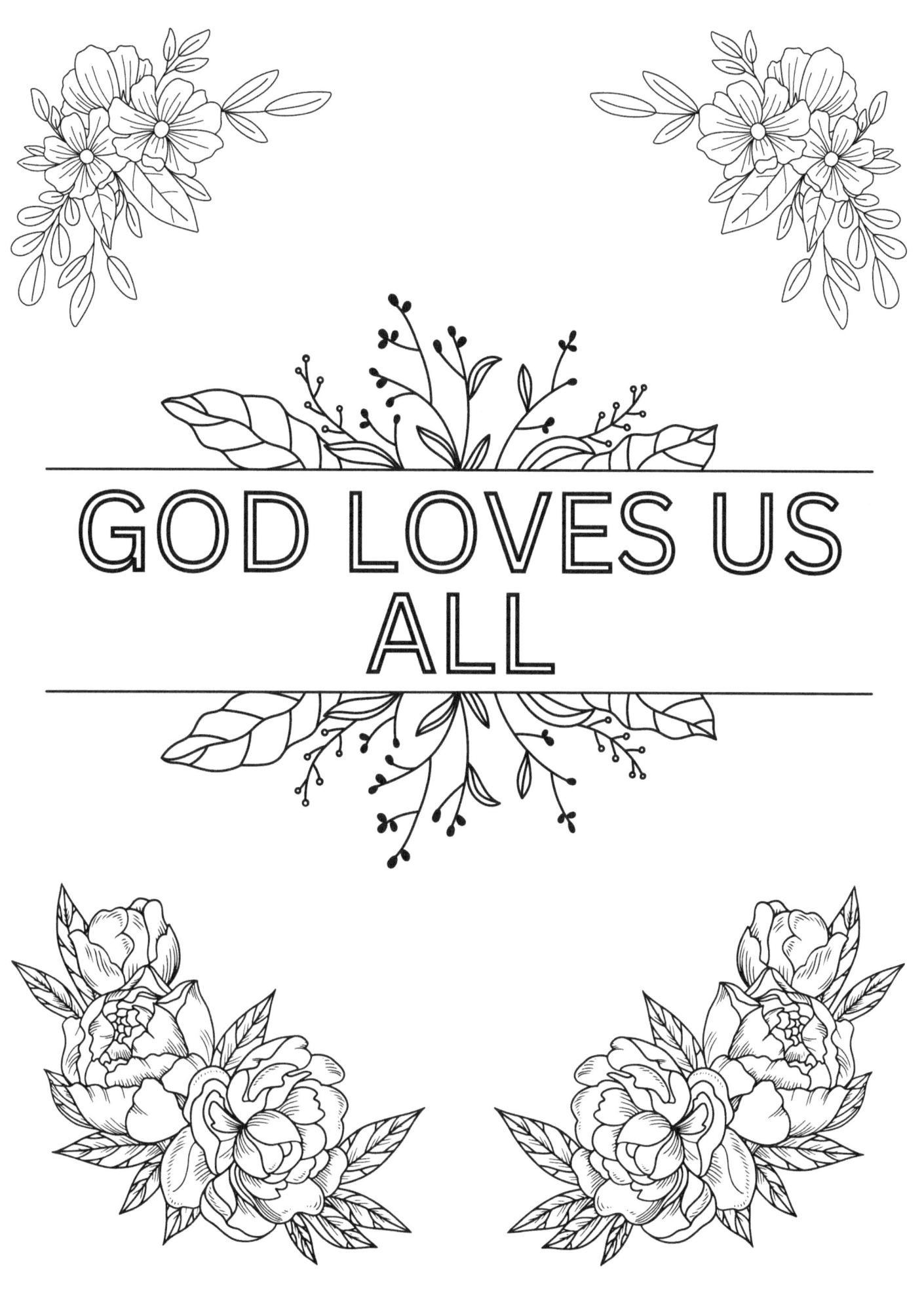

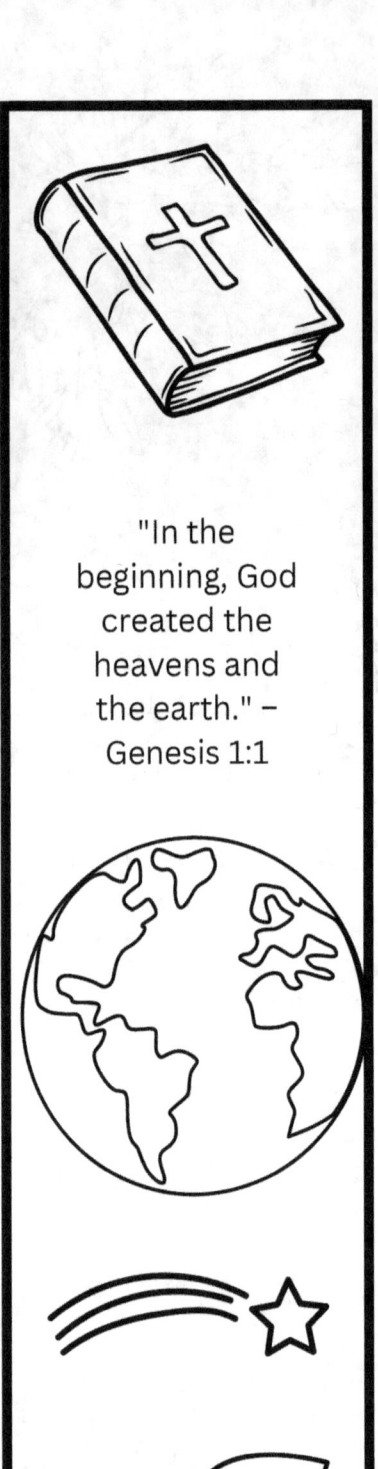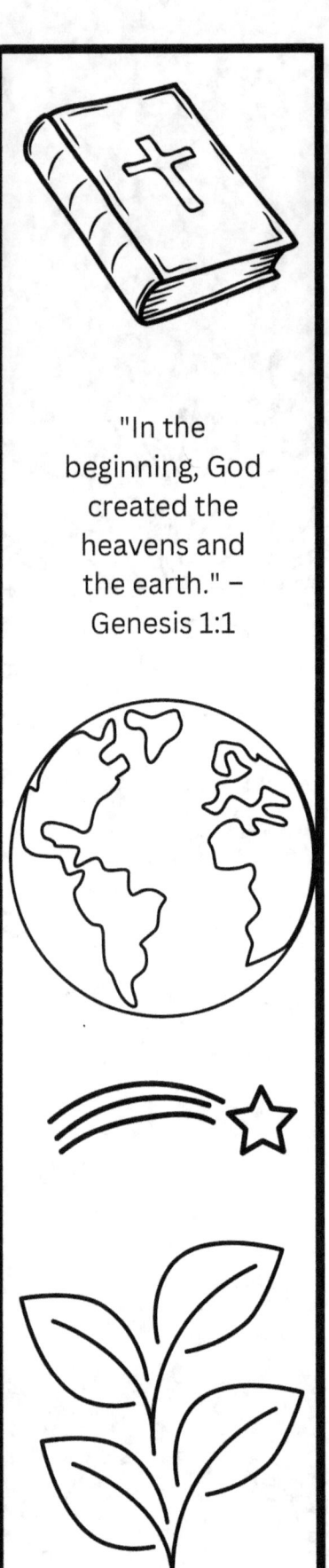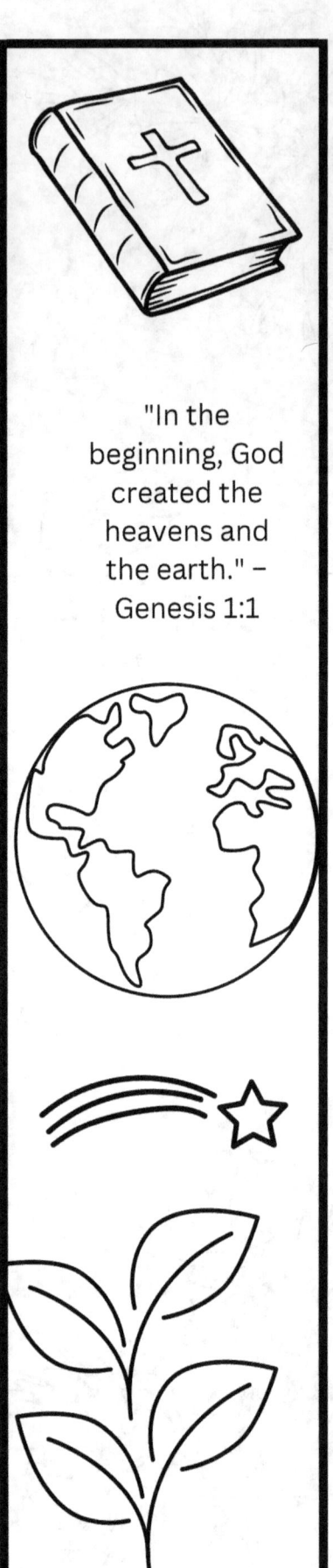

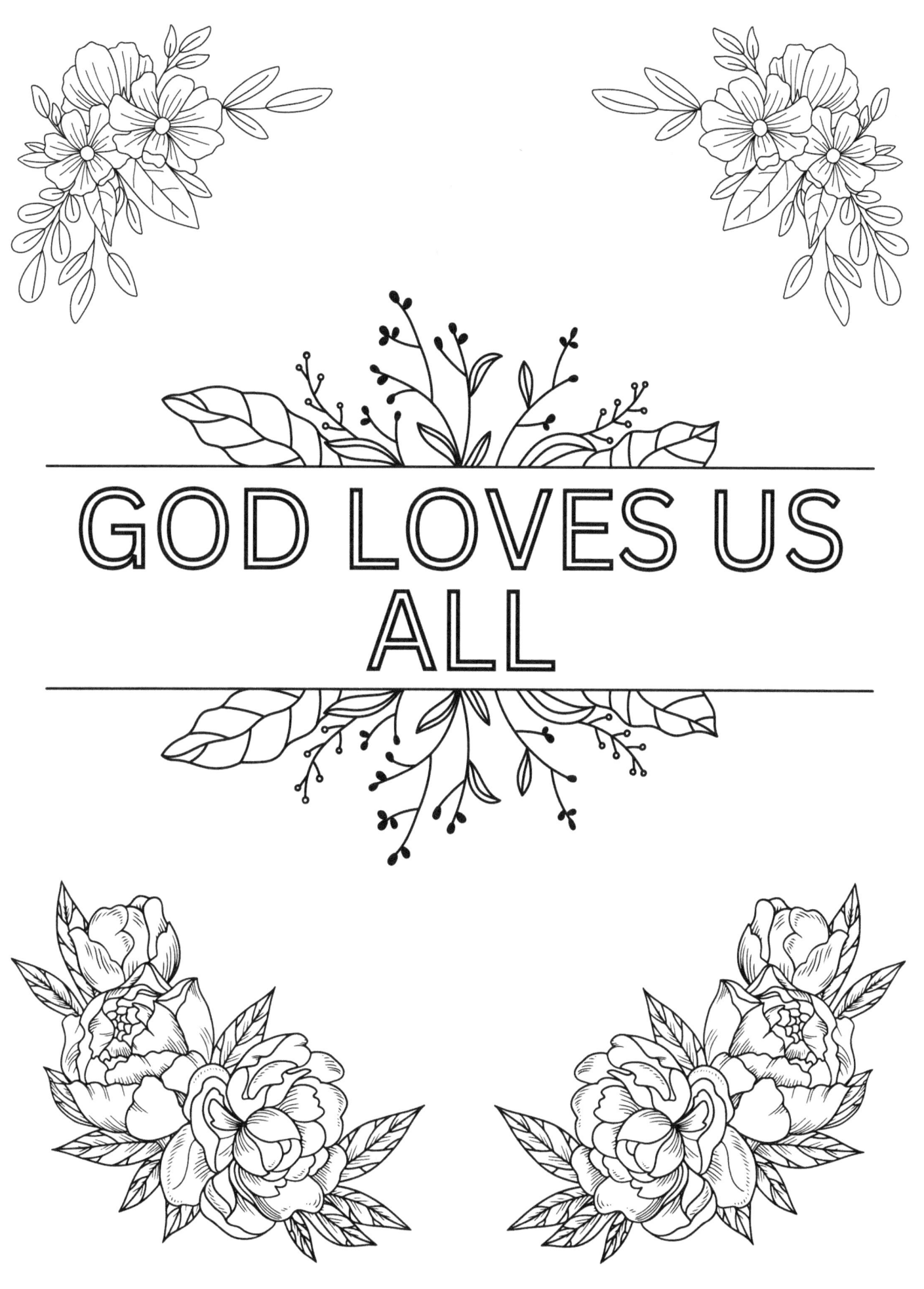

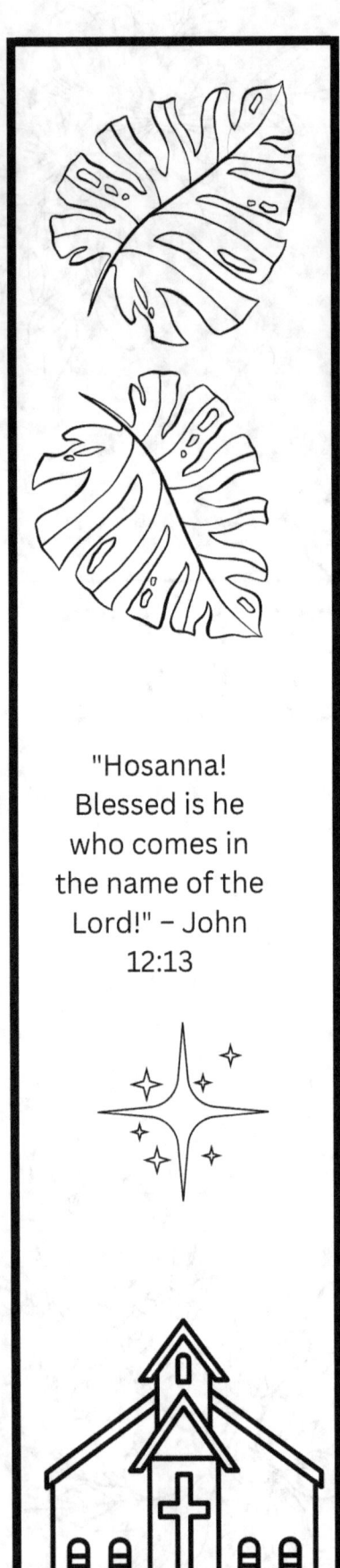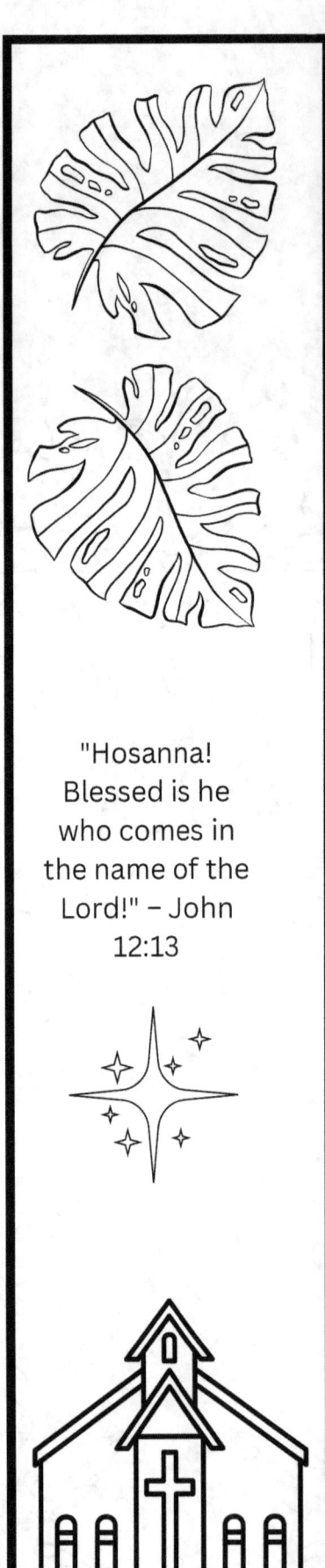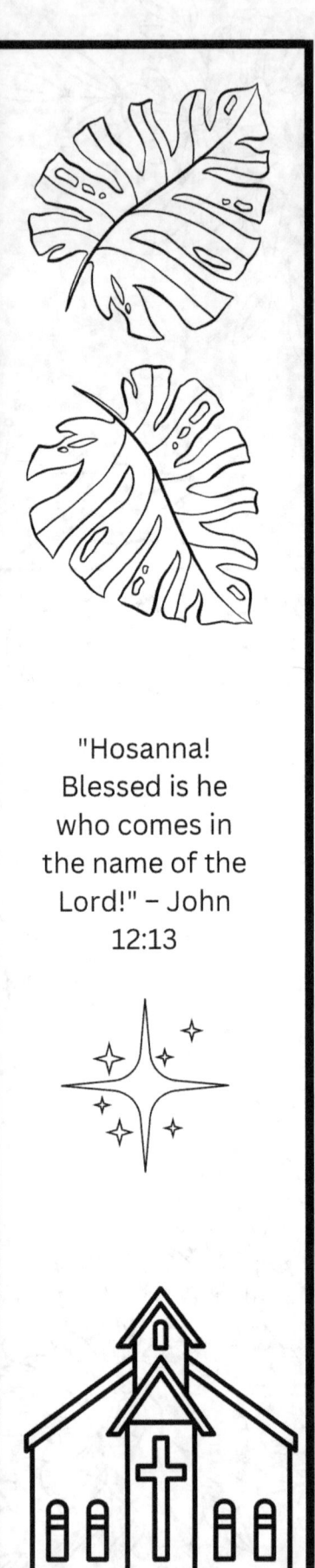

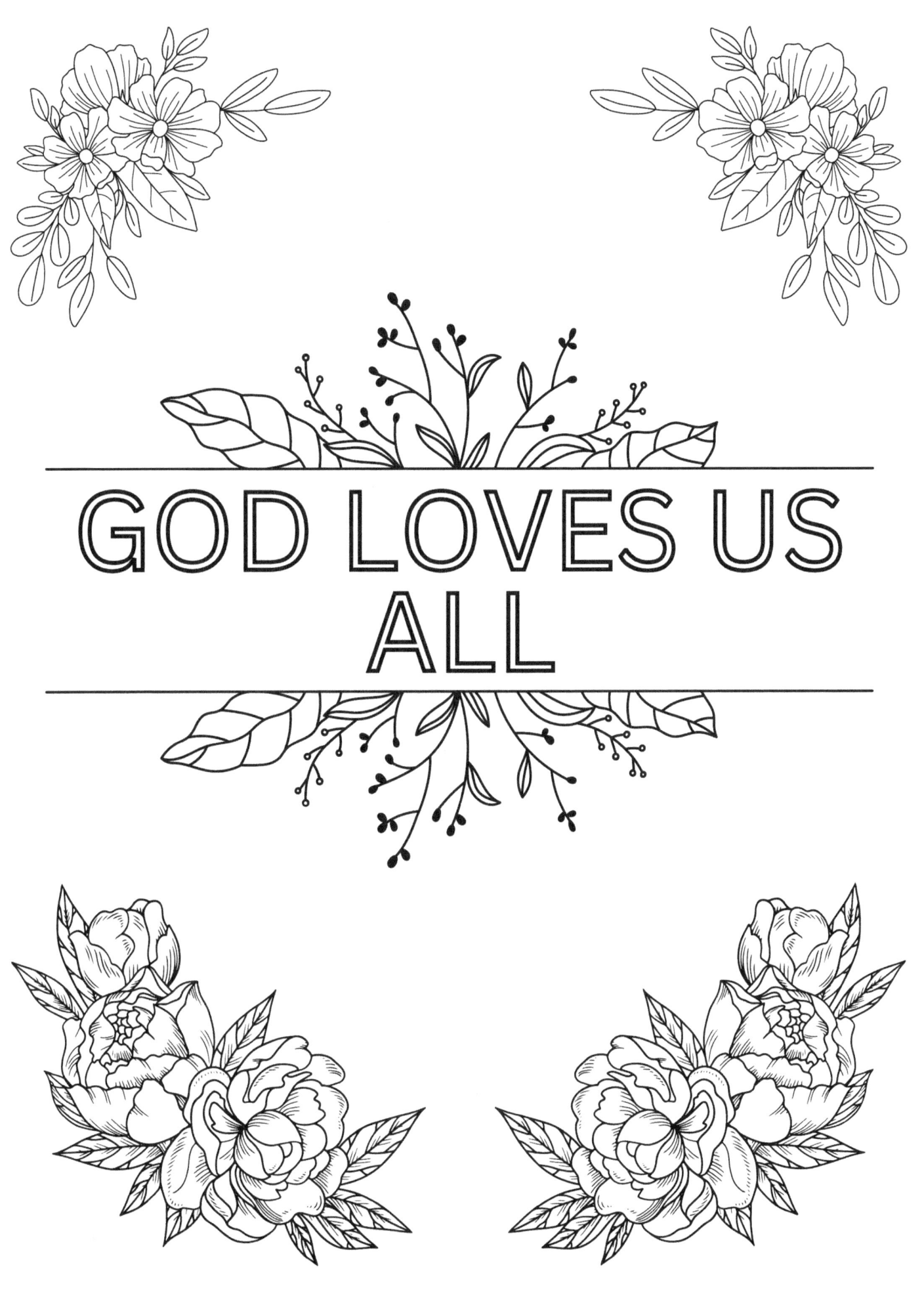

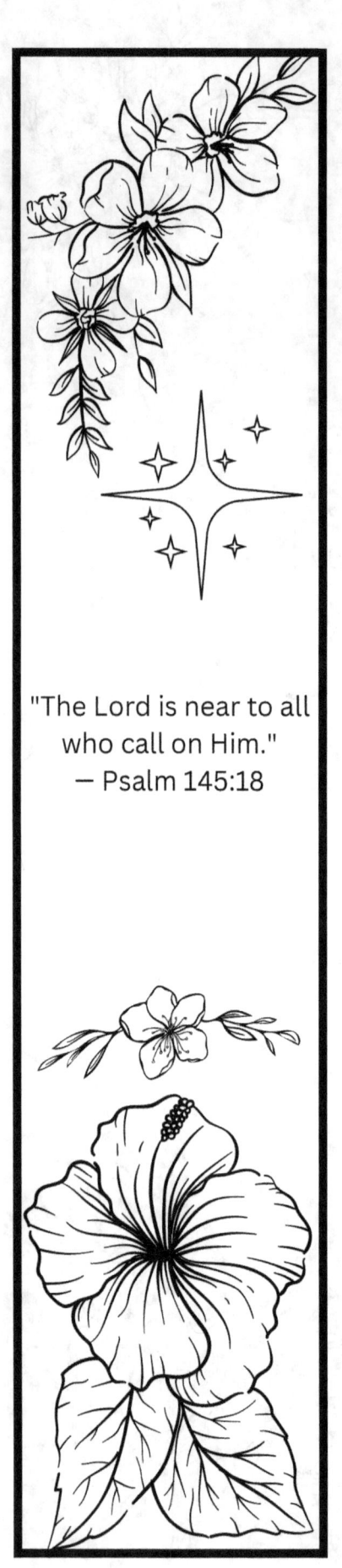
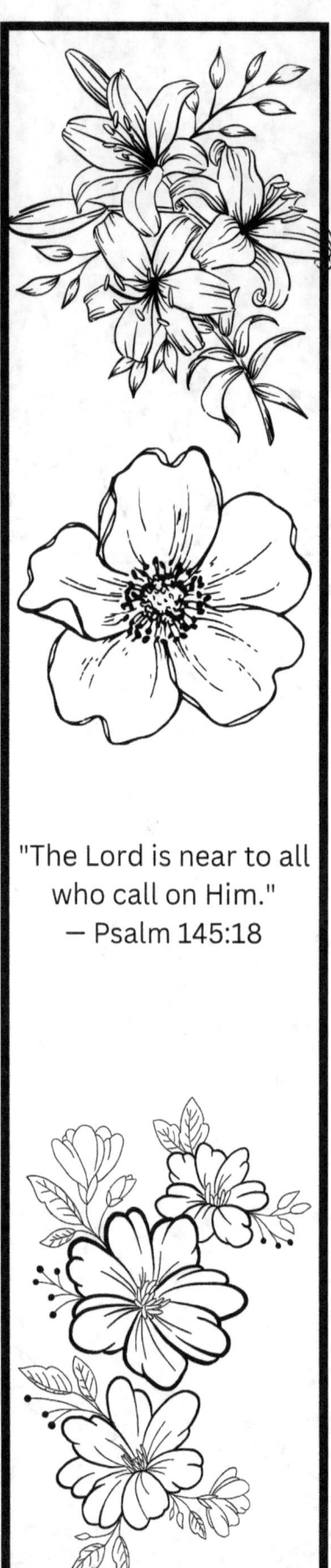
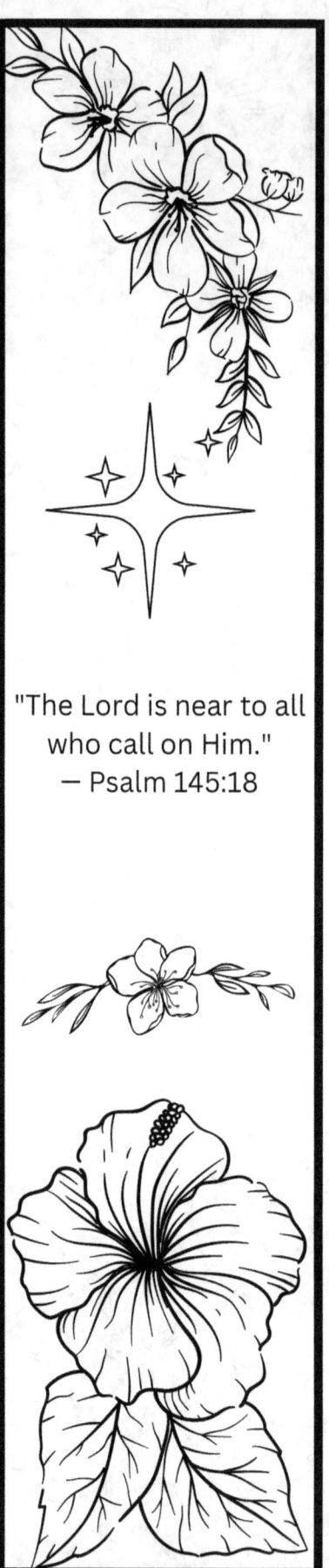

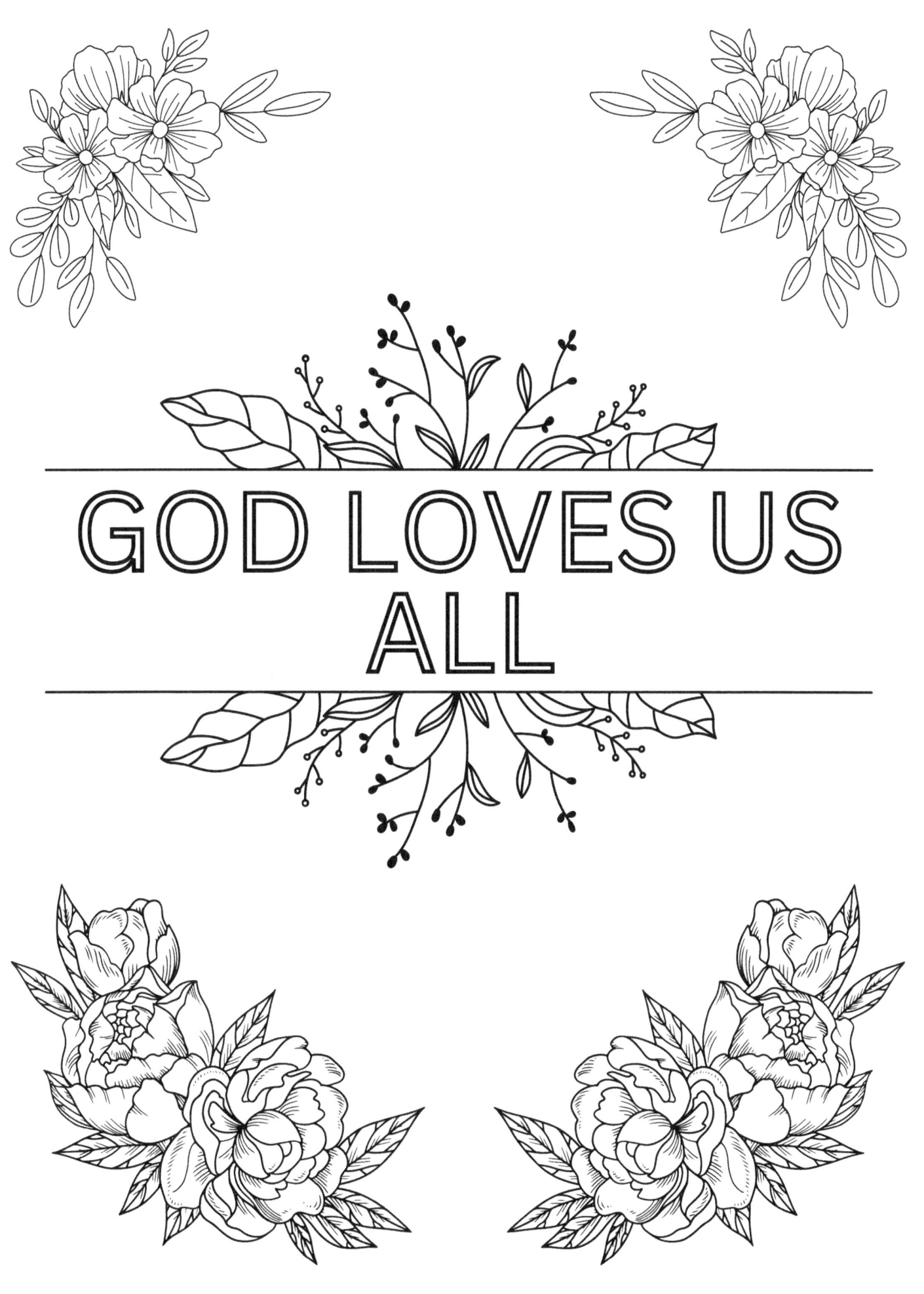

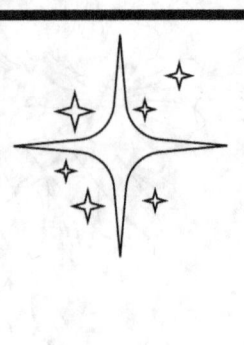
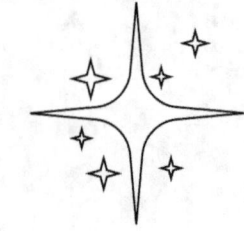
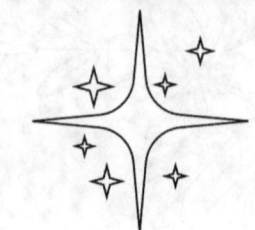

"Be still, and know that I am God." – Psalm 46:10

"Be still, and know that I am God." – Psalm 46:10

"Be still, and know that I am God." – Psalm 46:10

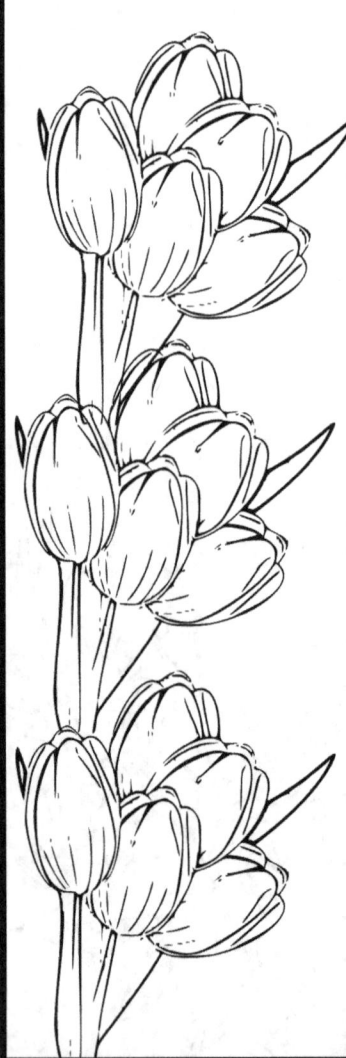
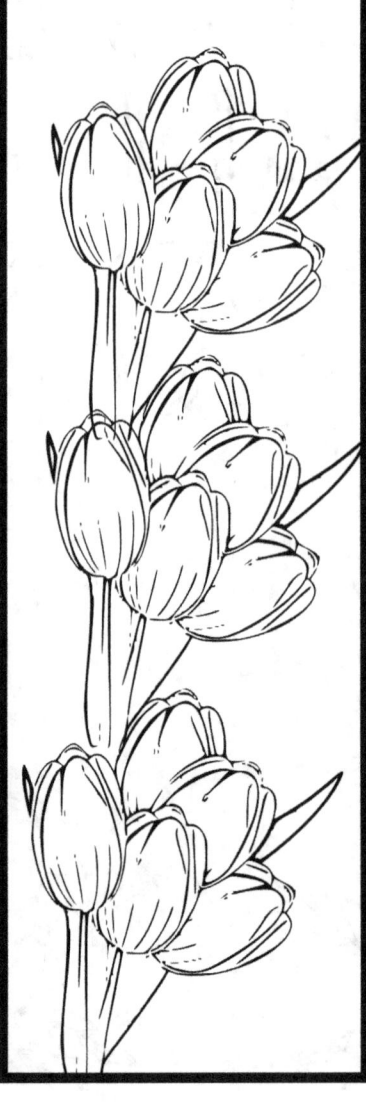
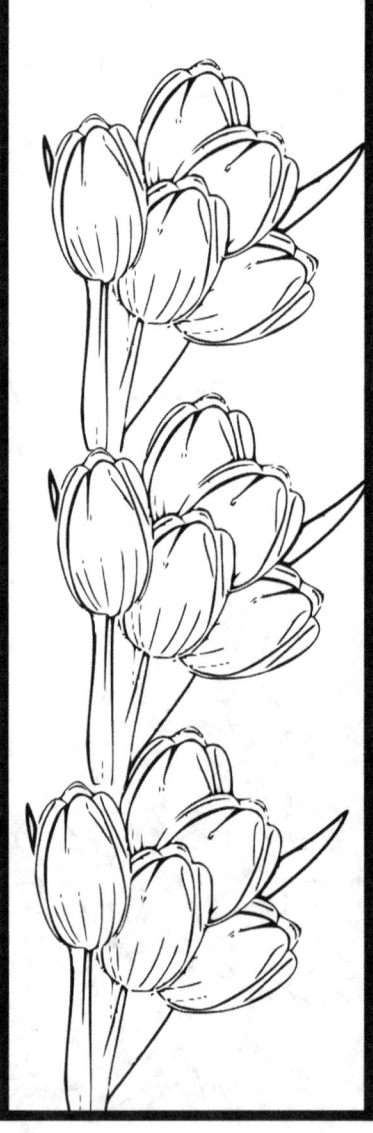

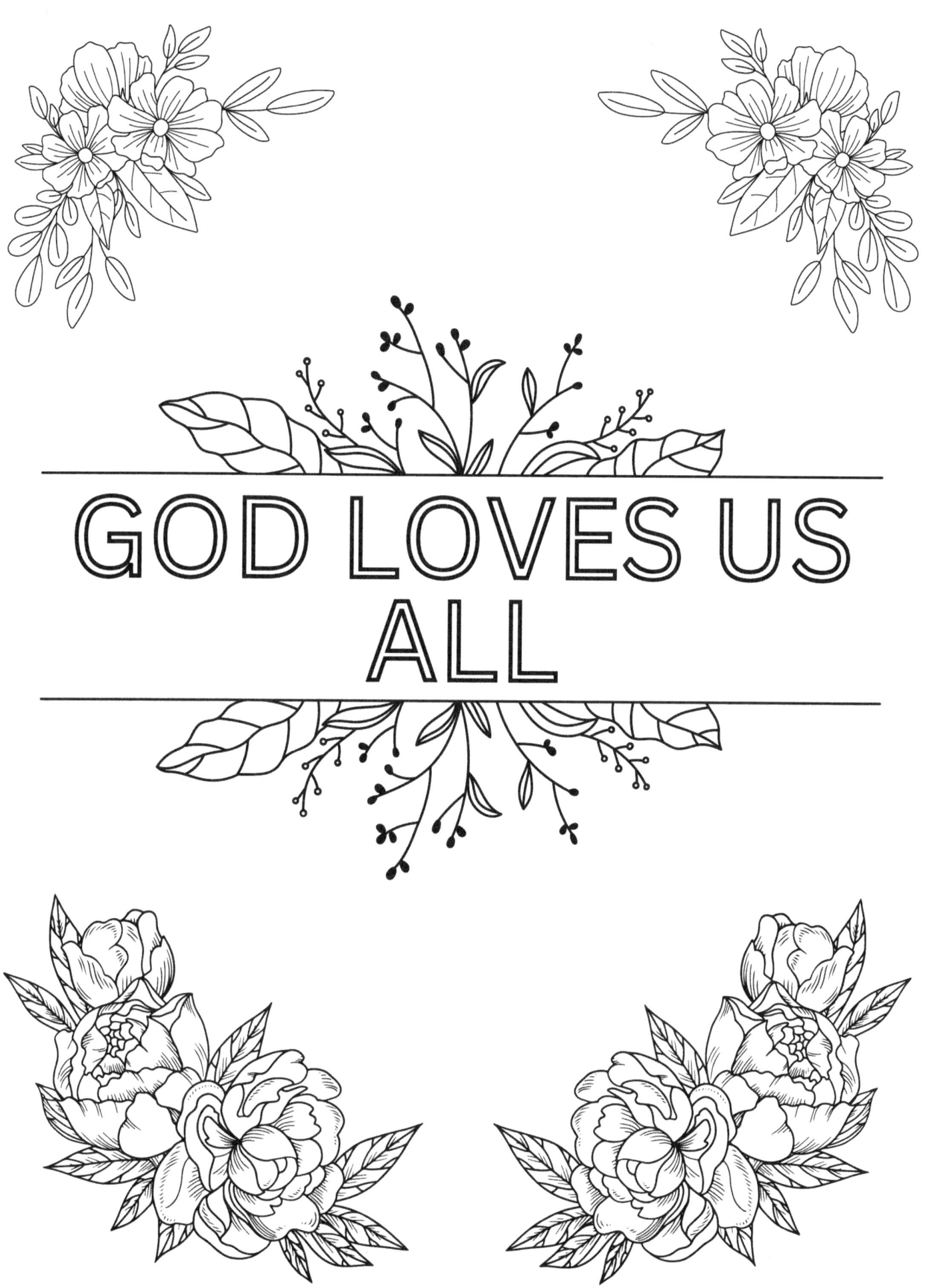

 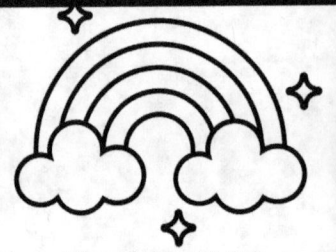 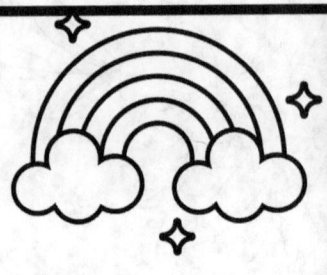

Matthew 6:26 (NIV): "Look at the birds of the air; they do not sow or reap or store away in barns, and yet your heavenly Father feeds them. Are you not much more valuable than they?"

Matthew 6:26 (NIV): "Look at the birds of the air; they do not sow or reap or store away in barns, and yet your heavenly Father feeds them. Are you not much more valuable than they?"

Matthew 6:26 (NIV): "Look at the birds of the air; they do not sow or reap or store away in barns, and yet your heavenly Father feeds them. Are you not much more valuable than they?"

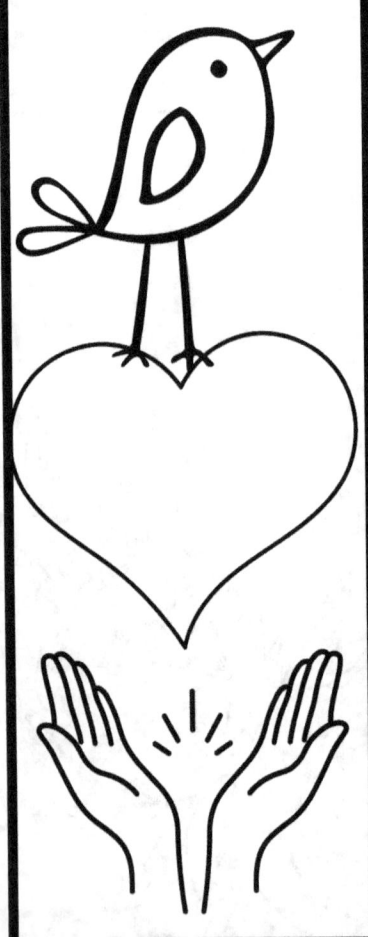 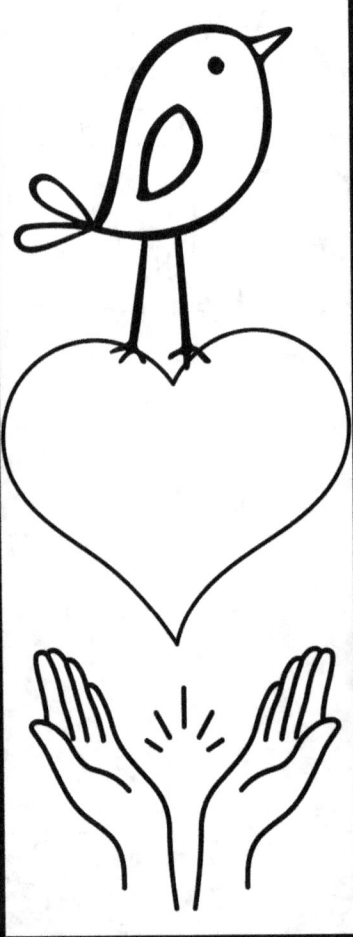 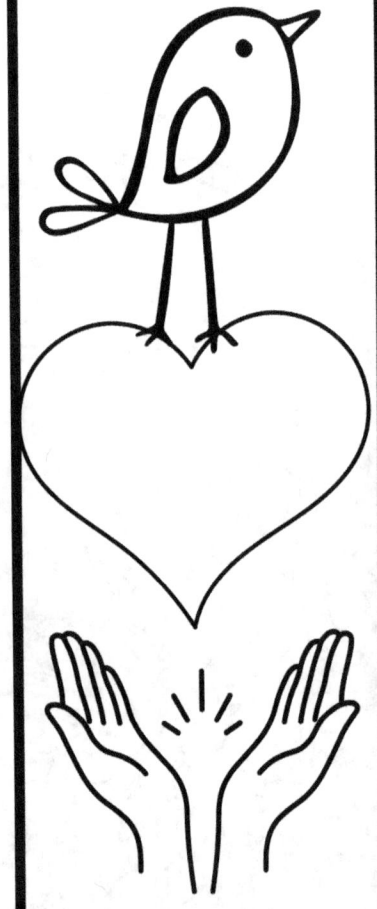

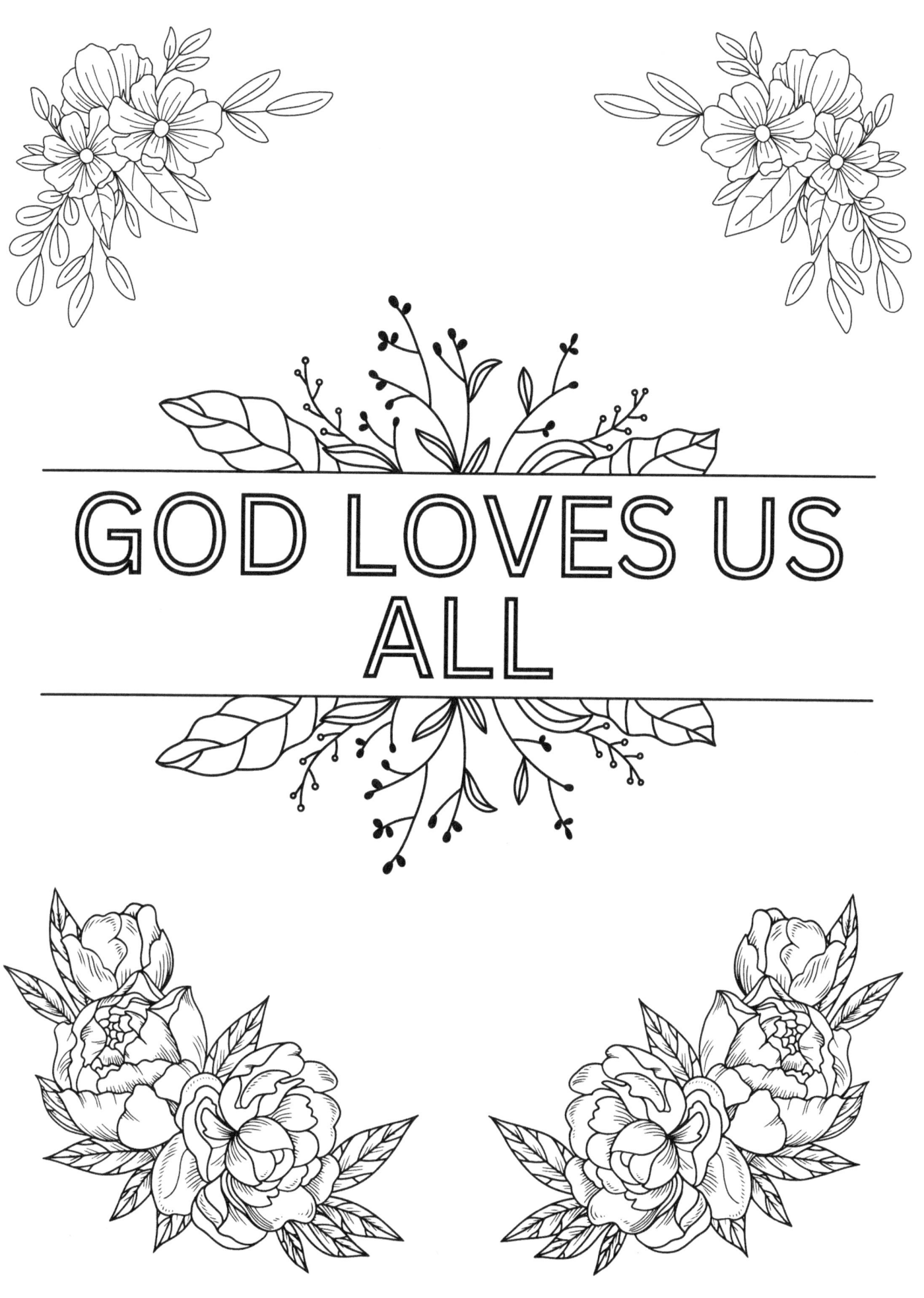

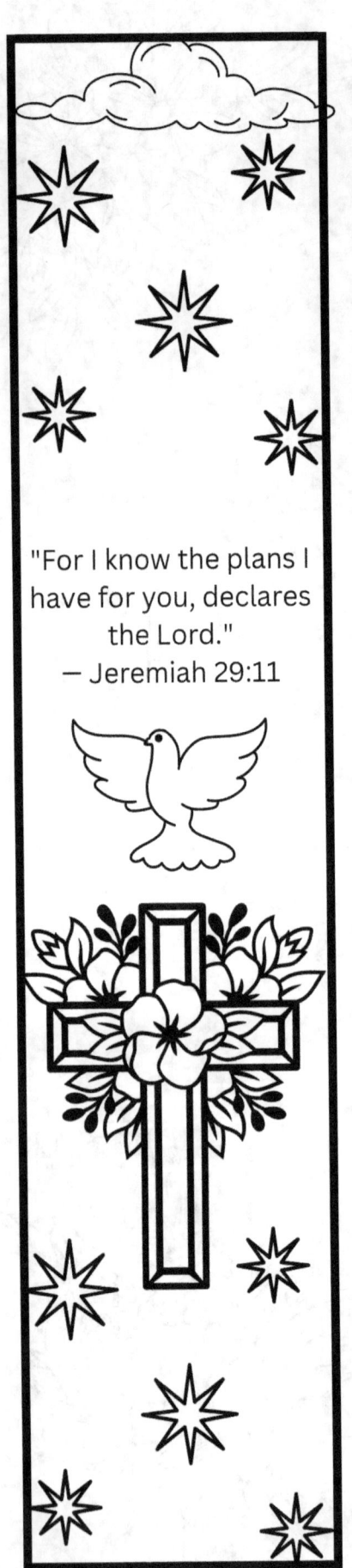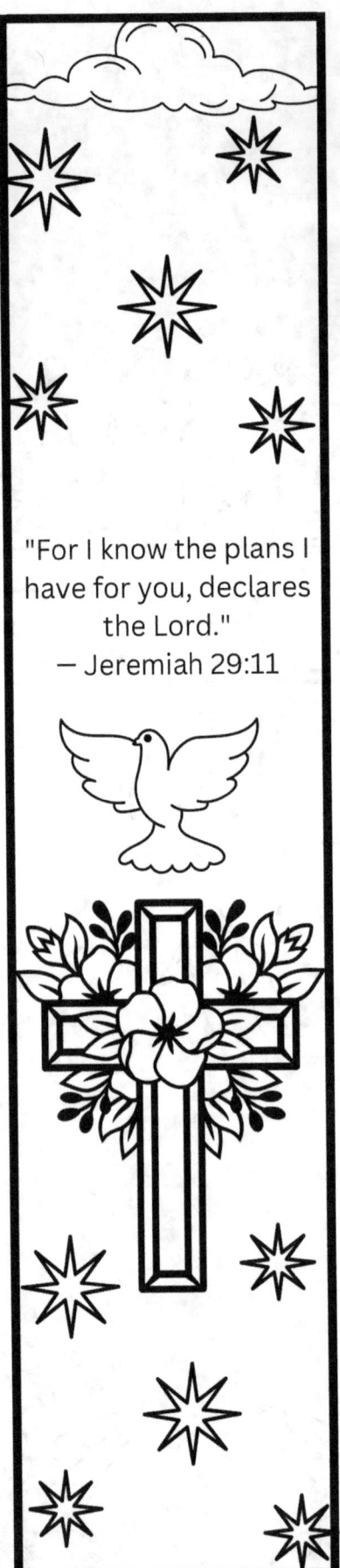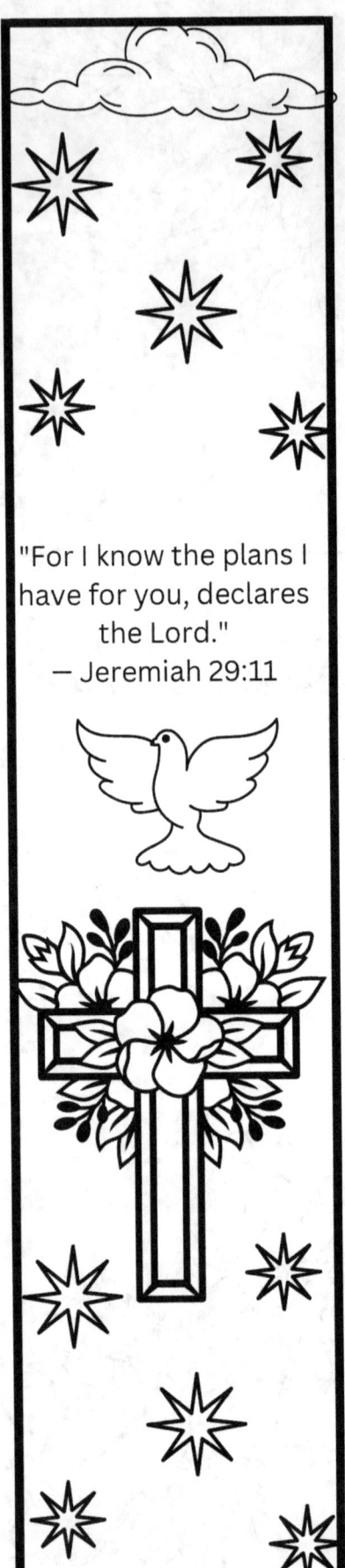

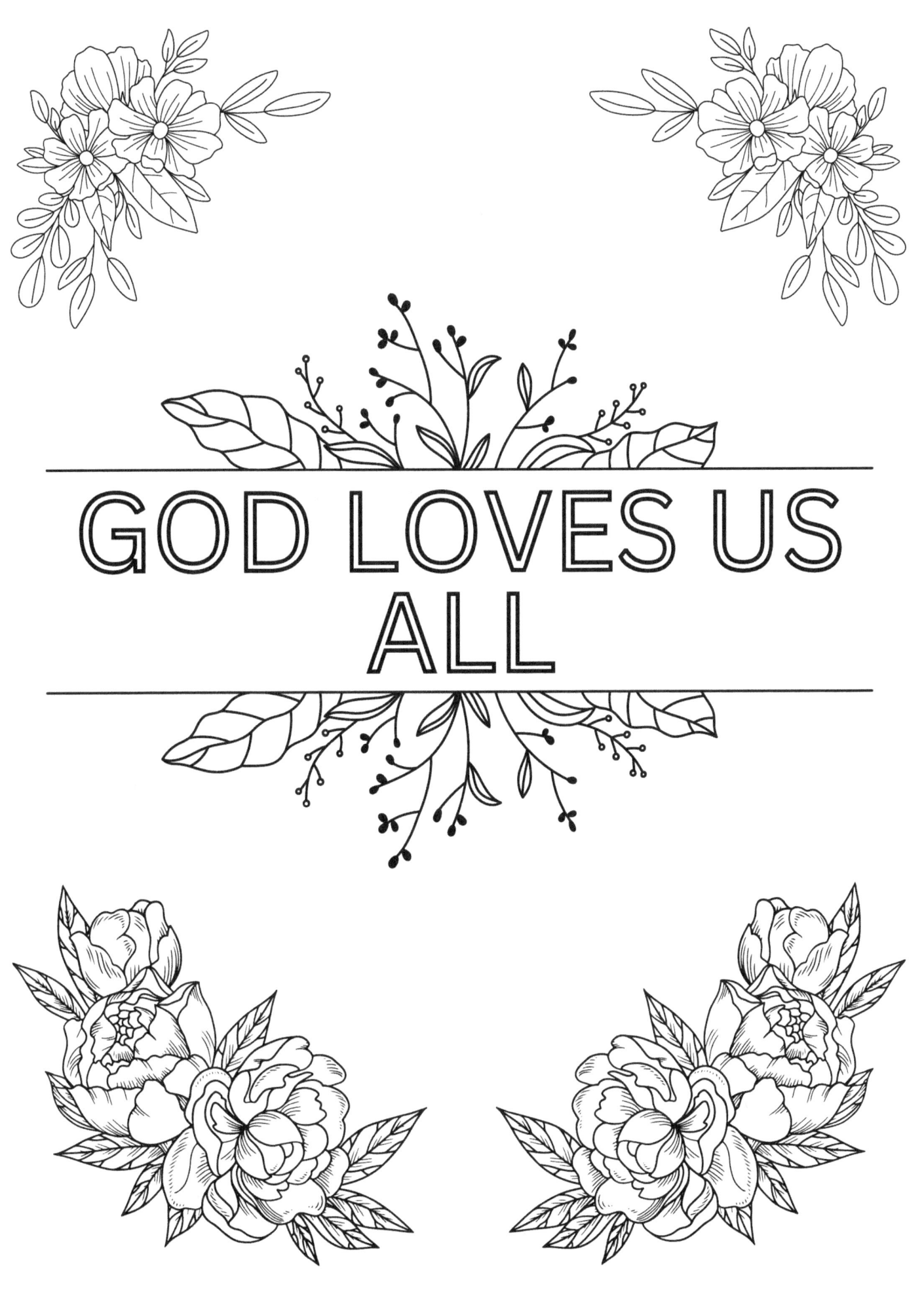

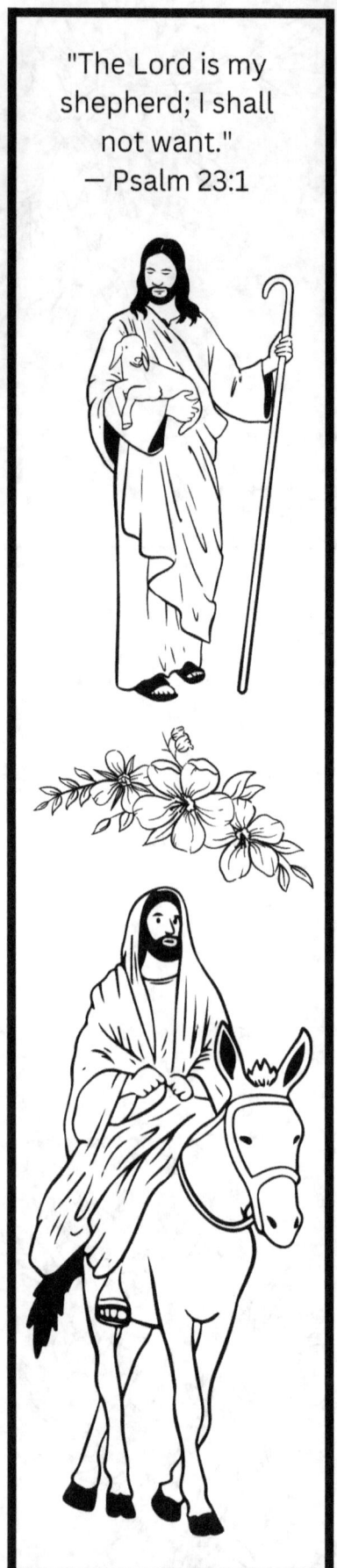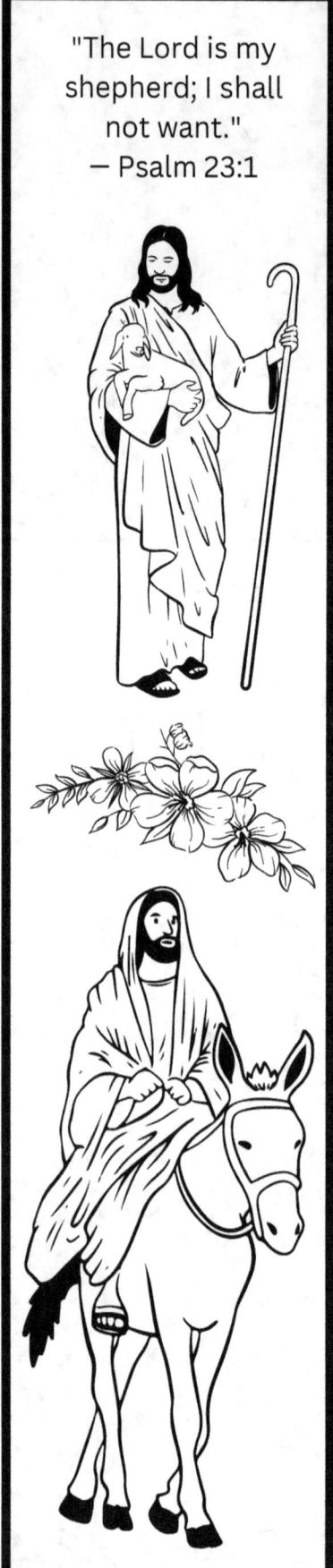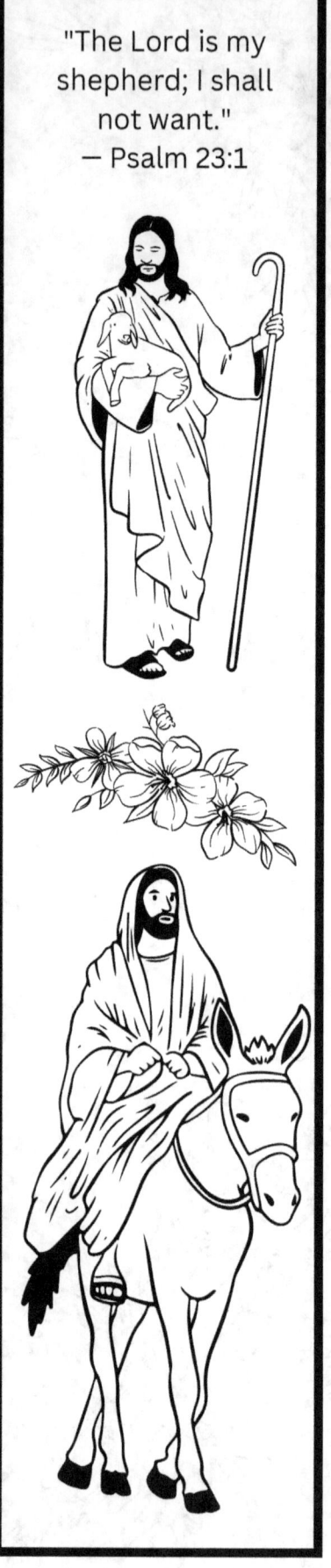

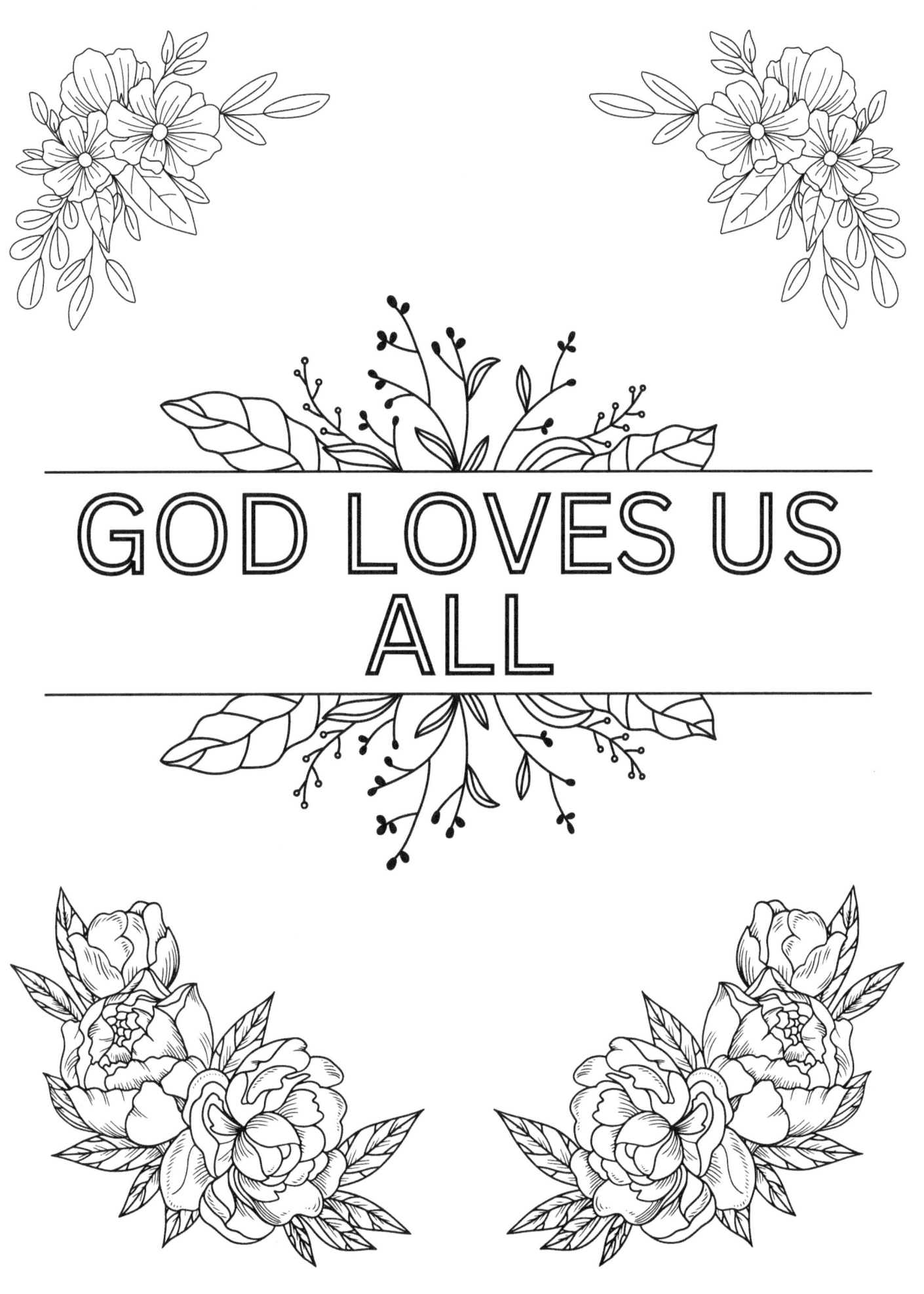

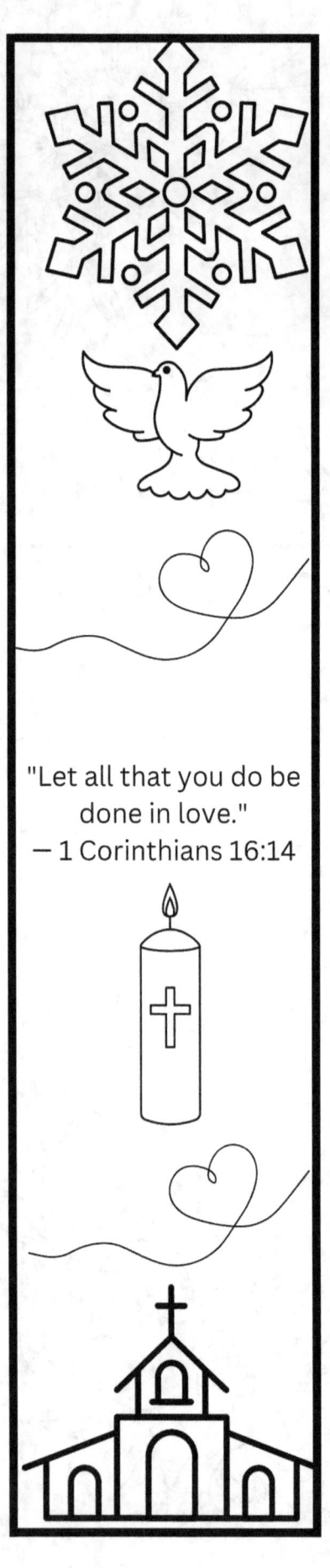
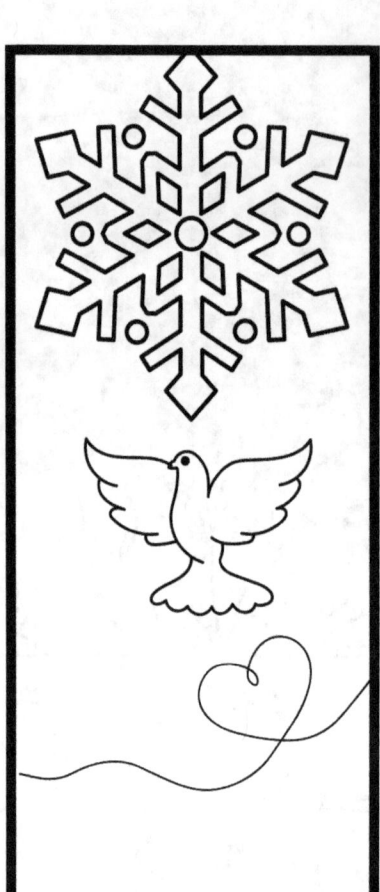
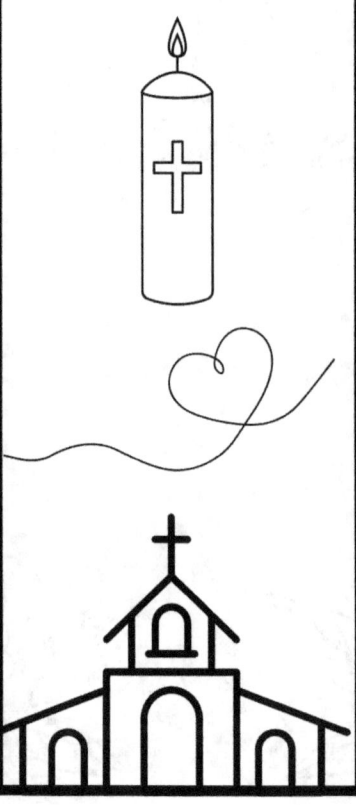
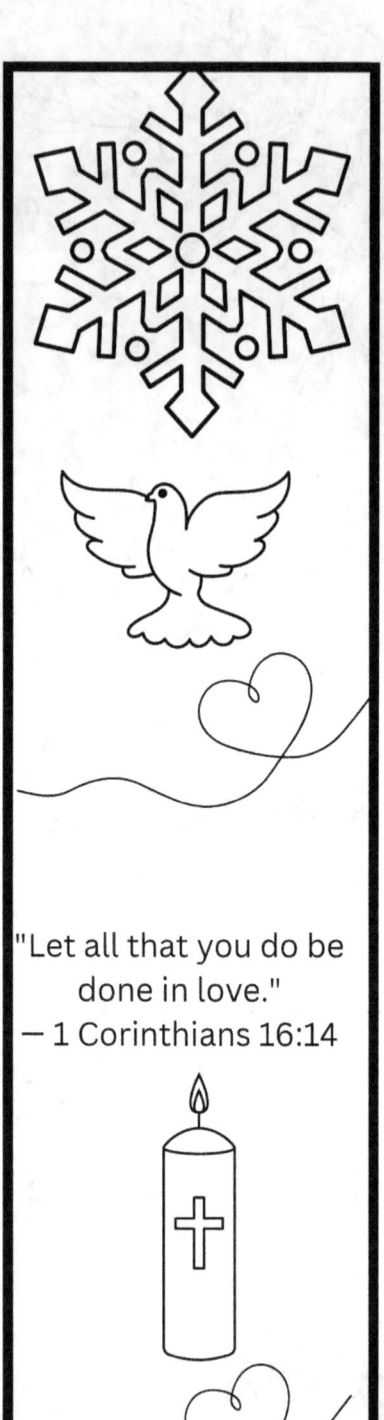
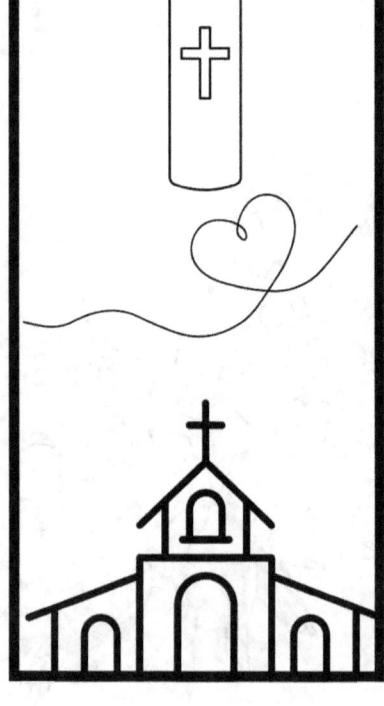

"Let all that you do be done in love."
— 1 Corinthians 16:14

"Let all that you do be done in love."
— 1 Corinthians 16:14

"Let all that you do be done in love."
— 1 Corinthians 16:14

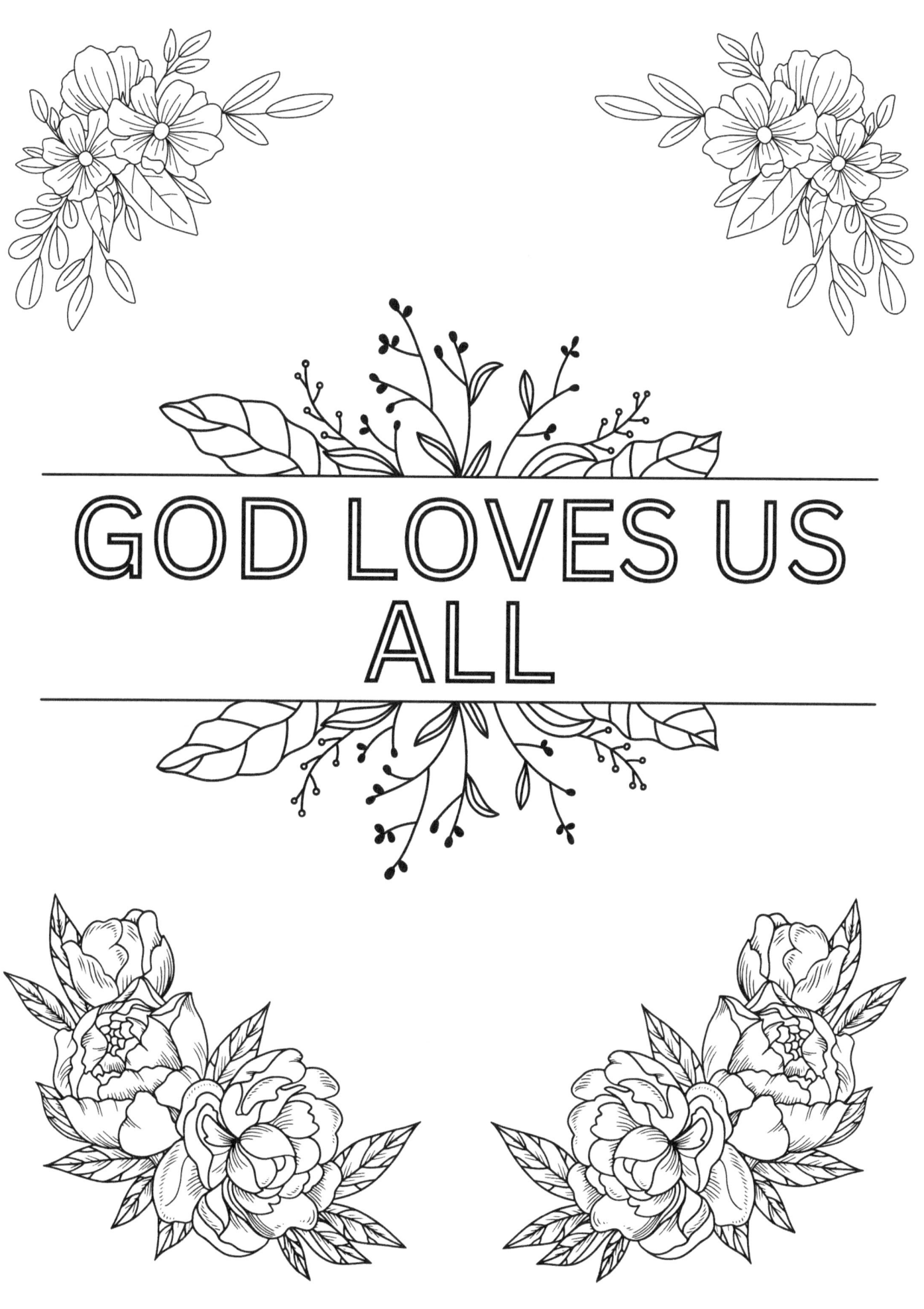

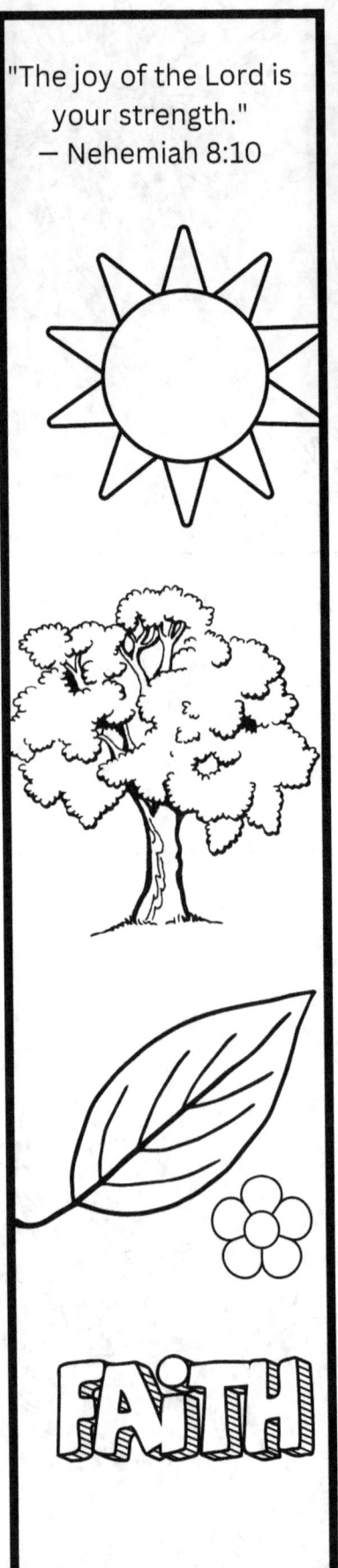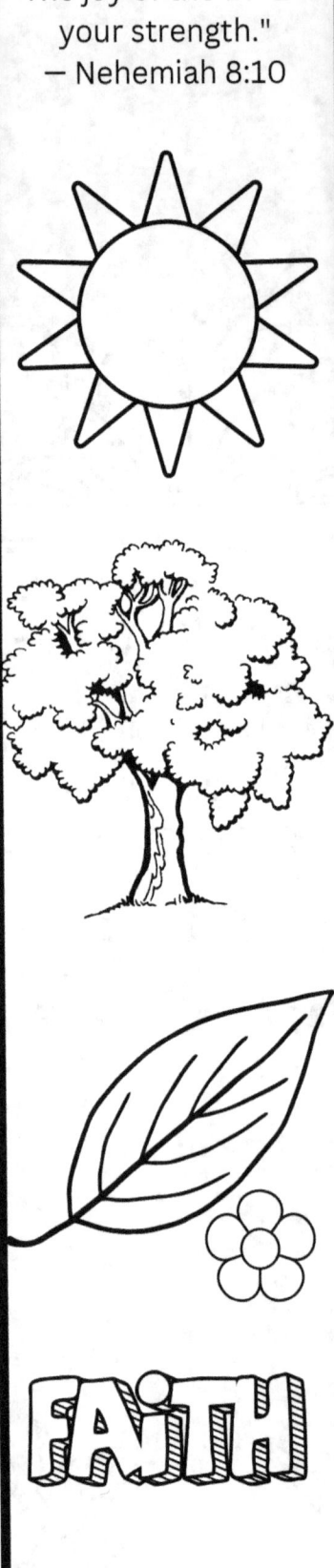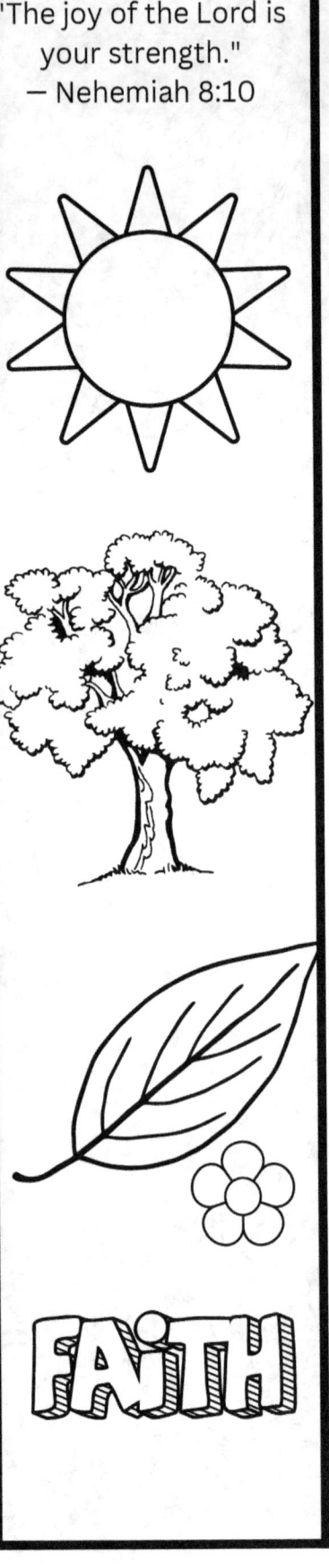

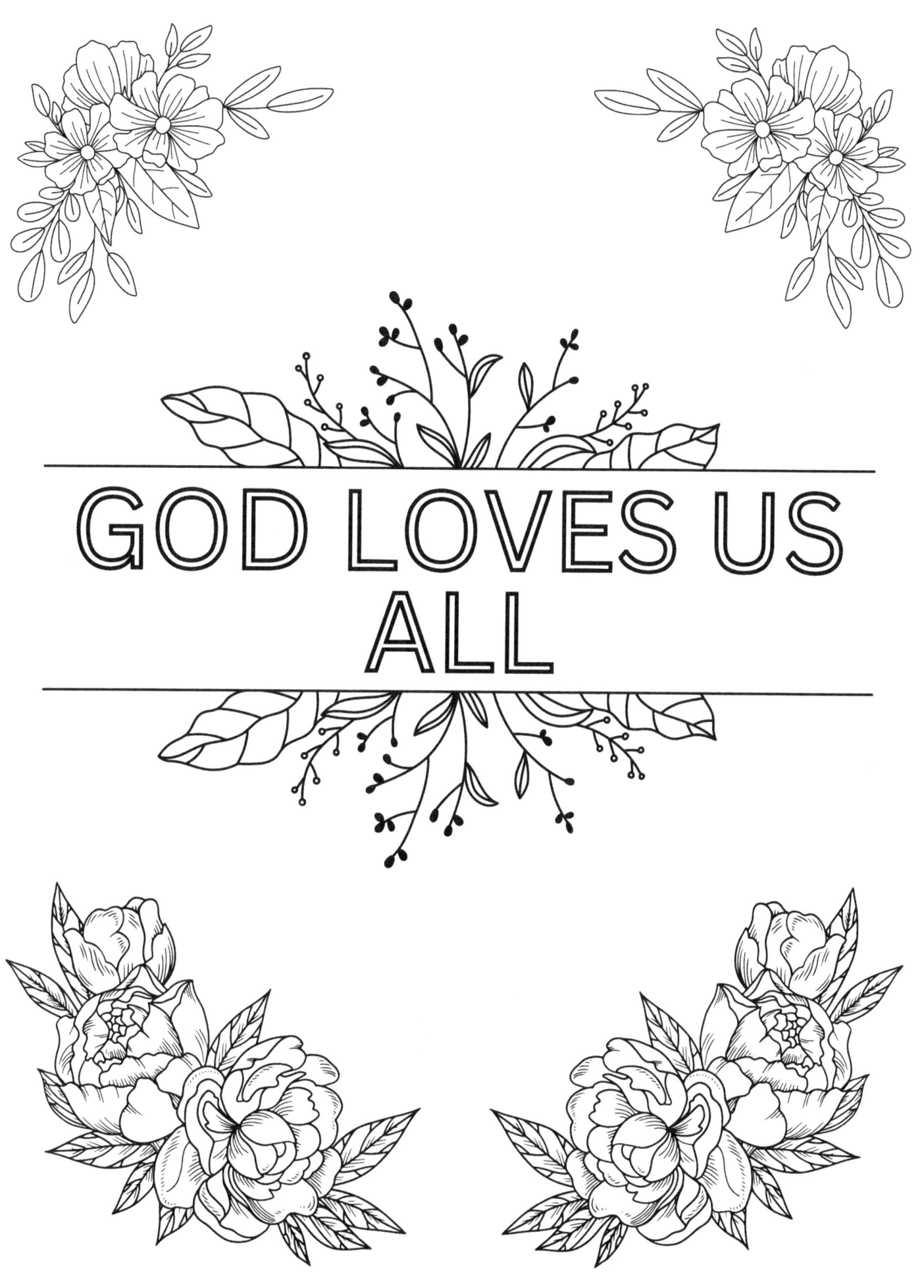

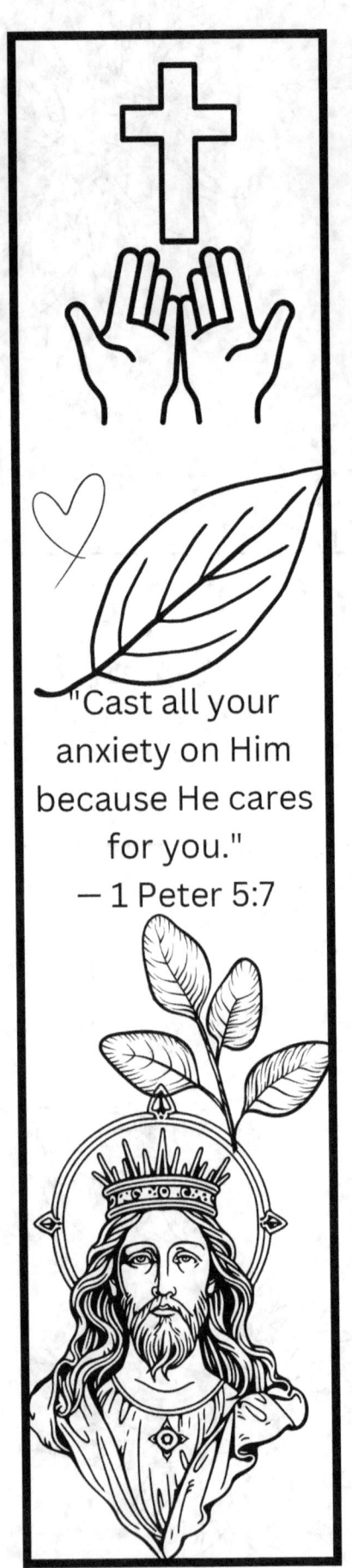
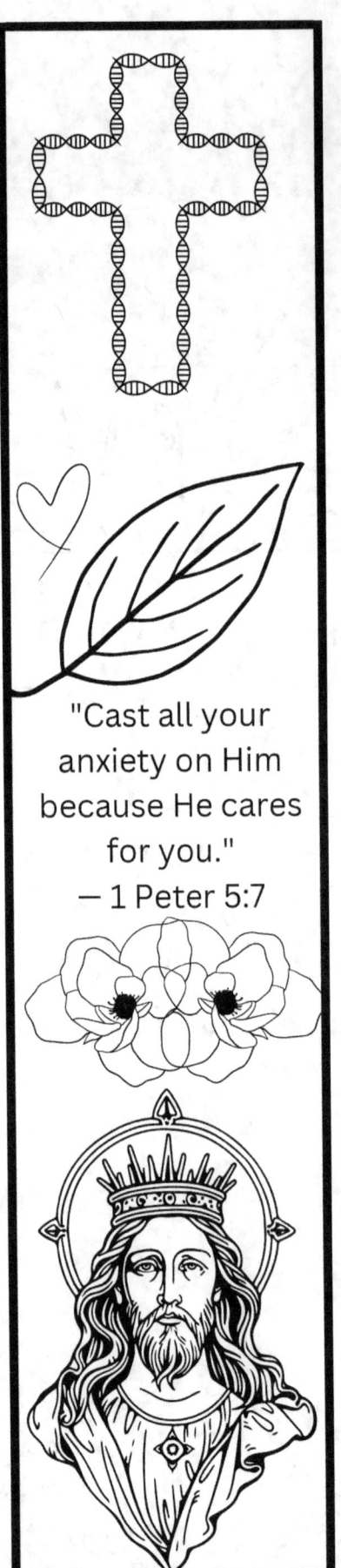
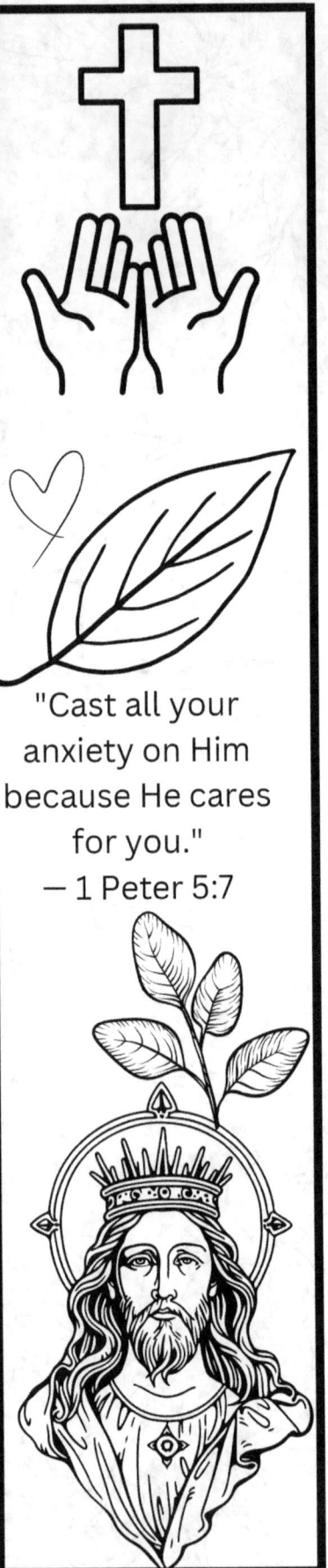

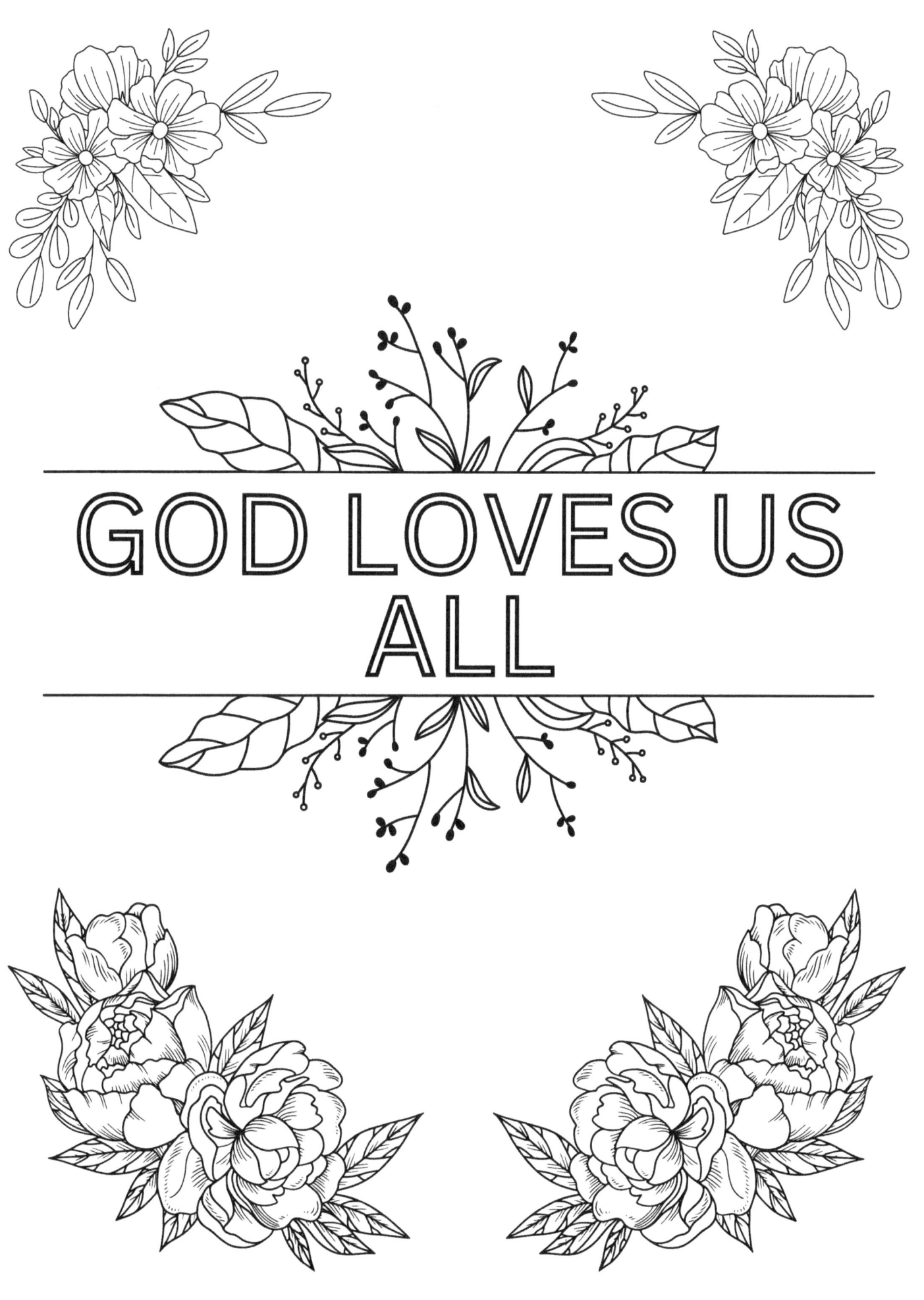

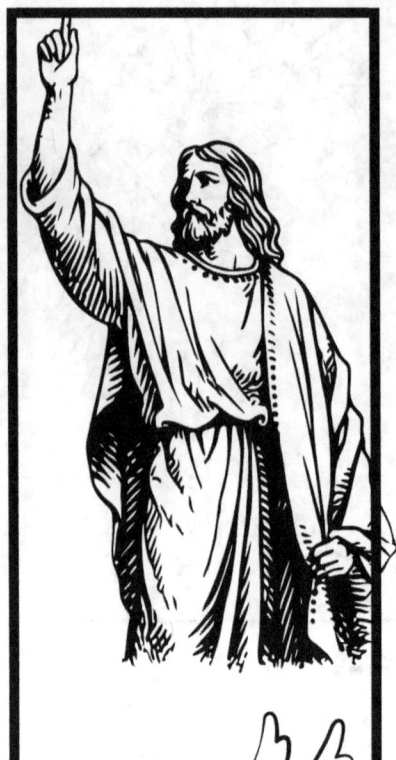
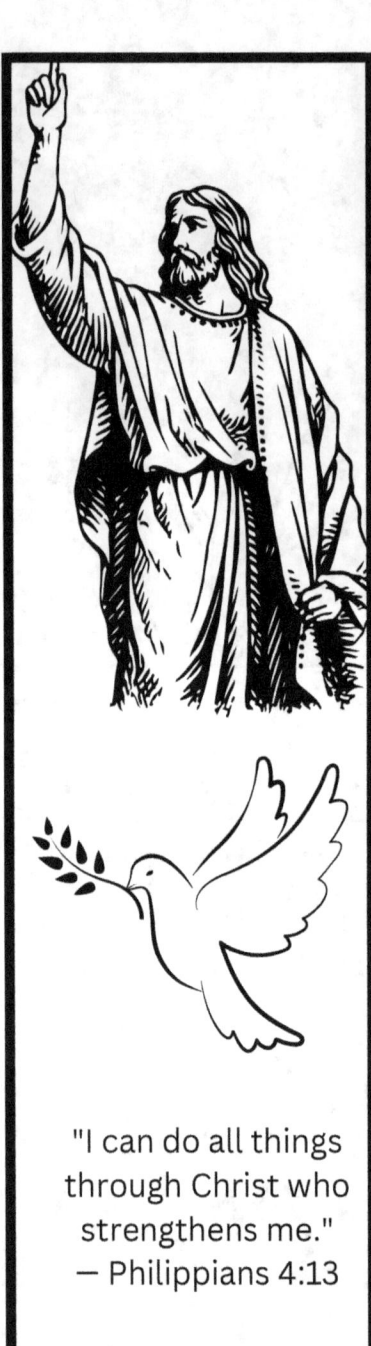
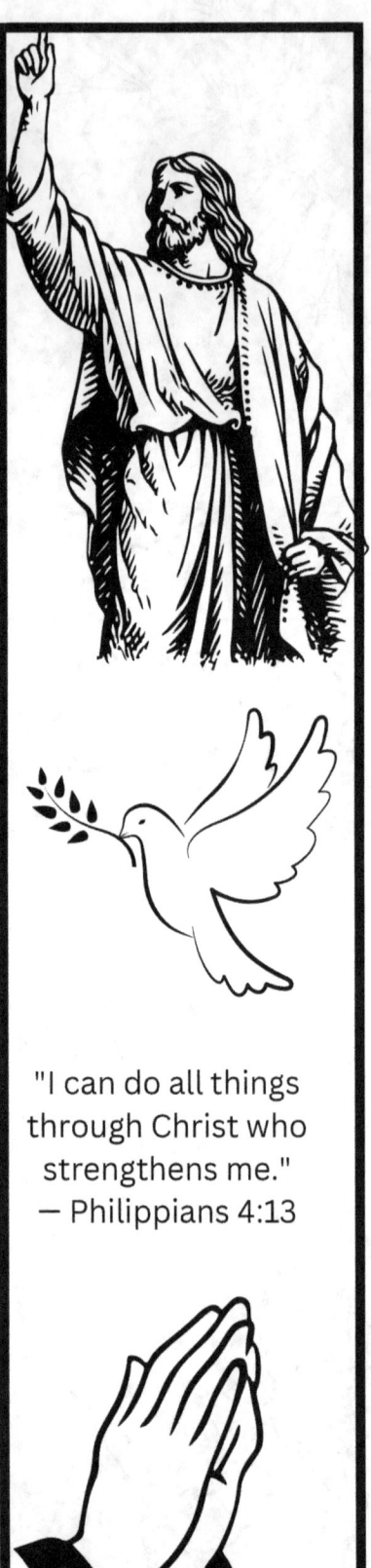

"I can do all things through Christ who strengthens me."
— Philippians 4:13

"I can do all things through Christ who strengthens me."
— Philippians 4:13

"I can do all things through Christ who strengthens me."
— Philippians 4:13

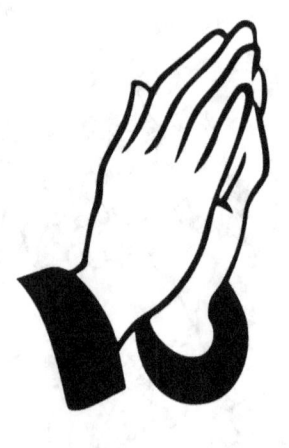
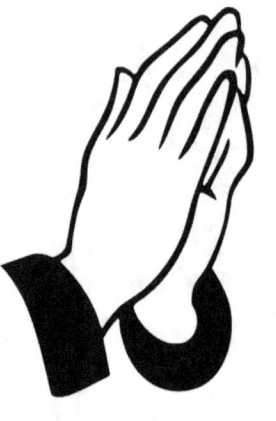

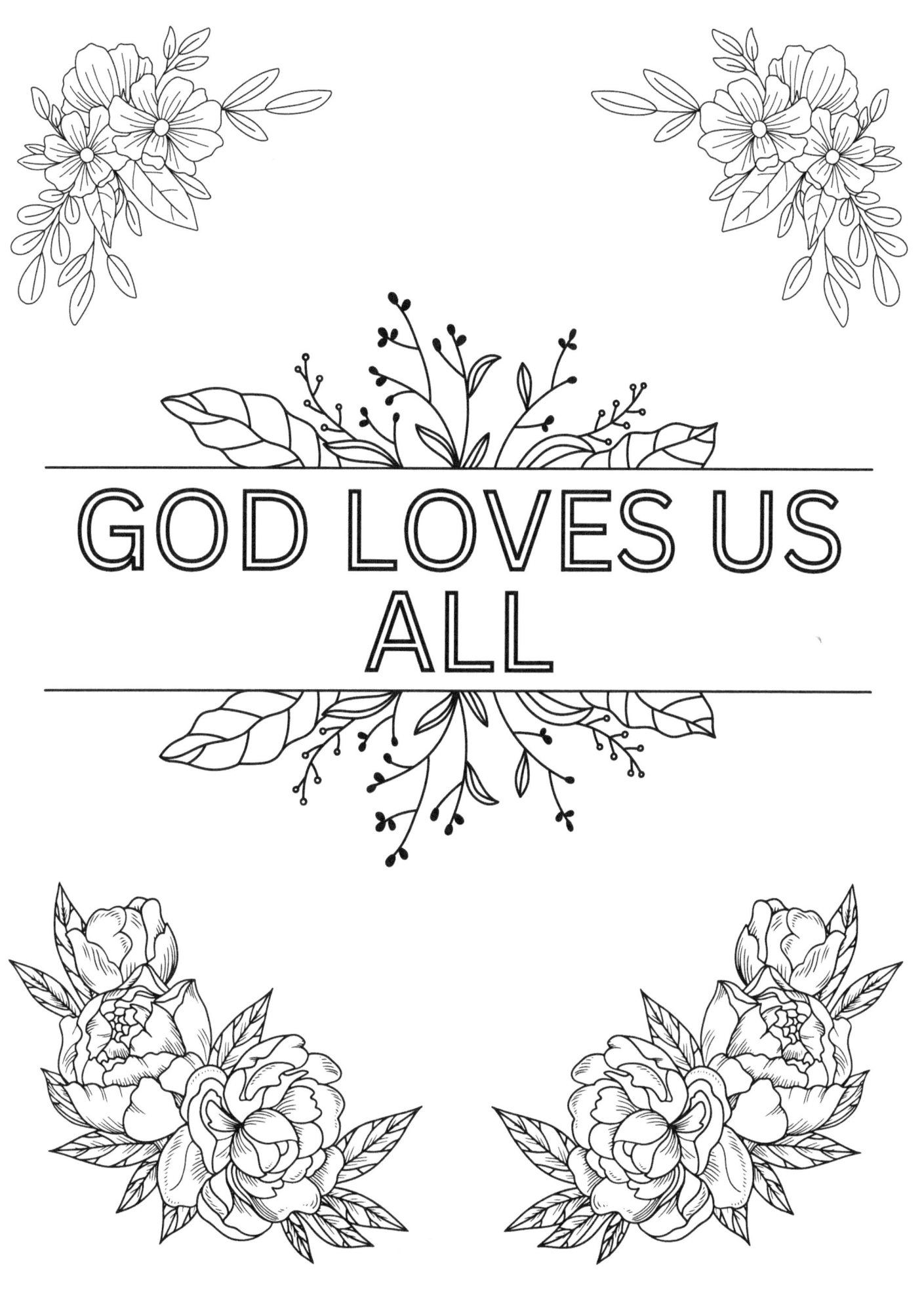

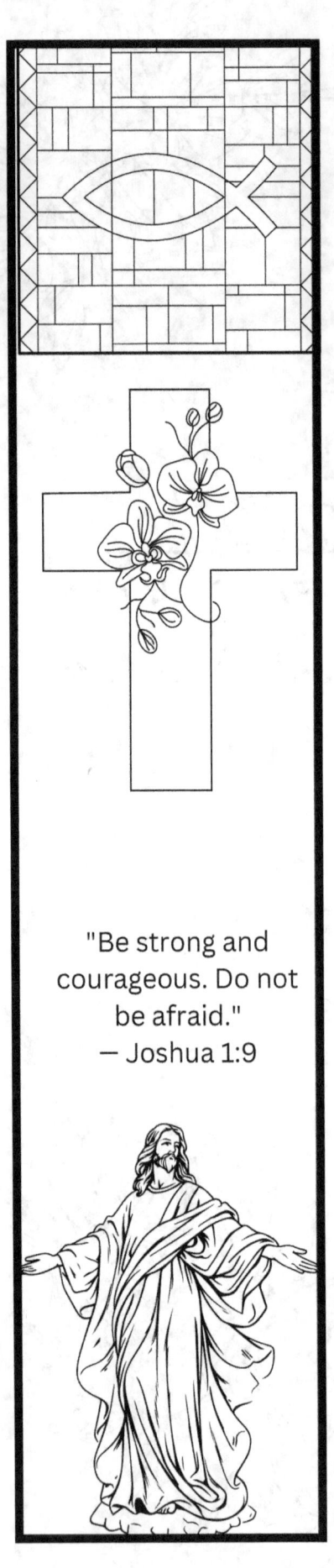
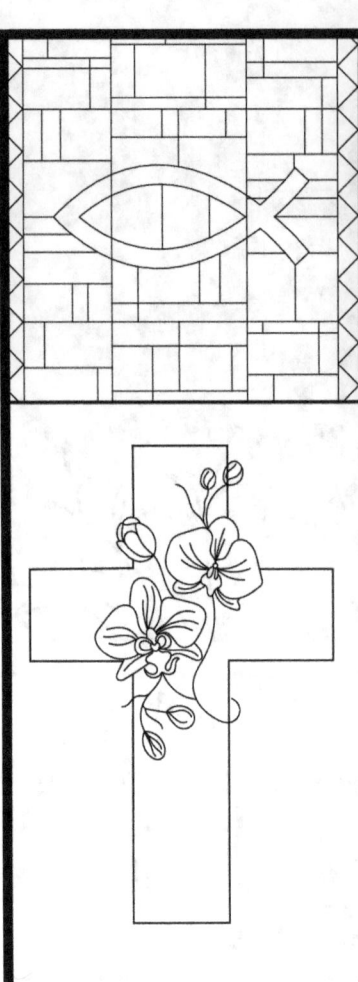
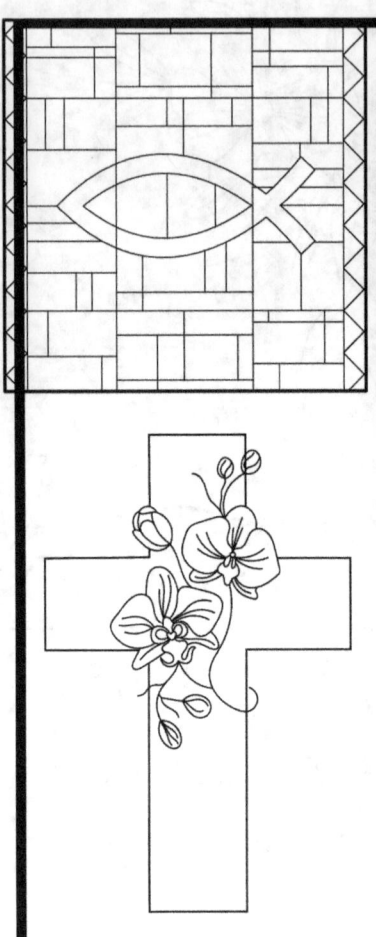

"Be strong and courageous. Do not be afraid."
— Joshua 1:9

"Be strong and courageous. Do not be afraid."
— Joshua 1:9

"Be strong and courageous. Do not be afraid."
— Joshua 1:9

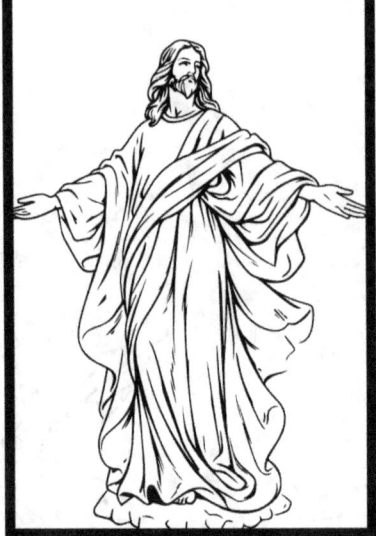
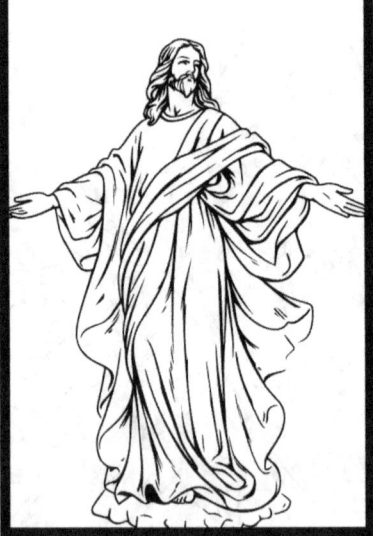

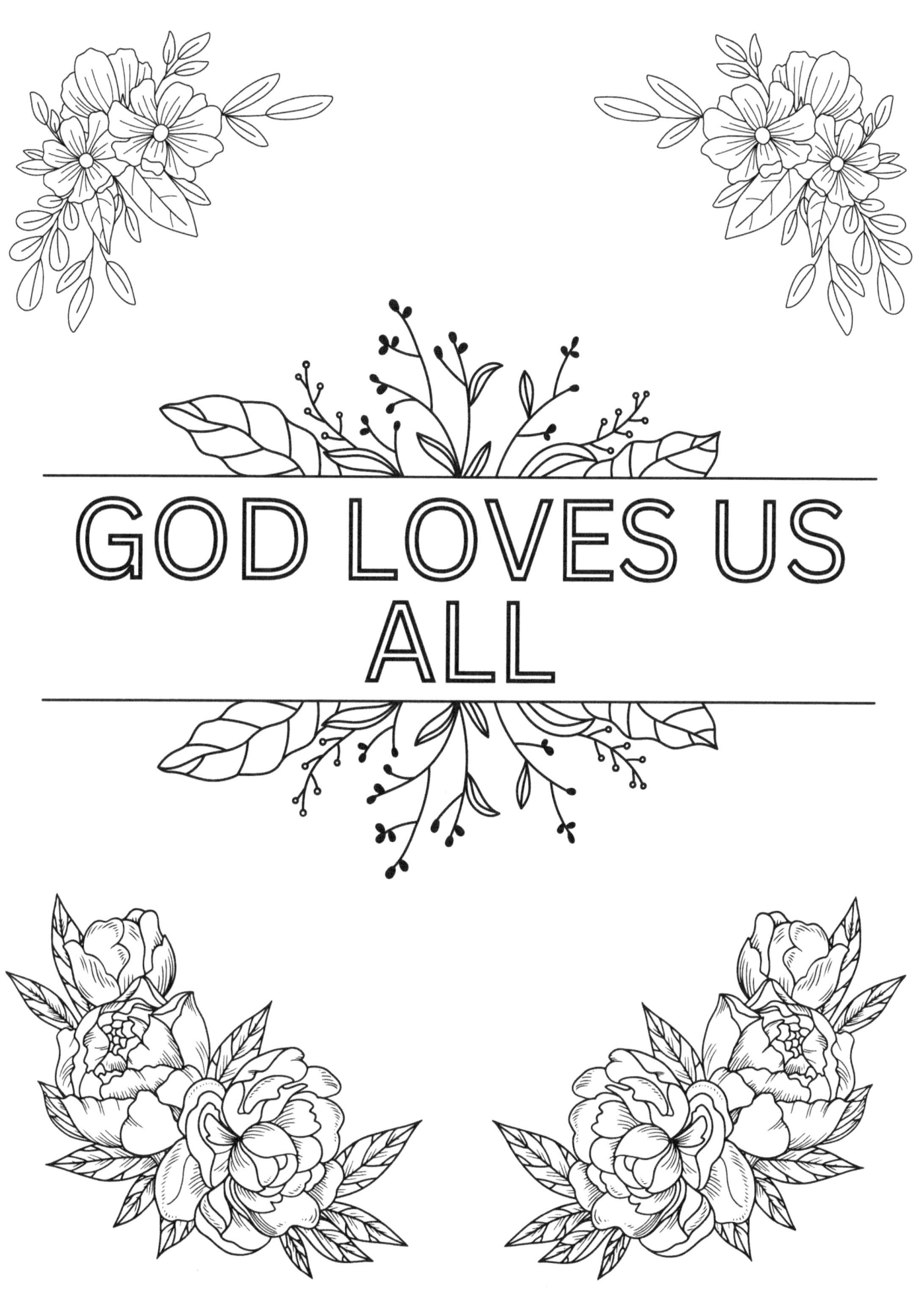

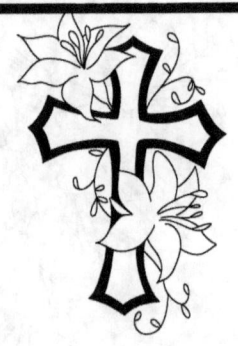
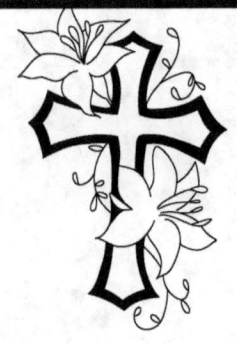
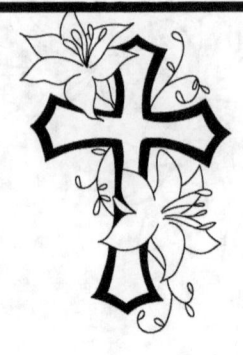

Psalm 23:1-4 (NIV):
"The Lord is my shepherd, I lack nothing.
He makes me lie down in green pastures,
He leads me beside quiet waters,
He refreshes my soul.
He guides me along the right paths for His name's sake.
Even though I walk through the darkest valley,
I will fear no evil, for You are with me;
Your rod and Your staff they comfort me."

Psalm 23:1-4 (NIV):
"The Lord is my shepherd, I lack nothing.
He makes me lie down in green pastures,
He leads me beside quiet waters,
He refreshes my soul.
He guides me along the right paths for His name's sake.
Even though I walk through the darkest valley,
I will fear no evil, for You are with me;
Your rod and Your staff they comfort me."

Psalm 23:1-4 (NIV):
"The Lord is my shepherd, I lack nothing.
He makes me lie down in green pastures,
He leads me beside quiet waters,
He refreshes my soul.
He guides me along the right paths for His name's sake.
Even though I walk through the darkest valley,
I will fear no evil, for You are with me;
Your rod and Your staff they comfort me."

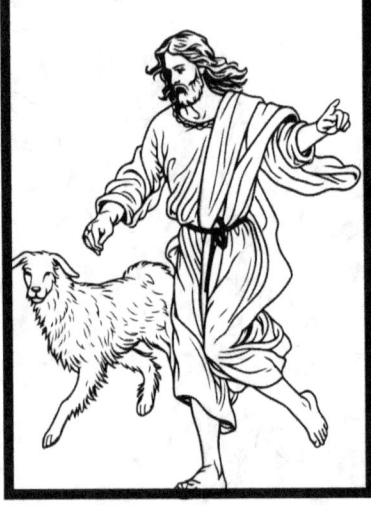
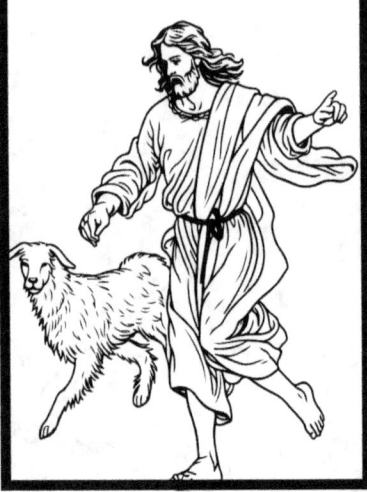
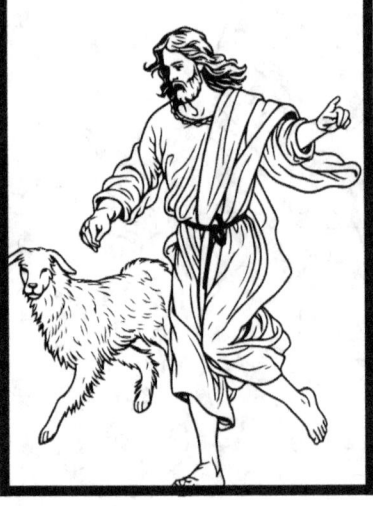

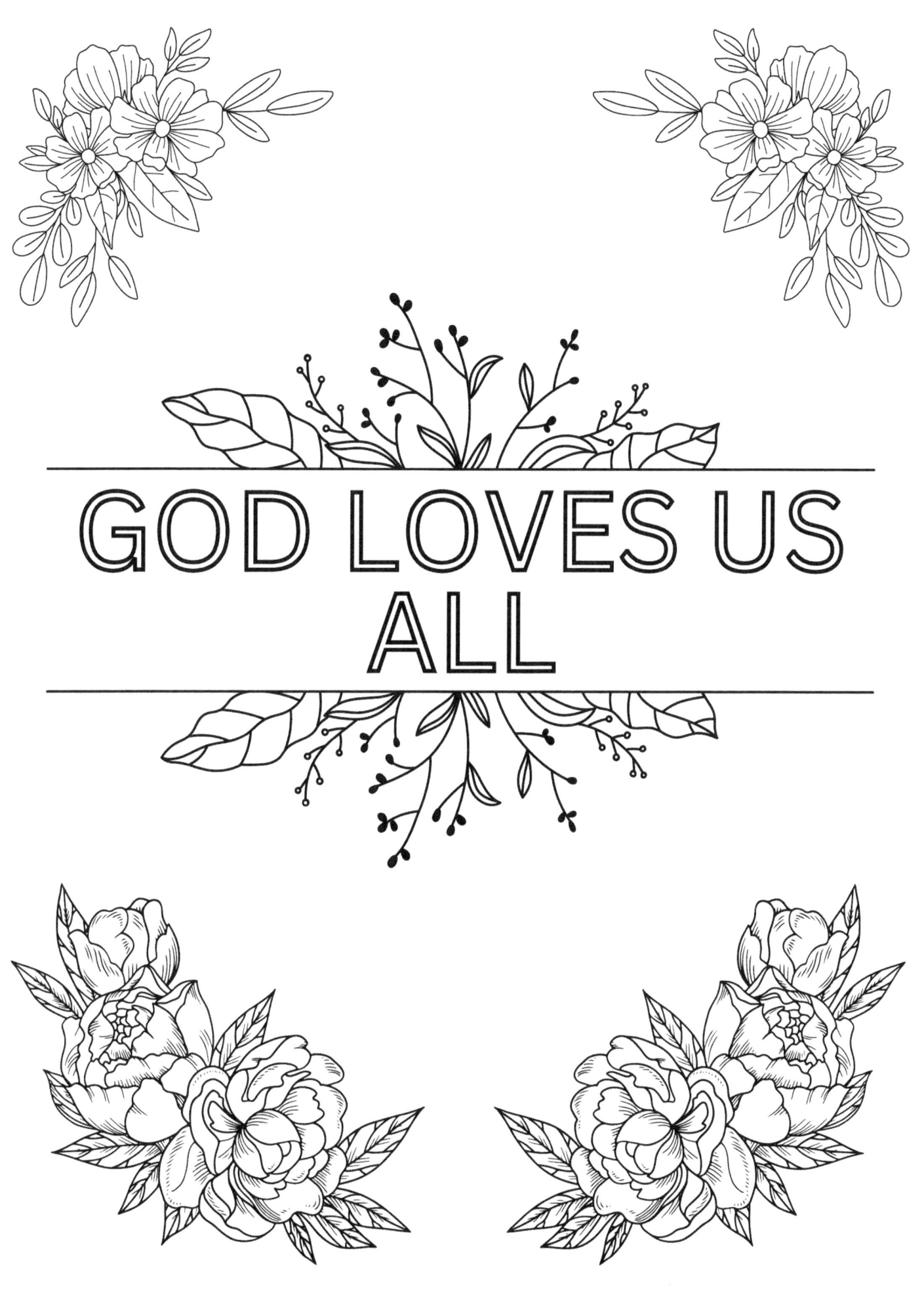

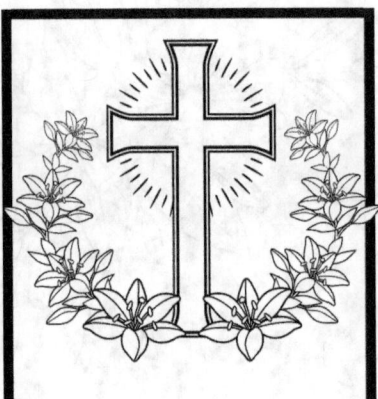 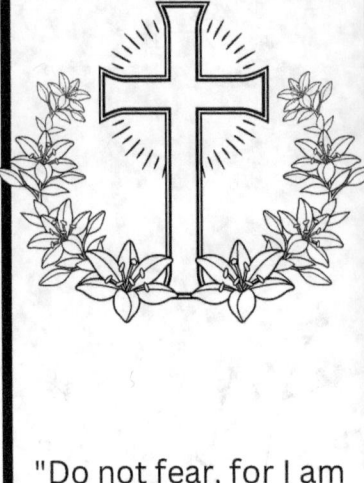 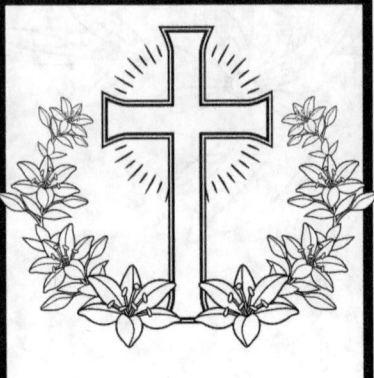

"Do not fear, for I am with you."
— Isaiah 41:10

"Do not fear, for I am with you."
— Isaiah 41:10

"Do not fear, for I am with you."
— Isaiah 41:10

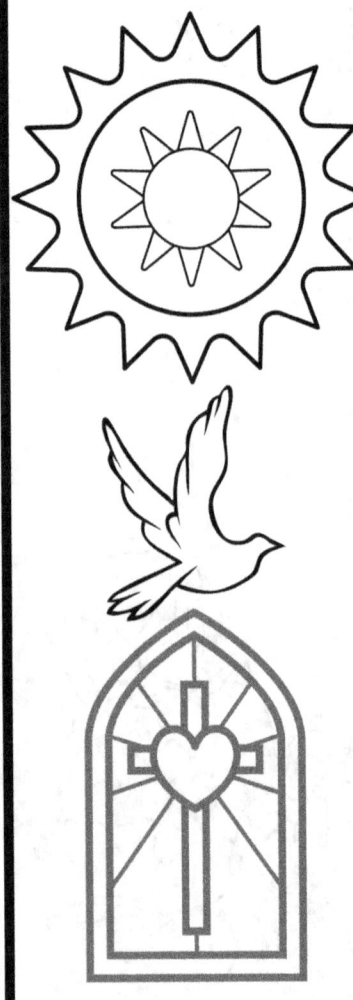 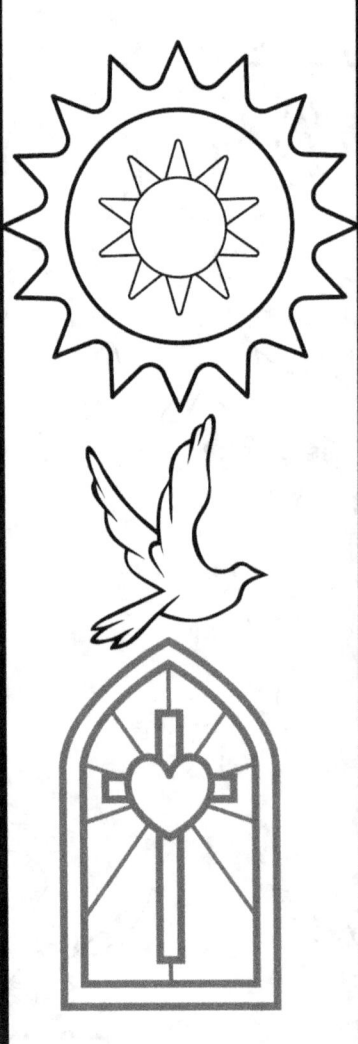 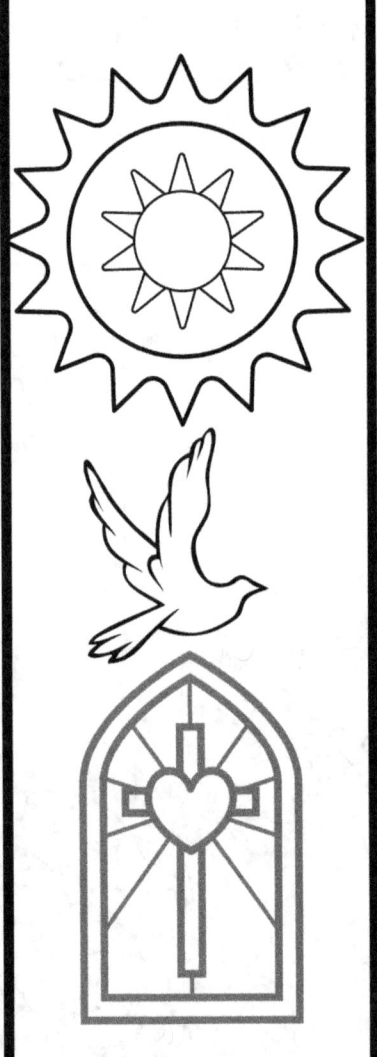

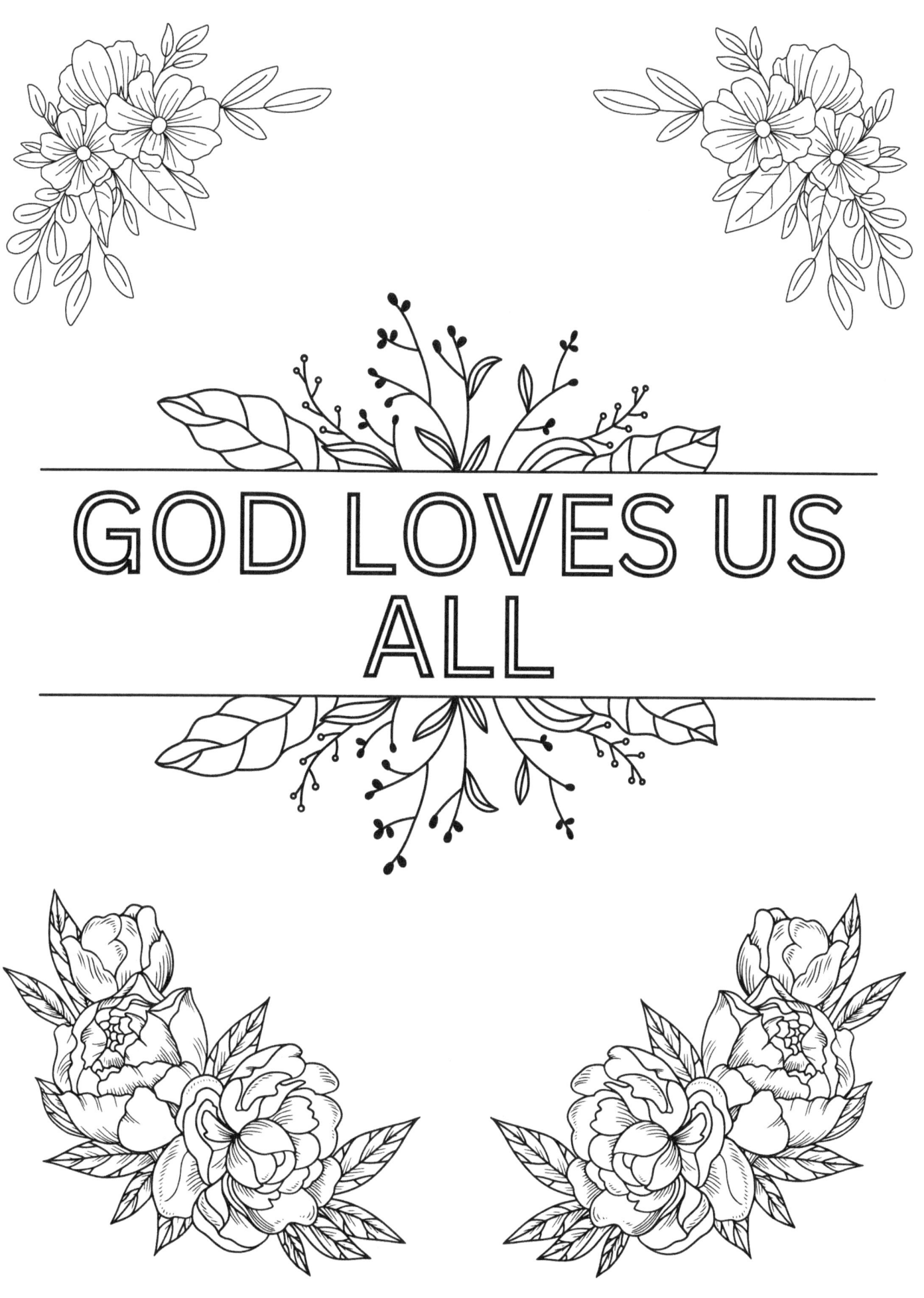

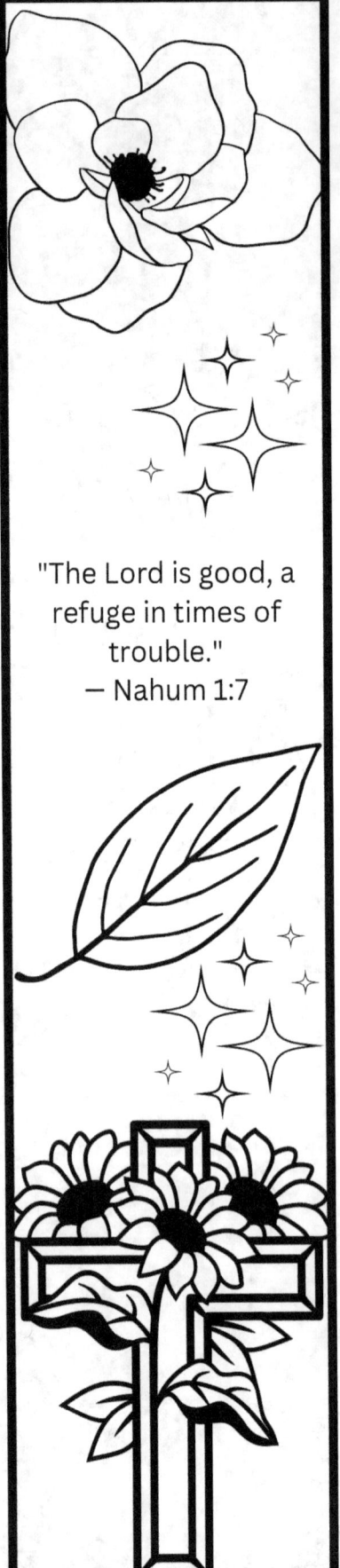

"The Lord is good, a refuge in times of trouble."
— Nahum 1:7

"The Lord is good, a refuge in times of trouble."
— Nahum 1:7

"The Lord is good, a refuge in times of trouble."
— Nahum 1:7

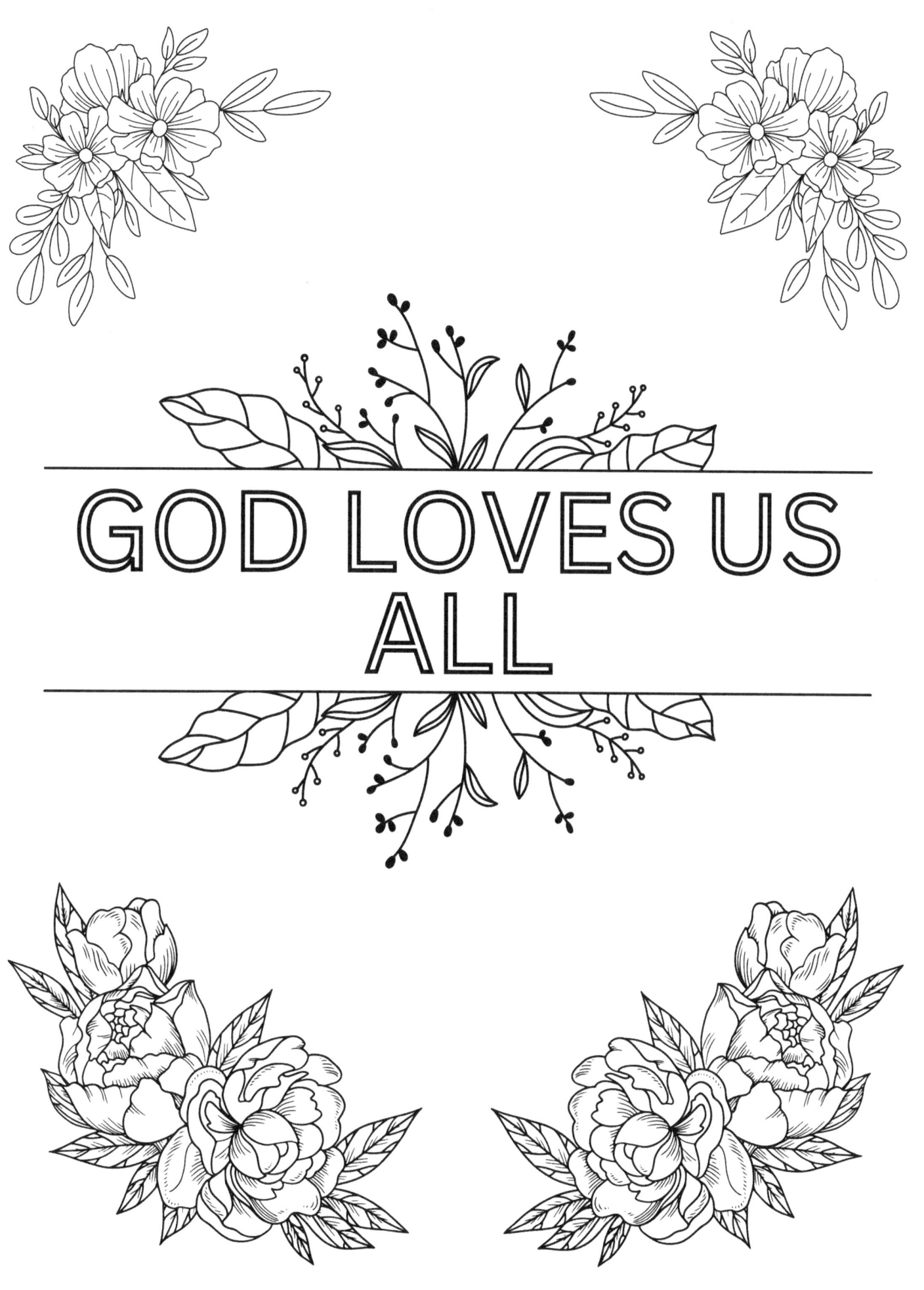

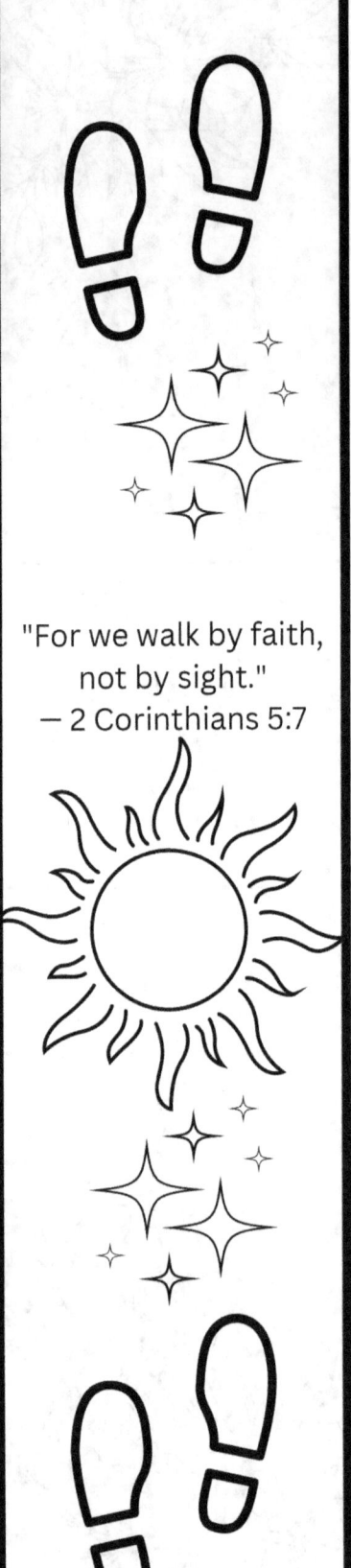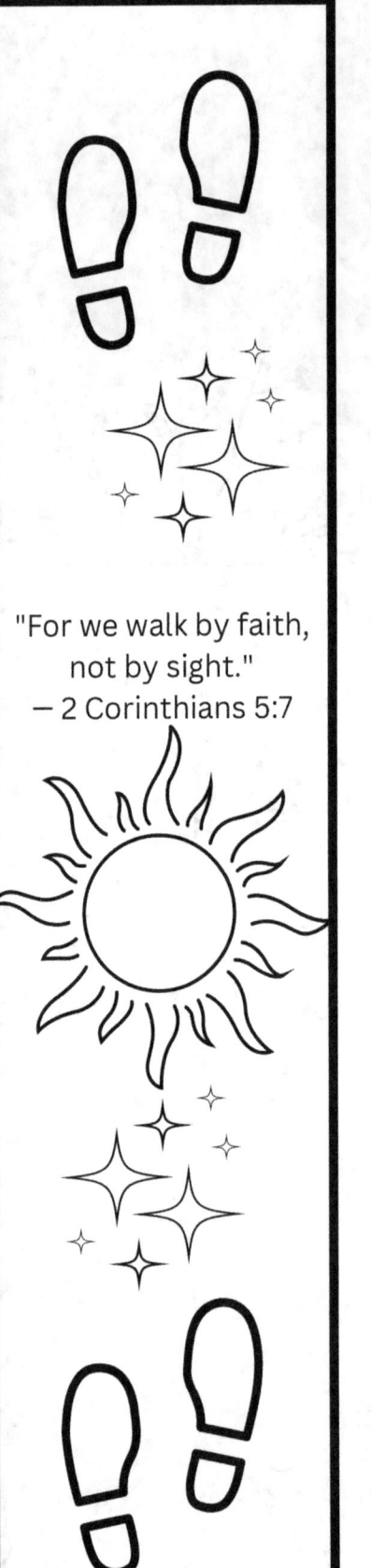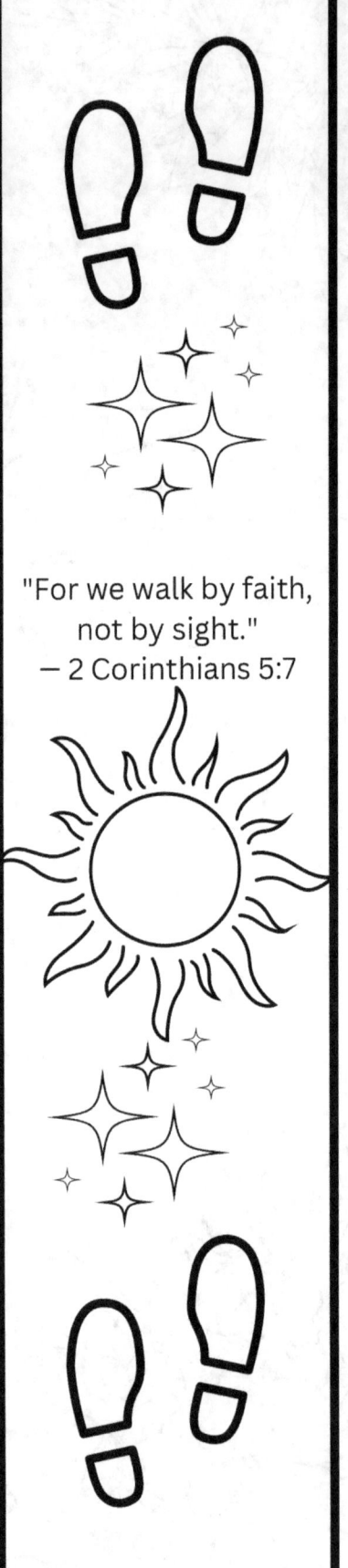

"For we walk by faith, not by sight."
— 2 Corinthians 5:7

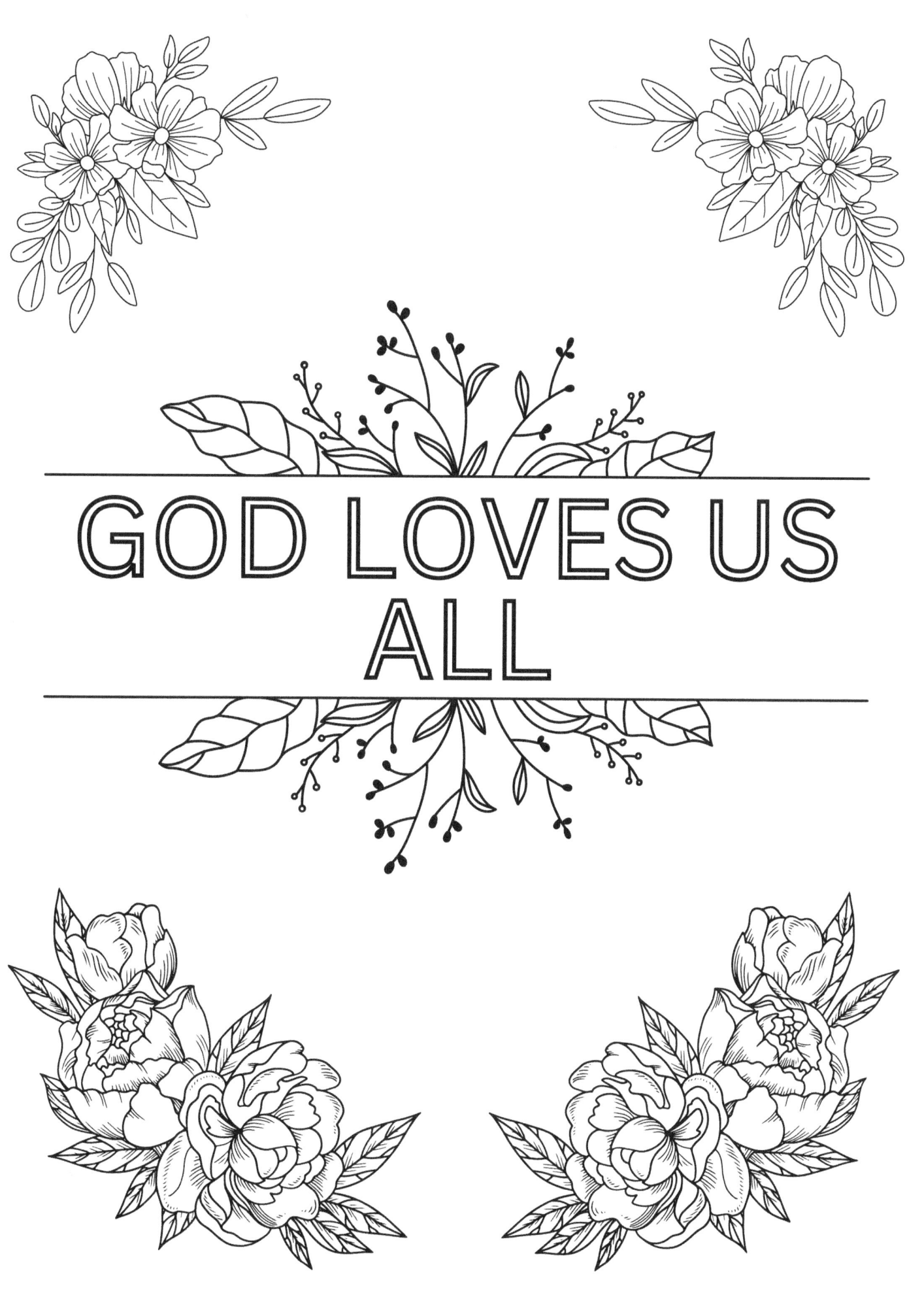

www.ingramcontent.com/pod-product-compliance
Lightning Source LLC
Chambersburg PA
CBHW062222220526
45471CB00009B/3312